FLORIDA GARDENING:
The Newcomers Survival Manual
Second Edition

by Monica Moran Brandies

How to make a great lawn and garden for your Florida home

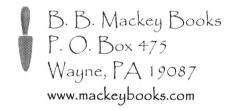

B. B. Mackey Books
P. O. Box 475
Wayne, PA 19087
www.mackeybooks.com

SECOND EDITION

FLORIDA GARDENING: THE NEWCOMER'S SURVIVAL MANUAL

by Monica Moran Brandies

ISBN 1-893443-09-4

Library of Congress Catalog Card Number: 92-075720

DEDICATION

To my daughter Catherine and her husband Adrian Merkey whose family have been Florida gardeners for generations.

ACKNOWLEDGEMENTS

Thanks to my publisher, editor, and illustrator Betty Mackey for encouraging me to do this book, to my family for living through my readjustment time, and to those who helped me relearn gardening in such a different climate: to my friends in Rare Fruit Council International, to those I have interviewed for Tampa Tribune and for hundreds of Brandon News articles, and to the people at the Hillsborough County Extension Service.

AUTHOR'S NOTE

I have since written other books that will also be helpful. *The Florida Gardener's Book of Lists* has more than 200 lists that make gardening here easier. Sunset's *Landscaping with Tropical Plants* has directions for growing these in both northern states and in Florida and has color photos on every page to help you learn to identify the new plants you will soon enjoy.

My website, **www.gardensflorida.com,** has loads of information. You can see many of my newspaper columns, lists, and photos along with seasonal tips and much more.

PUBLISHER'S NOTE

It has been my pleasure to work with Monica Brandies on wonderful Florida books for newcomers, for herb growers, and for flower growers for nearly twenty years. Books published by **B. B. Mackey Books** are carried at many Florida bookstores and garden centers, and may also be purchased by special order from any full service bookstore. For a book list and order form, including books for gardeners in other regions, visit my website at **www.mackeybooks.com** or see page 135. And if you want a really great read that lets you get to know Monica a lot better, be sure to get her autobiographical collection of stories, *Bless You For the Gifts* — Betty Mackey

B. B. Mackey Books
P. O. Box 475
Wayne, PA 19087   *   www.mackeybooks.com

CONTENTS

Books by Monica Brandies

A Cutting Garden for Florida, Third Edition. Use your Florida garden to fill your house with flowers. This book will introduce you to annuals, bulbs, perennials, flowering shrubs, and trees which have many uses indoors and out. Month-by-month planting guide, bulb chart, flower conditioning info, much more. 2001, B. B. Mackey Books. ISBN 9616338-9-1 $15.95. Betty Barr Mackey, co-author.

Bless You For the Gifts. A book of uplifting stories of blessings. Some gifts lie dormant for decades, as in "Seeing Grandma Naked", before becoming important. Others as in "Hence and the Haymow" take on new meanings over the years. "Cow Tails" and "Hit by a Train" will make you laugh and cry. Great gift book. 196 pages. 1997, B. B. Mackey Books. ISBN 9616338-7-5 $10.95.

Herbs and Spices for Florida Gardens. Grow herbs and spices for flavor, health, beauty, crafts, scent, and garden color. 250 pages. 1996. B. B. Mackey Books. ISBN 9616338-6-7. $15.50.

Landscaping With Tropical Plants. How to use tropicals and tropical look-alikes to create a lush and fascinating landscape in Florida or anywhere. 128 pages, all with color photos. 2004, Sunset Books. ISBN 03760345-7-2. $14.95.

Ortho's Guide to Herbs. One of Ortho's larger books on living with herbs in the landccape, the garden, the kitchen, the cupboard and closet, the bedroom and bath, and in decoration,. It includes an extensive encyclopedia of herbs with how to identify, use, and grow individual plants and has many color photos. 304 pages. 1997. ISBN 08972131-3-0. $24.95

Shade Gardening For Florida. A book with Florida methods and Florida plants. Tells you what and how to grow in the shade, how quick and easy it is to get shade here, how to manage the shade level, the difference in kinds of shade, and what to do if you get too much shade. 144 pages, 16 of color photos. Great Outdoors Publishing. ISBN 08200042-1-9. $19.95.

Sprouts and Saplings. Written when the author still lived in Iowa and had many small children at home, so there is emphasis on growing vegetables and small fruits, a garden for sanity, the importance of having a garden, birds and beasts, flowers, woodies, indoors plants, and methods. 208 pages. 1986, Strawberry Hill Press. ISBN 08940706-6-5 $9.95.

The Florida Gardener's Book of Lists. Amazingly useful, this book lists the kinds and varieties of trees, perennials, ferns, annuals, vines, shrubs, and groundcovers that will do best and just how far south. 186 pages. 1998, Taylor Trade Publishing. ISBN 08783390-8-6. $17.95. Lois Trigg Chaplin, co-author.

Xeriscaping for Florida Homes. A resource for creating a colorful, efficient, beautiful, water-saving garden. Charts of grasses, groundcovers, shrubs, vines, and trees. 181 pages. 1999, Great Outdoors Publishing. ISBN 08200041-8-9. $18.95.

Yankee Magazine's Panty Hose, Hot Peppers, Tea Bags, And More For The Garden: 1001 Ingenious Ways to use Common Household Items to Control Weeds, Beat Pests, Cook Compost, Solve Problems, Make Tricky Jobs Easy, and Save Time. Monica Brandies is one of nine of the nation's most frugal and inventive garden writers who worked together to produce this fascinating, money-and-plant-saving book. A Rodale Organic Gardening Book. ISBN 0-89909-394-9 Hardcover $29.95, Paperback $16.95.

Monica's Website

Many of Monica's weekly columns and feature articles can be found on her website, **www.gardensflorida.com**. It includes her biography, dozens of columns with photos and pictures, descriptions, and growing instruction for as many featured Florida plants, a schedule of her upcoming events, speaking topics available, and seasonal tips. Look there for color pictures for this book.

CHAPTER ONE
FIRST STEPS TO FLORIDA GROWING

You are about to move to Florida. Or maybe you just did. Or it still seems like you just did. What does it take to have a great garden?

Gardening in Florida is no harder than gardening elsewhere, but timing, techniques, plant selection, and insect control are different. When I moved from Iowa to Tampa, with forty years of gardening experience, I had to relearn gardening almost from scratch. Now, twenty years later, I am past the pain, but still learning. I understand the questions a new-to-Florida gardener will have. I hope that this book will help you to a quick and successful adjustment to the delightful mystery of gardening in the subtropics.

WONDERFUL WEATHER

If you are looking forward to pleasant, sunny days all year round, you will not be disappointed. Cloudy days are so infrequent that we transplanted people enjoy them as brief reminders of times back home. The same with cool days. Anything that involves frost is another matter which we will discuss later.

In any part of Florida, there are definite changes of seasons, sometimes subtle. Granted, the summer is hot, but most people have air conditioning and the use of their own or a neighborhood swimming pool. With these benefits, your first Florida summer may be, as mine was, the most comfortable of your life.

It is not too hot to keep right on gardening, working for short spurts in the morning and evening through all the steamy months. Don't overdo and don't worry if you can't keep up. Most of us don't. We just catch up when the weather cools. The cool weather plants will die out and should be removed, but some like nasturtiums will come back in the fall from self sown seeds and others will thrive

through the summer. Because of the heat and humidity, fruit trees leap into growth and coleus cuttings root in a week.

A YEAR-LONG GROWING SEASON

If you are a gardener, you will be looking forward to a year-round growing season. During the steamy summer, you can grow heat-loving annuals like amaranthus, begonia, celosia, cleome, coleus, cosmos, crossandra, gomphrena, impatiens, marigold, melampodium, narrow-leaved zinnias, ornamental peppers, portulaca, salvia of several types, torenia, vinca, and tithonia. Perennials like coreopsis, daisy bush, daylily, gaillardia, gazania, gerbera, shrimp plant, jacobinia, mallow, pentas, ruellia, and verbena do well. The vegetable garden may be on hold, but you can still pick okra, southern peas, sweet potatoes, cherry tomatoes, eggplant, peppers, and green papayas.

Summer is a great time to transplant trees and shrubs, prune a little, and gather and spread mulch. You can take cuttings to increase ground covers and many flowers, vines, and shrubs, for they root quickly with all the rain and humidity.

Then fall brings milder temperatures and a new beginning of the gardening season. Most flowers can be planted now. Sow seeds or buy plants of the ones that like cool weather, like alyssum, calendula and nasturtiums. You'll probably want to get blooming plants of dianthus, pansies, petunias and snapdragons. I have even had a little luck with poppies and stocks. Others such as larkspur and bishop's flower (Ammi) seem to grow very slowly through the short days, but will be ready to burst into abundant bloom with the first sign of spring.

Most vegetables can go into the garden in fall, especially the ones that like cold weather, like cabbage, lettuce, carrots, onion, beets, celery, radishes, and swiss chard. You can plant strawberries and rhubarb, both of which grow as annuals here. Beans and corn may get nipped by frost, depending on where you live, but try some

Tropical and semitropical plants such as these brugmansias like Florida growing and so will you.

Spring sneaks up on you in Florida. But once you are sure there won't be any more frosts, there may be some garden cleaning to do. If anything seems dead, remember, it may come back from the roots. Cut it back but don't dig it up for at least three months.

You can grow almost any annual in Florida's spring. Azaleas finish their long season of bloom with a month of glorious and varied color, and in the warmer parts of the state the citrus blossoms scent the air for a whole month in March, my favorite time. You may start the year picking citrus, but before you know it you are picking peaches in March and April and plums in May. April and May come the closest to northern summers with their abundance of flowers and vegetables, but you have to water so much that you are ready for the frequent rains to start in mid June.

FLORIDA CLIMATE FACTORS

Florida has special conditions to keep in mind. It is, as one expert says, "a desert where it rains three months of the year." Because of the hot, humid summer, some plants cook out by July. So we treat many plants as annuals and start over with new plantings in September. Do this for most vegetables, even rhubarb, for some herbs, and for flowers such as petunias, snapdragons, calendulas, and pansies.

From September until the return of the summer rains the next June, many plants require irrigation to thrive, sometimes even to survive. And the number and intensity of frosts varies greatly from one year to the next.

We arrived in Florida in mid-June, just at the end of the Florida growing season for most of the crops I then knew. That first summer was not the most encouraging, though even then it was much nicer than a northern winter. By the second summer, when the heat finished off my spring vegetables, I had fruit and ornamentals that jumped into such encouraging summer growth that the loss was more than balanced.

Plants in containers can be moved according to the seasons. Put them in the spotlight when they look best and remove them to the sidelines when they don't. Some fruits and other plants of marginal hardiness are best kept

early plantings anyway. Now that it's fall, you will start watering again, but it doesn't take too much water because the days have gotten shorter and cooler.

Winter varies from nonexistent to short and sweet, depending on both location and year. Make the most of January and February (the closest we have to a dormant period) to do necessary pruning. Move plants when they are as close to dormant as possible if you are going to rearrange any of your landscaping. Keep planting seeds of flowers and vegetables so you can make the most of spring when it happens.

Water and feed plants as needed. Azaleas take a lot of water year round and more water while in bloom. Their blossoms in midwinter are delightful, especially to your visiting relatives who will think that anything with green leaves is beautiful.

in containers so that when frost threatens in winter, they can be moved indoors or to protected places. When they get too large to move, you can turn the pot on its side and cover up the plant at ground level. This is much easier than trying to wrap it all the way to the top.

Many plants that liked full sun in northern states do much better with a little shade in Florida summers, especially afternoon shade. You can move some of those same container-growing fruit trees or shrubs into place for temporary summer shade. Move smaller plants in containers to shadier spots for the summer.

TERRIBLE SOIL

Whatever soil you have worked with before, Florida's sandy, infertile type will be different. The late nurseryman Robert Perry said, "It holds the plant up. You have to do all the rest." That means fertilizing and watering more often because the soil retains little. In most cases, Florida soil is almost pure sand, though some areas have muck. Near Homestead and in the Keys there are about two inches of fairly good soil on top of Miami oolite, a porous limestone. Growers there must use an auger to drill holes in the rock before they plant trees. Any of these soils can and must be improved constantly with heaps of humus. With help, all of them will produce amazing abundance.

Repeatedly adding organic matter is a good practice for gardeners anywhere. If you've already developed the habit, as I did years ago for Ohio clay, you are ahead. If not, you can develop both the habit and the enriched soil quickly by adding your own and some of your neighborhood's vast production of lawn clippings, leaves, and pine needles. Though I have been gathering mulching materials all my life, it has never been easier than here in Florida. In chapter 5 there are details about my methods.

A BALANCE OF BUGS

You may hear horror stories about Florida's bugs. There are some whoppers, but then there are hardly any flies, so I'd say it all evens out. Your first big palmetto bug may cause your daughters to scream, but even they

will get used to them. The mosquitoes are no worse than those in other places. You can garden here with no poisonous pesticides, or a bare minimum of them, if you wish. I do. We haven't had any spraying done by professionals inside or out in the years we've been here, in spite of people saying we must. But that is largely because I personally prefer the bug I can see to the invisible poison that may permeate everything.

Caution! Insecticides kill friend as well as foe.

We are grateful for the arsenal of insect control measures, especially the increasing number of biological pesticides that do much less or no harm to the environment. I had been using *Bacillus thuringiensis (Bt)* before we moved and have needed it no more often in Florida. I still pick off tomato hornworms if I can find them. For other harmful insects I start with a strong spray of water early enough in the day so it will dry off before nightfall. If that doesn't work I add soap. On very rare occasions I resort to something stronger. Mostly I just outlive the bugs as I did in the North. As with other aspects of gardening here, it's not more difficult, just different.

THE NECESSITY OF NEW METHODS

If you are dreading the idea of learning all new gardening methods from scratch, this book is for you. When I moved from Iowa in June of 1987, I had been writing a weekly garden column for the local paper and a monthly feature for the Des Moines Register for some years. They promised to let me continue as long as I did not say things that would make Iowa readers envious. The first summer it was all I could do to conceal my own envy and depression. I felt like a fraud sending advice to northern gardeners while mint died in my yard.

I also kept thinking that I had been gardening for so many years up North and had still not learned all I wanted to know, so how could I ever live long enough to start all over. But take heart. Trees grow faster in Florida, and determined gardeners grow fast also, in knowledge and experience. Along with some failures, which gardens produce everywhere, there will be some wonderful successes right from the first.

There are several things you can do before, during, or after your move to ease the transplant shock and assure survival and quick new growth.

ATTITUDE ADJUSTMENT

The most important thing to do is to adjust your attitude. Whether you've dreamed and saved for Florida living for years or had it suddenly thrust upon you by your own or your spouse's job, there will be certain misgivings.

During our last spring up north, I planted differently in the old yard. Instead of my usual experimenting, I concentrated on neatness and sure-to-succeed planting, two areas I tend to neglect normally. Instead of a large vegetable garden, I planted flowers in masses of the same color to make a better impression on potential home buyers.

Of course, you want to enjoy whatever you have in the old garden right up until you have to leave it. It would have been much easier to move in late fall because I don't miss winter at all. But the thought of never having lilacs and daffodils again seemed very sad at the time.

There is now a family of hyacinth-flowered lilacs, with varieties like 'Blue Skies', 'Lavender Lady', and 'Silver King'. These are supposed to grow in Florida, but I have tried two with little success. One died immediately, the other after months of sulking.

Several varieties of paperwhite or Tazetta narcissus grow outdoors in the garden in north and central Florida and there are a few large cup and others such as 'Carlton' and 'Ice Follies' that will do fairly well. You can even grow tulips if you give them cold treatment in your refrigerator. I am recently having some success

with certain varieties of the large flowered Clematis. The autumn flowering clematis is a native here.

But don't try too hard to reproduce your northern garden here. I'll never grow green beans and tomatoes here in the quantities I did up north. But having oranges and bananas is well worth the trade. You'll have much more success and satisfaction if you embrace more and more of the new plants you never could grow before. Once you get settled you'll realize that for every plant you give up, there are ten new ones to try.

Be aware, also, that some of the sorrow you naturally feel is transference. I couldn't bear to even think of the grown children and the little grandchildren I was leaving behind. I could express and control the idea of leaving the trees I had planted and nurtured.

The giving up of favorite plants, which was indeed painful, reminds me now of the priest who assured us that we could have anything we wanted once we got to heaven. We were school children at the time and wrote essays about the ball games we would always win and the pets who would never die, and he assured us that we could have all that if we wanted it. "But when you were babies you wanted bottles and rattles, and now you couldn't care less about those things. And that is how it will be in heaven."

One friend we met here greets every morning with "another day in Paradise." That is also how it will be in Florida once you adjust your attitude. You are going to love it so much that most of the things you no longer have

won't matter. Children and grandchildren are obviously an exception. But there is no place people would rather visit, so friends and family you leave behind will not be lost to you.

PACK OR TOSS DECISIONS

What you decide to bring along and what you give away will be greatly influenced by who is paying for the move and what you treasure most. It may be easier to discard garden items that you can cheaply and easily replace.

We have moved twice now at company expense. Both times I got rid of many things that I later wished I'd brought. I discovered that single employees moved larger amounts than our big family, and no one objected. Don't dis-card things you want to keep unless you have to.

PLANTS

Because the horticulture and citrus industries have so much at stake in Florida, there are laws that prohibit people from bringing some plants into the state, unless they have them inspected at their departure point. If you want to bring plants, check with the agricultural extension service in your northern home several weeks before moving and follow their instructions.

Most moving companies will agree to transport plants growing in containers if asked to before the contract is signed, but will give no guarantee of their health or even life upon arrival. So I gave away the vast majority of my houseplants. I kept perhaps six most treasured.

The people who came to pack us kept saying, "None of these will survive. You might as well throw them away." So I gave away as many more as I could get the gathering crowd to take. But there were some, like the orchid, I did want to bring, so we piled them, with all the other forbidden things, inside the car that the movers were transporting. And in spite of a full week in the moving van in 90 degree weather, they came through just fine.

Many plants that grow as houseplants in the North are lovely landscape plants in much of Florida. From the Tampa area south there are fiddle leaf figs, schefflera, rubber plants, pothos, philodendron, and the like growing as trees, large bushes, or ground covers outdoors. Some even become invasive. All of the common ones can be easily replaced, unless they were a Mother's day gift.

SEEDS INSTEAD OF PLANTS

I collected plenty of seed, the ideal moving method for plants because it takes less space and undergoes no inspection. You can

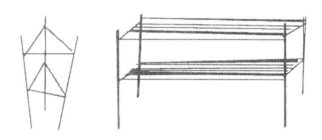

collect and label seed well before the move, and plant it well after. Once you get to Florida, store your seed in the freezer until planting time to protect its viability. Be careful to pack seed and garden supplies in well-marked boxes. I brought a trowel, spade, and hoe in the family's van and was digging for three days before the furniture arrived.

EQUIPMENT

No mover questions the necessity of moving a lawnmower. My garden cart, com-poster, hoses, bird bath, porch swing, garden benches, and statue of St. Francis made the movers mutter. But they were essential and I am glad I insisted. And if we had been paying for the move ourselves rather than through the company, I would still have moved those, even if I had to leave some furniture behind.

By the last morning of our Iowa packing we had reached the basement and yard. The movers spread across the front walk a great assortment of what they outspokenly considered junk. Much of it looked like junk. They wanted me to leave an old set of shelves that held can-ning jars. We had gotten it for free, moved it

from Ohio, and would have to pay over $100 to replace it. The same with my plastic compost bin, which I had washed out well. I finally bowed to the badgering and left my tomato rings behind, and it was 18 months before I found replacement wire that I didn't have to buy by the roll. Bear in mind not only the cost but the difficulty of replacing things in an area where you do not know the sources and where traffic may be too heavy for searching.

I gave away a truckload of canning jars and only brought the ones that were full. A family has to eat until a new garden gets growing. The movers who took us from Ohio to Iowa understood that but the Florida ones fussed a lot. If you get fussy packers or movers, ignore them. However, if you pack some of the smaller and more unsightly things yourself ahead of time and have the boxes sealed and labeled, this will save you explaining what non-gardeners can never understand.

You should pack any special flowerpots and planters, especially large ones, but don't bring more than a token few plain plastic pots. You'll be going to the nursery soon and you'll have more empties than you'll ever need.

Balance the cost of moving gardening equipment against the cost not only of replacing it but also the wear and tear of shopping, searching in vain, doing without, or going to a psychiatrist. You wouldn't throw away your child's favorite toys. Don't throw away all of your own.

ALL THE INFORMATION YOU CAN GET

If you are getting ready to move, you have a thousand other details to worry about, so you may not even think of writing to the extension service for bulletins. Someone else had to give me the idea, but then it took only a few minutes to scratch out a letter to IFAS

NEWSLETTERS AND MAGAZINES OF SPECIAL INTEREST

Florida Gardening Magazine. Florida's Own Home Gardening Magazine. Rich in Florida know-how and illustrated with color photos, this wonderful magazine is available on newsstands and by subscription. One year (6 issues) is $21. Send to P.O. Box 500678, Malabar, FL 32950-9902, or go to www.floridagardening.com.

Florida Market Bulletin. Free on request, this delightful publication includes unusual sources for plants, seeds, and equipment. Ads for pick-your-own farms. Write and request it from Florida Department of Agriculture and Consumer Services, Mayo Building, Tallahassee, FL 32304. www.florida-agriculture.com/fmb/subscribe.htm

The Palmetto. The statewide publication of the Native Plant Society, mailed quarterly. It features information and description of Florida's native plants, some of which are underappreciated and worth more notice. This newsletter goes to all members; dues start at $25 a year ($15 for full-time students). The state office at P.O. Box 6116, Spring Hill, FL 34611 will put you in touch with your nearest branch. Membership brings you the local chapter's monthly or bimonthly newsletter. Guests are welcome at local meetings. www.fnps.org/pages/fnps/join.php

The Cargo Report. Subscribe for $15 per year or view online, free. This newsletter features rare plants and fascinating information.Tropifiora, 3530 Tallevast Road, Sarasota, FL 34234. www.tropiflora.con/creport/.

PLANT SOCIETIES AND GARDEN CLUBS

There are many plant societies and garden clubs that meet in almost every county of Florida. Check with your extension office for a list of names, places, meeting dates and times, and contact people. Within driving distance of Tampa these include two African violet and gesneriad groups, two for orchids, two for bromeliads, one each for fruit, camellias, aroids, ferns, roses, native plants, rare plants, herbs, and more.

All societies welcome visitors to most meetings but you should call and check before you go. I once went a good distance and found they were on a rare field trip that month. If you join these groups, many will send a newsletter that alone will probably be worth the cost of dues even if you never get to a meeting. But meetings are a great place to make new friends, to watch and listen and ask questions for quick learning, to trade or buy plants or win them in a raffle.

Almost every town, even some developments, have at least one general garden club. Large cities have several to many. Some groups are relatively new and some go back generations. Some have members who are active gardeners but some have members for whom gardening is now a spectator activity, and this is okay, too. Find one or more and go to several meetings until you are feel comfortable making a commitment. If you can't find what you want, start your own.

Become a member of the Florida State Horticultural Society or of the botanical garden closest to you. This is a good investment with many benefits that often include a newsletter, a discount on plants purchased and workshop prices, early admittance to special shows and sales, and sometimes a discount at other gardens in the same state or area. The price of membership helps maintain the gardens, so it is an investment for the community and the planet as well.

More details are listed in the Resource section at the end of this book.

(Institute of Food and Agricultural Sciences, University of Florida, Gainesville, Florida 32611). If you have certain areas of special interest, such as trees, vegetables, lawns, flowers, fruit, or landscaping, mention them specifically.

Of course, you don't have much time to sit around reading, but you have to stop packing, or unpacking, and relax sometime. Reading about the exciting new plants you soon can grow and how best to go about it will restore your soul much better than TV will. The day my packet came from Gainesville, I cried with relief to read that I could still have dogwood trees. Iowa was too far north for mine to bloom except after the warmest winters. Tampa is on the southern edge of the dogwood's range, but the first March we were here the dogwoods were more beautiful than any I had seen since I went to college in Pennsylvania. They have not been as lovely since, but I haven't needed them as desperately.

It is because your time and energy are sorely taxed now that this book is small. It will help you bridge the gap. Although I have learned so much, I am still learning, and I still remember when I didn't even know what questions to ask. Florida natives cannot imagine the feelings we newcomers have, or the fears and uncertainties. After you get settled, you can buy or borrow many books on different aspects of Florida gardening,

IFAS can give you the address of your own county extension service. Find that building and stop in now and then to get free informational bulletins and ask the experts your most recent questions. Some extension sites also have demonstration gardens where you can observe or volunteer to help. If you have to live in an apartment for a time, this would be an excellent way to get your hands into a garden, meet other gardeners, and gain experience.

HOPE TO KEEP YOU GOING

There will be times during the first year when you will be frustrated by failures. Bear in mind that this was true during any growing season farther north, though not to such an extent. But then, you never had a better excuse. Also keep in mind that your gardening is now in some confusion, along with, rather than in contrast to, the rest of life. It will all get better.

At first it seemed to me, especially in vegetable growing, that there was as much color and production here as in the North, but it was spread out over twelve instead of, say, seven months, and never appeared to be as great. I still find this true for vegetables since they grow mostly in the cooler, shorter days of winter and only resemble northern production vaguely and briefly in May. Too many people give up because of that.

With trees, shrubs, and many flowers, growth has been so lush from the first that it more than makes up for problems in the vegetable garden. Keep trying and you soon will learn methods and plant varieties that ensure success.

Since later in that first year, my yard has looked as good, then better than any yard I had before. Within five years, I had fruit, herbs, vegetables, and flowers to pick almost every day of the year. And back then the fruit was just beginning. My front yard now looks great and I even have garden open days! In spite of seasonal weediness, the back yard is coming along well. I do not produce the 90 percent of our food that I once did (no cows or pigs here) but I do produce 75 percent of our fruits and vegetables. I know we will never go hungry. My workplace and my private park surround us. I am happy here, and it is a good place for my family.

Crinum lilies in a Florida shade garden.

CHAPTER TWO
FLORIDA LANDSCAPING FEATURES

Florida, along with California, is leading the country into a new appreciation of landscaping. And why not, when we can enjoy outdoor living all year? A nice yard can make a great difference in life if it opens up outdoor living space for you and your family.

Here in Florida, because trees and plants grow year round, or nearly so, new houses can be surrounded with fast-maturing plants that look settled and lush in no time at all.

Many new residents are likely to accept whatever landscaping features come with the house and location they have selected. Yet changes are easily accomplished. Here are features to consider for future landscaping improvements or to keep in mind if you are still house shopping.

SWIMMING POOLS

Many people who come to Florida do not consider buying a house without a pool. But, after seeing houses where the pool seemed to be most of the yard, even though surrounded by lovely shrubbery, we told our realtor not to show us any more houses with pools. About three days later we pulled into the drive of THE house that felt right and she said, "Oh, it has a pool, but it is above ground. You could get rid of it."

We looked anyway. We bought the house. The pool was only a fraction of a large, pie-shaped yard. We loved both the yard and the pool. The above-ground pool seemed safer for us because small children have to learn to climb before they can get in, and by then you can teach them to swim. Our youngest was only four years old at the time.

Our pool had a narrow deck and fence, and we never had any child-in-the-pool scares. We did not have wildlife falling in and drowning. One neighbor with an in-ground pool sometimes found drowned rats. Yuck! Someone on the news recently found a very-much-alive five foot alligator in his pool. Neither had screens surrounding it.

If our pool was not perfectly clean it did not show from the house, and when the time came that we wanted to get rid of it after the children grew up and moved away, we could do

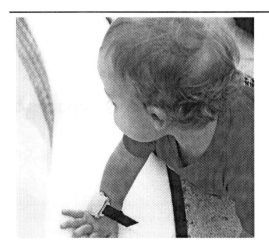

Pool Safety

There are some high-tech pool safety devices that everyone with a home pool should consider. One is a Wireless Wristband Alarm: a combination of wireless signal-outfitted wristbands and a wireless base station receiver that sounds an alarm the instant a young child or pet falls or ventures into water. The base station can be positioned anywhere between 200 and 1500 feet away from the pool (depending on model desired). This can be purchased online at or at retail stores, pool builders and fencing installers throughout North. America.

Another is a Wireless Gate Alarm that warns pool owners the instant a child opens the gate to a pool fence without adult assistance as well as if the pool fence gate fails to latch closed within 11 seconds of an adult entry (great feature for pet owners as well). A base station located as far as 200 feet away from a pool warns the adult(s) to come immediately to the pool area. The Safety Turtle Wireless Gate Alarm comes with an adult bypass switch which attaches near the gate latch so that an adult can enter without setting off the alarm. There are also pool covers with alarms attached.

so easily. In the beginning, it added much less to the price of the house.

Many yards with in-ground pools still have plenty of room for growing plants in other sections, and many of the best gardeners I know have pools.

Any kind of pool is often a lovely focal point for the house and yard, visible from the front door and most of the rooms. It certainly adds an air of luxury, but also quite a bit of upkeep. By the way, insist that your swimming pool be sparkling clean and swimmable on your move-in day. Ours wasn't and we were sadly surprised at how expensive corrective treatment was, and what a delay in swimming the strong chemicals could cause. It is hard enough to learn pool maintenance procedures without starting with green water.

Many Florida people live happily without pools. There are always neighbors who will share and community facilities, too.

SCREENED-IN POOLS.

Many Floridians consider screened pool enclosures necessary to keep leaves and debris out of the pool, and to keep bugs and other unwanted creatures out of the patio area. This has obvious advantages, but also some disadvantages to consider. The screen, especially on top, is prone to damage and difficult to repair. If you live near pine trees, the needles will stick into the screening and give it a furry look. Clean it out by spraying with the hose at high pressure.

Screening cuts the sunlight falling on the pool area. The added shade shortens the swimming season somewhat, though its good for growing plants under. We've had neighbors come use our pool because it was warmer than their screened pools. Most native or settled Floridians only swim in their pools from about May to September. Pools are costly to heat and, as a rule, only hotel or community pools do so. I swam in our unheated pool in every month, but one must be set for fast-moving exercise (or crazy) to follow my example.

PLANTING AROUND YOUR POOL

There are several requirements for plants surrounding the pool area. They must not be prickly, spiny, or thorny. These would hurt bare feet or skin. They should not be attractive to bees and wasps. They must be able to survive a certain amount of splashing. And they should be as litter-free as possible with whatever they drop being too large to get into the pool's filter.

The best thing I ever planted was the moonflower vine on the deck railing. I took to swimming in the evenings when I could watch the huge fragrant white flowers open. They don't pop open all at once, but over the time of a twenty minute swim, many go gradually from bud to full flower.

GARDEN POOLS

Fishponds, water gardens, clear reflecting pools, fountains with trickling water: all were once luxuries beyond the budget and knowledge of the average homeowner. With modern plastics, today we can put in a pool or fountain in one or two weekends at reasonable cost. A few evenings' study of water garden catalogs will tell you all you need to know. Maintenance is easy, and winter freezing is not much of a problem. Check building codes and consider safety. Locate your pool in the sun if you want water lilies. Check into solar powered pool pumps to keep the water circulating.

HOT TUBS

Hot tubs are popular in Florida either as part of the pool, or as a separate unit, instead of

Plants for Surrounding a Swimming Pool

The following are some that work best, look good, and cause few problems. N, C, and S indicate that the plant grows in northern, central, or southern Florida.

Trees

Bananas, edible (*Musa acuminata*) CS

Bananas, ornamental (*Musa coccinea, M. ornata*) CS

Palms, all kinds that do not grow too tall for you to reach for pruning

Vines

Jasmine (*Jasiminum* species) NCS

Jasmine, Confederate (*Trachelospermum jasminoides*) NCS

Grape ivy (*Cissus rhombifolia*) S

Herald's trumpet (*Beaumontia grandiflora*) CS

Marine ivy (*Cissus incisa*) NCS

Moonflowers (*Ipomoea alata*) CS annual N

Perennials

Adams needle (*Yucca filamentosa*) NCS

Butterfly weeds (*Asclepias* species) NCS

Calliopsis (*Coreopsis lanceolata*) NCS

Canna (*Canna* X *generalis*) NCS

Cigar plant (*Cuphea micropetala*) NCS

Fernleaf yarrow (*Achillea filipendulina*) NC

Gaura (*Gaura lindheimeri*) NC

Goldenrod (*Solidago* species) NCS

Hardy ageratum (*Eupatorium coelestinum*) NCS

Lantana, old fashioned types (*Lantana camara*) NCS

Mexican petunia (*Ruellia Brittoniana*) CS

Powis Castle (*Artemisia* 'Powis Castle') NCS

Purple coneflower (*Echinacea purpurea*) NCS

Rudbeckia Goldsturm (*Rudbeckia fulgida* 'Goldsturm') NC

Rudbeckia (*Rudbeckia maxima*) NCS

Sedum (*Sedum* species) NCS

Silver King artemisia (*Artemisia ludoviciana*) NC

Stokes aster (*Stokesia laevis*) NCS

Shrubs

Australian tree fern (*Sphaeropteris cooperi*) CS

Camellia (*Camellia* species) NC

Dracaena (*Dracaena* species) CS

Fatsia (*Fatsia japonica*) NCS

Fiddle leaf fig (*Ficus lyrata*) CS

Holly, Burford *(Ilex cornuta rotunda),* NCS

Indian hawthorn (*Rhaphiolepis indica*) NCS

Jasmine (*Jasiminum* species) NCS

Jasmine, Confederate (*Trachelospermum jasminoides*) NCS

Juniperus (*Juniperus* species) NC

Lantana (*Lantana* species) NCS

Orchids (*Cattleya* species, *Dendrobium* species) CS

Pittosporum (*Pittosporum tobira* 'Wheeler's Dwarf') NCS

Roses (*Rosa* species) NCS

Schefflera (*Schefflera arboricola*) CS

Spanish bayonet (*Yucca* species) NCS

Thryallis (*Galphimia glauca*) CS

Ti plant (*Cordyline terminalis*) CS

Viburnum (*Viburnum* species) NCS

hibiscus

or in addition to the pool. The hot tub alone is less expensive and easier to install and fit into the landscape. You can use it for a longer season than you would a pool because the water is heated. It doesn't offer the exercise that a pool does, but it is even better for relaxation and also for therapy for many physical aches and pains like a bad back. Florida hot tubs are often placed inside the screened-in patio or porch area to protect twilight and nighttime soakers from mosquitoes.

BIRDBATHS AND FEEDERS

Though Florida birds do not depend on people for winter help as they do in the North, birdbaths and feeders are still attractive garden features that will pay dividends, bringing you interesting winged visitors who will help with bug control. Put these where you can watch the birds use them. Keep them clean and full, and you probably will see both familiar and unfamiliar species such as blue jay, meadowlark, cardinal, swallow, ibis, martin, and mockingbird. Keep a bird book handy for identification.

DECKS, PATIOS, SCREENED-IN PORCHES, AND SUNSHADES

Paved or screened outdoor living areas are common here. Some houses have one or more of each type.

Decks are great for uneven yards or for houses that are above ground level. The deck on its stilts can be level with the floor of your home. You can build a deck into open air and have outdoor living without steps. You can also build it under the branches and around the trunks of trees for a natural roof and privacy without any harm to the tree. You can build storage areas underneath some decks. Florida decks often extend over water and combine with a pier.

A patio, screened or unscreened, may be more appropriate for a level area. It can be paved with brick, stone, tile, or concrete.

A screened-in porch or Florida room is ideal because it is almost another room of the house for many months of the year. It gives the best of both outdoor and indoor living. We have

one and eat there often from April until October or later. It is absolutely private. It is great to sit where you can see out but not be seen by neighbors or reached by bugs. I keep plants on our screened porch in winter to keep them from freezing. Curtains of Virginia creeper and other vines shaded it in summer until there was enough shade from trees and shrubs to make the vines unnecessary.

Some screened-in rooms have windows as well as screens and are useful for all but the coldest periods, especially if they are on the south side, receiving heat from the sun. Even during the coldest times, plants on such a porch will seldom freeze.

Some people prefer front porches from which they can hail their neighbors and visit with passersby. Even if you are not so sociable, front yard structures can be useful. Early on we built an arbor over the area around our front door and the bay window of the living room. Carefully selected deciduous vines and evergreen vines (grape, *Petrea* or queen's wreath, pipe vine for butterflies) then shaded the front room from the intense summer sun, but would let in some sun in winter. We hung that porch swing form Iowa to provide a place to sit with our Teresa while she waited for the school bus, and for the older girls to sit and say good-night to their dates, and for me to set sacks of groceries while I unlocked the door.

Muscadine grapes grow well here and are delicious.

16

The swing wore out, was followed by a bench, and the bench was replaced with shelves for my most treasured plants, but from the beginning and over the years that overhead sunshade made a big difference in air conditioning costs and indoor as well as outdoor comfort. It also gives us a feeling of privacy.

OUTDOOR ROOMS

Arranging spaces for outdoor living will give you outdoor rooms. No one understands their value and importance more than the parents of young children, for they add space to the home and provide healthy, safe play areas. Outdoor rooms are great for cooking and entertaining. Even a small yard can have several outdoor rooms that will increase the usefulness of both house and garden and offer delights not possible indoors alone.

Try to make outdoor rooms an extension of indoor rooms: a dining patio or deck should have easy access to the kitchen; an area for entertaining can be connected by French doors to the living or family room, and there can be a quiet balcony outside a bedroom. Consider the sun, shade, and privacy created when you select and place your plants.

Outdoor rooms need not be as well defined as indoor ones, but they need some of the same amenities: something nice to look at, maybe walls, trellises, or hedges for a sense of enclosure, and a place to sit or have a picnic.

As a first consideration, they need a floor, which can be grass, mulch, or a solid, preferably porous surface such as gravel, flagstone, or modern pavers that permit water to drain through. Then comes seating. If your outdoor room consists only of a bench, put mulch under

it for convenience. A bench on the grass is going to be in the way every time you mow.

For most of us, outdoor rooms are fairly simple and inexpensive. Eating, reading, and resting areas can be achieved with seating, garden art, and partial divisions. You might need to work on areas such as the entranceway, the parking area, the garden work area, the service area (garbage cans, dog runs, clothesline), the herb garden, etc. Use your imagination. Give names and themes to the various parts of your own garden, and good ideas will evolve.

It is possible to add an overhead covering, a wall or partial wall, or other structural elements to turn a simple patio into a gazebo, a pavilion, or a pool house with dressing rooms. This can often be done with much less cost and almost as much reward as building a conventional room addition. Be sure to get any permits and professional help you need and to check with local building codes

The garden of Sue Powers, Hillsborough County Master Gardener, is only a quarter of an acre, but there are nine different outdoor sitting areas, not counting the front porch or the breezeway, all of which are full of plants and have lovely views. One is a trellised area near the kitchen where 50 people fit comfortably in the shade when the Camellia Society has their annual potluck luncheon. She even provides a fan there on hot days or a fire nearby on cold ones. When she had the annual graduation and Christmas party for the county's Master Gardeners, they set tables onto the largest bit of lawn and seated nearly a hundred people.

She tells a great story. Years ago, her parents' family property contained several houses, and when Sue found herself living with a big young family in one of the smallest houses while her parents finally were alone in a much larger house, she suggested they exchange. "What! And leave my garden," said her mother. So instead of moving the families, they moved the houses and stayed with their own gardens.

A MIRROR?

Among my neighbors, one couple with a long, narrow yard has a mirror hanging on one wall of the lath around their patio. It expands

Sit down in the shade and make yourself comfortable!

their view to include much of the yard that they could not see from their chairs otherwise. The mirror is so filled with the reflection of foliage that it blends right in.

GARAGES AND CARPORT

"We'll have to find a house with a garage whose door does not face the street," I told David when we were house hunting. We hadn't seen or heard of any basements, so I could imagine what my garage would look like with the door open. Since then I have known many people who could never put their cars in their garage because it had become their storage area. Only a few people keep garages neat enough to dare expose them to public view.

We found a house whose garage had been replaced by two rooms: a large study and a storage area. A carport had been added outside.

Carports are great because they hold a bicycle or two, but not enough junk to shame a person. They keep the rain and sun off your car and off you on your comings and goings. They shade the adjoining room and therefore save on

air conditioning. Our neighbors were so impressed with the convenience of ours that they built a carport in addition to their garage. Ours is open, but theirs has decorative lattice on the sides. This might be restraining when loading or unloading, but it is very pretty.

PRIVACY, HEDGES, AND FENCES

Our house came with a privacy fence surrounding the entire back yard. If it had not, I might have hesitated to spend the money to install one. But I will not hesitate for a moment to say the privacy was and is wonderful. From the first, I could go out in my nightgown to feed the rabbits. I could make garden mistakes and no one could see. I could swim without anyone seeing me in my bathing suit. Well, a few houses did look over the fence, but I trust they found us too dull for their entertainment. By now the trees have grown up and our privacy is complete. But we still had the fence replaced when that became necessary.

There are some disadvantages of fencing: cost for one. Consider it as property improvement. Upkeep is minimal until it starts to fall down. At that point we propped ours up until we could arrange for replacement. Ours is natural wood. Check out the alternatives. There are vinyl fences now that last indefinitely. There are others made from recycled plastics. They cost much more but might be worth it.

There was always a large gate on the widest side of our privacy fence between the front and back yard. When we replaced the last of the old privacy fence, we put in a large, wide gate with a wheel so that we can close it easily. The old gate with two narrow sections wore out from being moved so frequently. This one is holding up much better.

We also had a smaller gate, just wide enough for a wheelbarrow, put in on the other side of the house, so now I and my visitors can make a complete circle. This is a great improvement. There is a latch on the front side and a string through a hole on the back side so I can open and close it from either side.

I consider privacy the number one requirement for making a yard into an outdoor living space. It can be achieved instantly and at some expense with a fence or screen around the yard, around part of it, or only as a privacy screen between your own and a neighbor's patio or window. Fences do not seem unfriendly in Florida, where they are common. A fence gives a measure of privacy to the families on both sides.

A fence does mean that you may never meet neighbors in back that you might otherwise enjoy. In some cases, a partial fence or privacy screen may be preferable. It will also be less

A succulent wreath is easy to maintain.

expensive. And that way the kids can still play a ballgame that covers more than one yard.

Plants too can provide privacy. Well chosen and situated shrubs, trees, or planter boxes are less expensive and can seem more friendly than fences. The plantings grow to maturity very quickly in Florida. Shrubs can grow six feet tall in only one year. In places where width is unwanted, select narrow or columnar ones.

Most people don't mind at all if the neighbors see them working, but would rather rest in some seclusion. So a green screen of shrubbery that is only chair height is still comforting. A raised bed or row of pots full of impatiens can do the job in color.

Many people plant formal hedges around their yards, and they are certainly effective for privacy. But constant clipping can be a hard chore. One neighbor's son gave his mother a hedge clipping for her birthday and worked for three days to get the job done. And in six months it needed trimming again. I would rather spend that time on other gardening chores. Be aware of the work you are getting yourself into if you choose to plant anything that needs constant trimming.

FOUNDATION PLANTINGS

If you are building a home or buying one before the building is complete, pay close attention to whatever standard planting the builder will include. In some case you have a choice of plans and plants. If you have no such choices, you can still ask that certain parts of their standard package be omitted such as sod where you know youll have to remove it for other plantings, trees or tall shrubs that will block rather than frame your best views, or shrubs under windows or near walkways that will need constant pruning or clipping to stay in bounds.

We had to clip the pittosporum that came with our house at least twice a year to keep it from covering the windows and the front door. With such pruning it was attractive, but I would rather have something that kept in bounds naturally, bloomed, or bore fruit. When we had our first visit from the tree trimmers, taking the shubs out and hauling them away was a job they could do quickly at little extra cost. For us it would have been difficult and time consuming.

Styles have changed, and foundation plantings no longer have to be moustaches all around a house. They can include small trees, open areas, edible plants, flower gardens, a bench or birdbath under a window, a basketball court by the garage, and almost anything else, as long as it harmonizes with the landscape, the house, and the people who live there.

TURF

For many decades, grass has been used as a cover-up for any spot nothing else claimed. No more. Common sense, shortages of energy (both human and fossil), and water shortages are turning grass into a design element instead. There is more about this in the lawn chapter. My spouse said Id better cut our lawn down to size before all our children got too old to mow it. I used tons of mulch material collected in the neighborhood to surround trees, make new beds, and remove turf from areas for future plantings.

We did have a lawn man for a few years after the children had all grown, but eventually the lawn shrank until we could mow it in 15 minutes so we took over the chore. I'm now replacing that last little bit with ground cover.

The rest is now trees, shrubs, flowers, fruit, herbs, and vegetables in casual beds with paths between. Be sure to make your paths at least wide enough for a wheelbarrow and remember that the plants on the edges are going to be constantly growing, so set them back accordingly. I use mulch for most of the paths, low groundcovers such as ornamental peanuts for some. I also realize now, in some cases too late, that some areas of very low groundcovers or just mulch are needed to set off the other plantings and prevent the jungle look.

FRONT YARDS

At one time, front yards were considered more formal and public than back and side areas. They were mown and groomed more for show than for enjoyment. That is no longer necessarily so. If the front yard has the best microclimate for fruit, go ahead and plant your fruit there instead of using the space for the same ornamentals that everyone else on the block is using. Just bear in mind that some fruit is going to drop. Place fruit where such drop can be mulch rather than mess. Even flower petals are best kept from walks or patios where they can get slippery.

Dooryards and entryways are spots that people see first and most often, so my most pampered flower garden borders the front walk. Why should flowers all be in the back where they don't show? They look great in Florida most or all of the year.

Service areas are best kept out of sight. Some subdivisions require clotheslines and vegetable gardens to be hidden from the street, others forbid them outright. Check neighborhood association rules before you buy, if possible. Some are reasonable but some are ridiculous. I've heard of one that forbids any citrus trees at all; perhaps they are worried that dropped fruit might look messy. I would not live in such a place, though I do believe in cleaning up messy dropped fruit. We use most of ours before it gets a chance to hit the ground.

Vegetables can be cleverly mixed in with flowers and shrubs, or grown in containers, so that they are too attractive for anyone to notice or complain about.

Our one big shade tree was on the border of our front and side yard, so I immediately started a shade garden beneath its branches on the front side of the fence. It has looked pretty good from the first, and I am proud of it. On the back side of the fence that separates our front and back yards were, for a time, the rabbit cages, a shed, pots and potting soil, and an "intensive care unit" for plants I was nursing along from seeds and cuttings. It was not as lovely. But it was private, and I had a bench in it, surrounded by ferns, where my visiting friend sat every morning to drink her coffee. She is the kind of friend who thinks rabbit cages are interesting. The neighbor children thought the rabbits smelled, but they seldom did: never did to people used to Iowa hog farms.

The rabbits and that shed are long gone and I'm gradually replacing the wild ferns with more interesting shade loving plants.

My intensive care area now hides beneath the branches of a huge loquat tree beside the carport where it is hardly visible but very handy. I can even work there at night if I wish and I don't forget anything because I am reminded every time we use the car.

DRIVEWAYS AND PARKING AREAS

These service areas are often a necessary part of the front yard. Be sure to keep plantings low near the road or street so as not to obstruct the view of cars entering or leaving. Make driveways wide. If there is room, a circular drive will eliminate the need for backing into traffic. So will an L- or T -shaped turnaround area that can double as a play area or entry way or a place to park extra cars (especially while your children are teens). If you do not want to have all of this in hard surface, consider an area of bark or woodchip mulch for turning around or parking extra cars out of the way. The only disadvantage to such mulch is that parts may stick to shoes and be tracked into the house unless there is an area of grass or porous paving in between where it can drop off before you reach the door.

The paved road and the blacktop driveway have come to be considered signs of civilization, but there are more ecological choices we can make in our home landscapes. For several decades there have been open blocks or what looks like concrete lattice instead of solid concrete. With these the water can seep through and go back to the aquifer where nature recycles for free rather than into the storm sewers where man recycles half as well at great expense. Yet you still have a firm paving material for automobiles.

One could use these rain-friendly materials on the entire driveway or on parts. Many people prefer the look over asphalt. You can put grass or gravel in the openings. When grass is used, that is a lot prettier and cooler and blends in with the environment and allows a house or garden to be more visually dominant than the driveway.

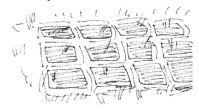

GARDEN PATHS AND WALKWAYS

Paths provide access that opens up a yard. Have you ever watched a small child try walking on grass after a long winter of learning to walk on solid floors? That soft, oddly textured, sometimes dewy surface goes against the grain. Our feet like to follow a path with a predictable surface and direction.

Hard paving, cement, brick, or stone, usually leads people from the street or sidewalk to your front door or from the parking space to the back entrance. Other paths around the rest of the yard also lead to these areas. Side paths can be stepping stones, or mulch of pine needles, pebbles, bark chips, or wood chips, or anything else that will keep the feet dry and set out the direction.

Part of adjusting to a new garden involves planting certain plants that you want to see or pick often, in places where you can reach them easily. Parts of the garden that require early morning access should have paths with a solid or at least a mulched surface. Grass walkways may suffice for getting to distant areas after the dew dries off.

Some portions of most yards are doomed to neglect by their distance from or lack of connection with anything important. When we no longer had our pool on an automatic timer, someone had to walk to the pump morning and night to plug in or unplug the motor. Any plant along this well-traveled path got attention.

Plants out by a back shed may only be noticed when someone gets out the lawnmower. Since that was usually an otherwise non-gardening teenager or Dad in our case, those plants still got little attention. Any plant near the back or front door or the mailbox is sure of constant notice and care from me!

The principles of xeriscaping (gardening with a minimum of water waste) come into play here. Plants that need frequent watering should be grouped together as near where the hose turns on as possible. Plants that need only occasional watering can be at the far reaches of the hose. Those that are native and will survive on natural rainfall can go as far out as you like. But even those will need water for several weeks or months when they are newly planted.

Paths should flow with the natural route of traffic. Curves and crossways should have a purpose. If a path meanders around without a good reason, just watch how children or even your own feet will make a new one to get more directly where you want to go. If foot traffic wears paths in your lawn, add pavers where the need for it has been so clearly shown.

Plantings and walls near walkways should be low and far enough from the walk that they do not crowd it. Make paths wide enough for carrying groceries, wheeling a garden cart, or whatever use you foresee for it in the future.

MULCHING MATERIALS

Weed growth in Florida is no more insidious than in any other place I've gardened. But the grasses are especially tough and rampant. And vines can quickly get out of hand. I often pull vine weeds in late summer that are 20 feet long and they can cover your whole yard. Some of them, such as passionflowers and black-eyed Susan vines, have beautiful flowers but the first threatened to cover our pool and the latter once did cover my whole tall banana patch like Kudzu. Be ruthless to keep them in check. And be glad that you can pull vines standing up, not stooping over.

On his first visit from Iowa, our son Mike (who has long since moved nearby) laid out a path to the pool with paving blocks set in a bed of sand. Within a year, the path was entirely lost in encroaching grass. David dug out the blocks, removed the weeds and grass from the area, put black woven mulching cloth underneath the sand and black plastic edging along the sides, and reset the paving stones. David used a little Round-Up™ along the sides as needed and it stayed clear for a long time.

He hasn't done that lately and I don't mind edging once a year and pulling a few weeds out from between the stones. I've also learned that there are different grades of mulching cloth. Some last a few months and that worked to kill the invasive wedelia I wanted to eradicate. I was glad enough after that to be able to easily dig through and plant other, better behaved plants. The heaviest barrier cloth will cost a bit more, but it will keep plants from growing through for years and this is what you want for paths and patios where you never intend to plant anything in the ground. A few weeds will still root in the debris that collects above the cloth, but these will be shallow rooted and pull out easily.

The previous owners of our house put in a sandbox/ play area larger than the living room, and surrounded it with railroad ties. We wish they had used mulching cloth under the sand, because grass grew right through, and we could never keep it clear. The neighbors have a similar problem in a bark-mulched parking area in front of their house. It looks nice, but the weeds are constantly creeping through. Mulching cloth would prevent most of these weeds.

When we first moved to Florida, I was thrilled to collect dozens of bags of grass clippings, pine needles, and leaves set out for trash collection. Since then mulching mowers have largely eliminated the supply of grass clipping through the summer months. This is good for lawns. But it means I have to get extra leaves during the fall and winter. See chapter 5 for details. If I keep telling people they are throwing away their treasure, this source will disappear, too, but already we are producing a good amount of mulch with our own falling leaves and pulled weeds and the soil has greatly improved.

In most areas there are landfills where yard waste is composted and sold to homeowners at a very reasonable price. Many places will load it for you if you have or can borrow a truck. The last batch I got was so well composted it could be added to potting soil and planting holes as well as used for mulch. Call your landfill or local government for details. To collect municipal compost we have to take along a record of our latest tax payment and something to prove our address.

Tree trimmers have to pay to dump their wood chips at the local landfill and will often be glad to dump them closer. These can be coarse, but they break down quickly. I've known great gardeners to turn their entire yard into a garden quickly with these. I got several truckloads free and always felt rich when I had

Mulch Materials

Kind	Availability	Comments
leaves	All you can carry home, already bagged, from December through March.	Leaves work well. Add lime if you worry about soil getting too acid though it is not likely. Pulverize with lawn mower for faster decomposition and neatness.
newspapers	Free, made from wood.	Overlap thin sections of paper and cover them with more attractive mulches. They break down quickly and improve the soil.
black plastic	Inexpensive	Can be messy and bad for environment.
mulching cloth	Worth the price.	Various grades for various uses
grass clippings	Bag your own.	Mulching mowers have made these rare.
pine needles	Free where pine trees abound or purchase them by the bale.	Attractive and useful but can be slippery when wet. Do not use on paths.
compost, partly decomposed	Free or low-priced at many landfills.	Adds nutrients and improves soil, can be added to potting mix and planting holes.
wood chips	Available from tree trimmers and stump grinders.	Some coarse, some fine. Can deplete nitrogen in soil. Add N if plants indicate need by yellowing or poor growth.
other mulches	Can be purchased.	Some are very attractive, some require raking or blowing away leaves constantly.
old carpets	Free from rug companies	One man used these upside down on his 40 acres of fruit. In my yard, though, weeds grew over the carpet. Also I could not plant anything through it without cutting it.

Mulches to Avoid

Red mulch: this is used extensively. I think it looks artificial. It might look better in the panhandle where the soil is red or in Georgia, but in most of Florida it stands out, not what you want mulch to do. Wae Nelson, publisher of *Florida Gardening Magazine*, says it's bad for the environment.

Rubber mulch comes in many colors so it can blend in. It is almost permanent, though it adds little humus to the soil. It makes use of used tires that are otherwise a problem. But Wae Nelson says that nothing will live in it, no bugs or mice, so how can it be good for plants. It seems old tires were used to make an artificial reef in the ocean years ago and everything in that part of the ocean died. So I would advise using rubber mulch only on paths you are sure you will not want to move or ground where you **never** want anything to grow.

I have long discouraged gardeners from buying **cypress mulch**. If you already have some, use it because there is nothing wrong with it as mulch, but it depletes a natural resource that we should be protecting. Use eucalyptus if you are buying mulch. It is treated to do no harm and uses the eucalyptus trees we need to get rid of.

a woodchip pile. When our children were small they loved to play there and never seemed to get splinters. Once I made the mistake of having the chips unloaded where I only realized later that the load blocked the gate.

Resist any heavy charges for what they should give you for free, but it is nice to give the drivers a tip. Some neighborhoods get a truckload and share it, in which case it disappears quickly and is not in anyone's way for more than a few days.

LIGHTS FOR OUTDOOR LIVING

Garden lighting is no longer a new trend but a pleasant reality. Both low-voltage systems and solar lights are inexpensive to buy and use, and easy enough for even an unhandy person to install. With them, you can work, eat, entertain, or walk in the yard and garden through the long dark evenings of winter as well as the twilight ones of summer. Lights allow you to accent the good points of a garden or dramatize architectural features. Less attractive parts of the yard add mystery by being in the shadow. Even if the weather is bad and no one goes out, lighted views or pool lights shining beyond the large windows or glass doors give added elegance.

When I put in my first set of low voltage lights, (I suggest using a kit for starters), it was more fun than Christmas. Son Tom helped me figure out how one set of six tier and four floodlights could light three front gardens.

They lasted for several years while I moved them as far as their wires would allow to keep them from being lost in the foliage. I weeded carefully around the wires.

Please note that the wires of outdoor lights must always be grounded, and the fixtures should be rated as "water-resistant/UL approved for outdoor use." Also remember that lights rated for indoor use should never be used outdoors. Whatever other lights you do or do not have, bear in mind that a bright light on your house number could be important in an emergency.

Solar lights have no cabling to worry about and can be freely moved about around the garden as your plants grow and plans change. They automatically turn off during the day and turn on at night and use the sun for energy, thereby burning no fossil fuels. Solar lighting can be set in places that, up until now, were not practical or even possible to light.

But they must have several hours of direct sunlight during the day to give off a soft diffused light at night, so they must be carefully placed in a mostly shady garden such as mine has become. Still there are spots along the driveway, walks, and path where there is enough sunlight for much of the year.

There are solar light fixtures for posts, columns, walls, flood, security, and more as well as for placing throughout the best parts of the garden. Some have handblown glass globes. The taller the solar fixtures stand above the foliage, the more sunlight they will get. With optimum sun, the best of them can now be expected to give 12 hours of light per night with the output of a 20 watt bulb. This is very low if you were planning to read beside them, but surprisingly bright in an otherwise dark landscape. The diffused light seems more natural in the garden and does not attract insects as brighter lights do.

STORAGE AREAS

Garden sheds can be as attractive as they are handy. They are almost a necessity if you don't have a storage place in the house or garage for at least a lawn mower, wheelbarrow, tomato cages, and/or a few other bulky garden tools. They do not need to be large in most cases. Situate them for convenience, add racks and hanging space, shelves, a potting bench, and a place for pot and garden product storage.

Lath siding, windowboxes, or other design features that harmonize with the house and landscape help them blend in. One of the sheds we inherited lacked a door. To screen the unattractive entrance, we put up a section of crisscross lath to support a flowering vine several feet in front of the open doorway.

Ours are the standard metal kind you can buy at many garden and home improvement stores. But I have seen some that are custom made and charming focal point in the garden. A

sound foundation is essential or else set them up on blocks. The lack of blocks caused the shed closest to our house to rot away while two others are still in good shape twenty years later. The greatest problem with storage areas is that we tend to store things we'll really never need and before we know it the place is too full to store the things we do need. Clean out ruthlessly at least once a year.

POTTING AREAS

If you garden as I do, you'll spend a good deal of your time making cuttings and potting, repotting, and grooming plants. This time will be even more pleasant and productive if you have a well organized potting area in a handy location and at a height that will save unnecessary backache. Shade is especially important in Florida not only for the gardener but for the plants at their time of intensive care. Nearness to water is also important, but in this case it can be a faucet or a rain barrel.

I do my potting on the side of the carport so I don't have to drag bags of soil very far. One lady I met made portable potting places by putting a broad board across her wheelbarrow, the soil mix in the bottom, and the pots on top of that. So inspired, I put the top of a broken table across the top of a garbage can for my first potting bench. David offered to buy me a beautiful one that someone had made and was selling at our church festival. I was so tempted I started noticing every potting bench I saw. You can buy plastic ones or wooden ones at many places. One lady kept hers in her screened-in Florida room with arm chairs and a TV surrounding it, but I am not that neat about my potting.

I stuck with my board until we replaced the fence. Then David had built a long potting table with shelves above and room below for pots and potting soil and it is wonderful.

If you can't lift those 40 pound bags of potting soil or cow manure easily, some places (Home Depot) do have these in 25 pound bags. That is my load limit lately. Now I get the store person to stack the 40-pound bags on the back seat and tip him gladly. At home I can pull the bags over and empty them halfway into a bucket. Rather than risk pain and medical expenses, you can have these things delivered.

RAIN BARRELS

Nothing saves a gardener so much work and gives such a feeling of assurance as does a rain barrel. Having one, or seven, is handy beyond belief. They allow you to conserve water for the planet and always have rain water handy for your own newly set and thirsty plants.

Most Florida county extension offices now offer rain barrel workshops where you learn how to assemble and use them to the best advantage and come home with your own barrel.

Inexpensive barrels are easy to find. There are other sources listed in phone books under Barrels & Drums. What you want to look for in a drum depends on how and where you are going to use it. You want one that has been used for food, not chemicals, so there will be no worry about residue.

The Extension Office has directions on how to lead your downspout drain right into a hole you cut-to-size in the lid and how to install a spigot so the water can be used through a hose or an irrigation system. You can also connect several barrels together to save more water.

Since my rain barrels sit open except for a screen cover on top and I dip out the water, the width of the top is important. My best ones let me dip any bucket or sprinkling can without crowding. The dipping is not that difficult and is healthier than lifting weights for exercise.

Color of the barrels may be a concern. I thought they would stand out like eyesores.

Actually, they blend in well among the plants. If you have fragrant plants around them, the dipping is all the more enjoyable. I also tend to plant the thirstiest plants near the barrels. You can paint your barrel, even with lovely scenes, if you wish.

Mosquitoes. Mosquitoes are most people's main concern. With lids left on, you have no worry about them. Even at the worst, I have found no more mosquito bites with than without the barrels, especially if you use the water often and thus pour out any larvae that are floating on top.

But there are several ways to be sure you have NO mosquitoes. Cover open tops with two layers of porch screening. This also keeps out debris.

Adding a small amount of vegetable oil makes a film over the top that stops the bugs, but won't harm the plants you are watering. It will just shine them up a bit. You can also add a tablespoon or less of liquid dish detergent. Mosquito Dunks also do the job. These round, hard bricks of *Bacillus thuringiensis* are a safe, natural biological control that kills hatching larvae. You can find them in larger garden centers and mail order catalogs.

Fish-in-the-barrel is another mosquito control. I started with guppies from a friend's pond but they soon disappeared. A piece of wood floating on the water to give frogs a landing for going and coming will encourage them to lay their eggs in your barrel and the tadpoles will keep the water and the barrel clean.

My most delightful mosquito control involves goldfish. If you feed them, they soon come to the top at the sound of your voice. But they don't really need feeding, I found, when one survived in a barrel I thought was empty of fish for months before I saw him again. Do not leave fish food outdoors because raccoons will carry it away.

The fish seem to go to the bottom during rainstorms and when I am dipping out. Only once in all these years have I found one in the dipping bucket, and being gold, he was easy to

see and return. I've never found evidence of their washing over the rim, even when I forgot to put the screening back on for a day.

Comet goldfish are the best because of the way they breathe. "Feeding size" ones cost as little as 15 cents each. Now and then some die for me, usually after much runoff of debris from the roof, but two dollars worth restores my supply for all barrels.

When you first bring them home, let the bag float for 15 minutes or more so that they can adjust to the water temperature. Don't add anything to the barrel that might harm the fish. When you use the water, always leave enough for the fish, about a third of the barrel.

Spouting that came with our house proved, after many years, to be a problem as leaves packed down and caused rotting of the surrounding wood, no matter how often we cleaned them out. So we removed most of the spouting, leaving only a bit over the doors to prevent drenching people and a bit around the downspouts to fill the barrels. This has left me with more places to put buckets for additional collection, plain old 5-gallon buckets lined up under the eaves. I begin to use this water within a few days of a rain for container and newly set plants. I also add fertilizers, manure, or soil activators to these for watering certain plants that need extra help or for the heavy drinkers like the roses. And I keep one the large barrels without fish for manure tea.

There are other ways to use the rain barrels as well. The rain water is great for washing dirt off hands and vegetables before going inside to wash under the tap. It gives quick relief to ant bites. I stick bags of cuttings over the edge to keep them fresh, or use the water to rinse the kitchen compost bucket after I empty it on the compost pile. You can use the water in it to wash tools or flush toilets if your water is ever cut off. Master Gardener Patty Bruda uses the chlorine-free water to top off her in-ground fish pond.

Rain barrels will fill up in a 10 to 15 minute shower. Master Gardener Cindy Paulhus has hers hooked up to their air conditioner and

it fills up once a week, even when it doesn't rain. Only in the worst drought do the barrels ever go dry and then you can fill them from the hose if you want.

GREENHOUSES

I have had a weekly garden column in our local Brandon News since 1993 and have interviewed hundreds of gardeners. I find that most people in Florida get along very well without a greenhouse. Orchid enthusiasts are one of the exceptions. They need one for winter, and one of my friends who downsized from a country home to a neighborhood with a rule against greenhouses, found a way to get around that. She designed and her husband built her what looks like a lovely arbor. Actually it has a fiberglass roof and rolls of plastic that come down in the dead of winter to make a snug small greenhouse that keeps the orchids safe and the neighborhood association happy.

Another orchid grower had a greenhouse built into the side of her house that was so like another room that they ate there most of the year surrounded by the blooming orchids.

There are great new materials for greenhouses. One of my friends has one with roof and sides of Aluminet thermo-reflective screening, an extremely lightweight material that takes less of a framework for support, lets in light and rain, and never needs to be removed for it keeps the area several degrees cooler in summer as well as warmer in the winter.

Some of my friends from the Rare Fruit group grow quite a few fruits of marginal hardiness and have greenhouses that are tall with a wide door for dragging in large containers of trees in the winter.

EDIBLE LANDSCAPING

This idea is such a natural for Florida yards that I can hardly believe how few people consider it. It must be the farmer in me that still says, "Plant something you can eat." The same plants can be beautiful, and are certainly more interesting than the privet hedges and hibiscus shrubs that you see in every yard.

Plant the edibles just as you would any other ornamental plants. There are edible annuals, perennials, shrubs, vines, and trees. Keep in mind all the features of the plants you choose. How large will they be? Will they give shade or privacy? How will they look and smell in flower and fruit? Can fruit drop without mess on mulch or grass, rather than staining the driveway or patio? Are the plants likely to suffer frost damage or have other times of looking less than lovely? If so, for how long and how often?

Chapters 7 through 10 discuss the individual edible or ornamental plants in detail.

Most of us want ornamental plants as well as fruits, herbs, and vegetables. And there are some people who don't want dropping fruit anywhere, and pay extra for fruitless mulberries and such. But for those of us who have genes that remember the Irish famine, and don't mind a little extra chopping in the kitchen, edible plants are preferred. A dual purpose tree, shrub, or ground cover, or flower is what we look for first, before our growing space is all used up.

There are many easy-to-grow fruits that you will never find even in the best fresh markets because they don't have shelf life or bear shipping without turning to mush. People who have never stood under a mulberry or a loquat tree and eaten to their heart's content have missed one of the great pleasures in life. Yes, mulberries grow in Florida, too, though I had three that produced no fruit (very unusual) before I bought a 'Tice' that has long, delicious fruits. Mulberries are coarse-looking trees and drop leaves in winter, so put them out of the spotlight. Mine does well between citrus trees. However, I learned too late that all mulberries should be pruned back drastically to keep them low and in bounds. I have talked to people who prune theirs constantly and, probably as a result, have fruit for many months of the year. Mulberries are easy to root just by sticking a branch into the ground. My theory is that mulberries taste better than blackberries, take no stooping to pick, and have no thorns.

I have about 15 different kinds of citrus at the moment and love it all. Ponkans are my favorite for eating out of hand. We make orange juice that is so far superior to anything you can buy that it is unbelievable. We freeze all but the

half gallon we are drinking at the moment to preserve the flavor. Our best is red, made with blood oranges and Valencias for many months of the spring. And I take the huge, sweet pommelos, the ancestors of the grapefruit, to sell with my books because so many people like them and can't find them often.

When I first moved here citrus canker was a threat. Now there is a serious disease called citrus greening which threatens the whole citrus industry in Florida. At this time there is little that can be done about it, but I talked to an experienced citrus grower who assured me that it, too, will be overcome. I hope so because enjoying fresh citrus is one of the best parts of living in Florida.

If you are buying citrus, buy grafted stock from a reputable dealer. If you buy a larger plant, as in a three gallon or larger pot, you will have fruit almost at once that will quickly make up the difference in the cost, and you will continue to have fruit, we hope, for years to come.

If I had to do it over, I would plant only the best varieties of any fruit. My starfruit is sour, though I have tasted many that are sweet. My loquat is good but an improved variety would have larger and even sweeter fruit. There is only so much room in any yard. I waited a long time for my jaboticaba and grumichama to bloom. And I once had a calamondin orange that grew quite huge but had no fruit. Plant seedlings only if you have time and land to spare. Many will turn out well, but you can't be sure of that.

Joining an organic growers club like the Barefoot Gardeners (you can join online) or the Rare Fruit Council International (check them out online also) will quickly get you to the point where you'll have something to eat from your garden every day of the year.

YARD CARE SERVICES

Lawn mowing is a big business in Florida and many people who don't enjoy mowing themselves use this service. If you are searching for a reliable lawn service, ask your neighbors for recommendations. You can sometimes all get a slight break in the price if the company has several yards to do on the block. We had such a person for a few years. He charged no more than we had been paying our teen-age children (who had all left home), did the job whenever it was needed without complaint, and never asked for the car on Saturday night. We thought he was a wonder.

Many gardeners would much rather work with their other plants and let someone else take care of the mowing, which must be done at least weekly through the long summer and monthly through the winter. Our mowing man did a great job and was very careful about my other plants. But most mowers are not gardeners. Many know only about grass and only how to cut it, not how to keep it healthy. We have some who work at the church where I tend the flowers who clip hedges and sometimes trim the palm trees, but in doing so they think nothing of stepping on a lily. If you need a garden helper for jobs other than mowing, you might check with the extension office, your favorite nursery, or the FFA department of the nearest high school. And plan to work alongside anyone you hire until you are sure of their knowledge and carefulness.

CHAPTER THREE
AVOID COSTLY MISTAKES

I have now been living in Florida for 20 years. My entire yard has changed drastically from a burning plain of burdensome grass to a woodland of fruit and flowers with some sunny spots of brilliant and ever changing color. I love every nook of it. But...

I have made some big mistakes. There are quite a few things I would have done differently if only I had known better.

TREES GROW SO FAST HERE!

I certainly would have been much more selective in which trees I planted and which seedlings planted by birds or wind I would have allowed to grow.

Who would believe that even oak trees grow five feet taller and ten feet broader every year, and that they would grow more in a decade here than in fifty years in northern states! Especially since, as the old saying goes, the first year they seem to sleep, the second to creep, and the third year, when their root system is well established, they leap. After that, stand back.

Since that is true, it is very important to find out as soon as possible what kind of trees you have and what they are likely to do in the future. Some cities will send an arborist to tell you this and you can get much information from the county extension service. But even if you have to hire an arborist, the information is worth more than the price of his visit.

When we arrived there was one large oak in the corner of our yard that was the largest tree we had ever had owned. We loved it then and we love it now, even though we have to spend a good bit periodically to have it trimmed for both its health and our safety.

There were four other oaks that were still fairly small. I could perhaps have cut them down myself in those first days, but back then we were desperate for shade and I never would have considered it. I was hoping they were live oaks rather than laurel oaks, and it was a long time before I was sure they were all laurel oaks.

Now, all these years later, they are large and spread shade over too much of our half acre. If I could go back to the time when the landscapers were putting in those trees, I would trade all of the laurel oaks for one live oak that would spread just as much shade, would be more storm resistant and more beautiful in its shape, and would possibly live for hundreds of years. The laurels only live for about 80 years.

This live oak spreads over the street near Orlando, Florida.

By the time our neighbors built beside us, a good 17 years ago, I already knew I had at least one too many of those oaks. I considered offering them one, but it would have been too difficult and expensive to move even then to be worth the trouble. I should have had it cut down then, but I didn't.

So now we have some of the lower limbs removed every time the tree trimmers come. We enjoy the shade and add more choice shade plants beneath them. Gardening in the shade is much easier and more comfortable, especially in dry times. And in spite of our high yearly rainfall, most of it comes in the summer and there are many dry times in every year.

BEWARE OF SEEDLING TREES

Many tree seedlings are going to sprout in any Florida yard from trees both near and far.

29

Birds drop seeds. The wind blows them in, and some cling to your shoes and clothes. If you have oaks, you will have many oak seedlings to pull out, if possible, or cut to ground level again and again until they give up the ghost.

On rare occasions you may want to keep or relocate a seedling you find in your yard. I did that with a loquat and was thrilled by its amazing rate of growth. We have had to have it topped twice already and have enjoyed much fruit. But if I were to do it again, I would remove even the loquat seedlings and buy one good, grafted variety that would produce fruit of larger size and sweeter flavor.

Presently in my yard I have one seedling maple but no room to let it grow, and dozens of seedlings of Queen palms and golden rain trees, none of which I want, so I keep pulling them out or cutting them back. If you put a tin can or a black bag over the stub to block out the sun, you can kill the roots more quickly.

It is very important to identify and be sure you want any seedling tree before it gets too large for you to remove yourself.

PROPERTY LINE CONSIDERATIONS

A homeowner has the right to cut away any branches that hang over his property line from the neighbor's trees that he does not want. When our neighbors began building, they politely asked first if they could cut away part of our largest tree and I suggested they cut the limbs from the trunk rather than leave stubs. They did so gladly and did a good job. Nevertheless, the day they trimmed I cringed and feared the tree was ruined. It did look shorn for a while, but it soon grew full again.

I must admit to enjoying oranges that dropped in my yard from a neighbor's tree. But I made a grave mistake by ignoring the seedling trees that quickly grew large right on the other side of our back privacy fence. I considered them someone else's trees, and indeed they may belong to the county since there is a very small canal back there. They may even be ours since they are so close to the fence. Before we knew

> It is very important to identify and be sure you want any seedling tree before it gets too large for you to remove yourself.

it, they were large and shading much of our back yard. We now pay for trimming our side of them higher and higher every time we have the tree men come.

So I tell people to be aware of what is growing beyond their property lines that will soon be hanging over, especially if that property is NOT someone else's yard. In such a case, it is wise to ask whoever owns the land before you go over there and prune away unwanted seedlings. But if you can't find anyone to ask, prune anyway.

When you are planting near your own property lines, consider what that tree or shrub might mean to your neighbor and how it will look if shorn at the boundary. And remember that neighbors are not necessarily as permanent as trees are.

SHADE IN THE SUNSHINE STATE

Because we have so much sunshine in Florida, shade is very important. Especially through the hot months from April through September, shade can make a marked difference in air conditioning costs and general comfort indoors and out. Gardening in the shade is more pleasant and takes much less water. By planting deciduous trees in selected spots, we can enjoy the summer shade and the winter sun.

If you do not have enough shade, don't worry. You can get it very quickly. You can even get too much.

I couldn't imagine that until we were looking at houses in Florida and I saw it for myself: houses that were too dark even on a sunny day. The house we chose seemed in no danger. But within ten years, I was paying a lot to remove a lovely tree that I had planted, a golden rain tree.

PLANTING TOO CLOSE TO THE HOUSE, DRIVEWAY, OR ROAD

Planting too close to the house is one of the biggest mistakes people make. I planted one tangerine too close to the house in the back yard, moved it when a visiting horticulturist pointed that out, and still had it too close. It has had to grow crookedly to fit. Living through several years of serious hurricane threats has made this positioning much more important to us.

Most trees will grow about as wide as they will high and their roots will spread much farther. As a general rule allow as much as 65 feet between tall spreading trees and 35 feet between more columnar shapes. Any tree that will grow over 20 feet tall should be at least 15 feet from buildings.

Tree branches meeting over a driveway can look very nice and give a sense of privacy, but consider what kind of litter such trees may drop. Every tree drops something. Flowering trees drop more because both petals and fruit or seedpods are involved. Be sure that trees over a driveway drop only fruit like acorns or such that will be easily pulverized by passing cars, not squished and leaving stains. Monkey puzzle trees can drop solid, conelike fruits that can weigh ten pounds or more.

At the entrance to a drive, even shrubs can obstruct the view of approaching traffic, so plant accordingly. Your life may depend upon it. And close to the road, overhanging low branches are going to be broken off by trunks and vehicles. I've even had to duck under some palm fronds on my bike ride and been very grateful when they were removed.

PLANTING OVER PLUMBING

We knew we had a septic tank, but weren't even sure where it was for the first 15 years we lived here. Then one Christmas Eve there was a stench in the yard and everyone wanted to know what I had spread on the garden this time. A few days later we found the opening and had the tank drained. But a few months later troubles returned and it was obvious we would need a new drain field which would mean digging up much of the front yard. The plumber gave me the boundaries.

I paid to have a pine tree removed, moved everything else myself, and fretted considerably. I fretted much more when the plumber returned with heavy equipment and announced that the dig would have to be much larger than he planned due to the inspector's

permit. I dug some more, but not as fast as they did, and I lost a good many plants either into the hole or buried in the soil piled up around it. I would have settled for an outhouse in the back yard by then, but we were in the process of planning a big party for my father's 95th birthday and David didn't think the guests would appreciate it.

So now I know not to plant any trees over a drain field and to keep the path to the septic tank open. We had a good 15 years, but suddenly all of the houses in the neighborhood were having the same kind of breakdown.

The plumber said it was okay to plant shrubs and flowers on top of the new drainfield, but even so I am careful to keep my treasures well away.

GUARD YOUR PLANTS

Speaking of choice plants, I must admit that for many years I would hover in the house and pray when painters, plumbers, and repairmen were needed in my yard. Until... I had managed to save my rarest plant, an orange-flowered Vireya rhododendron, from the brink of the plumber's hole, but when a single plumber came back to check the pump, he stepped right square in the center of my rhododendron and broke it into pieces, all of which died a slow death too soon thereafter.

Lost to a careless plumber, my treasured rare Vireya rhododendron.

31

So now I go out and cover each untouchable plant with one of the sheets I use when frost threatens. Then I explain that such plants must be saved at all cost and I stand by and watch the people work. It isn't fun, but I haven't lost anything important since.

CARE AND TRAINING OF YOUNG TREES

Thank goodness trees are so self sufficient. A plant that is going to grow for a century or more would be a problem if it needed constant care. But a baby is a baby. The mortality rate among newly planted trees is enough to make a tree planter take extra care.

The first rule of baby tree care is not to lose the tree. When we lived in Iowa, two of my future towering oaks were so small they arrived in an ordinary envelope in the mail. One of these tiny trees got lost in the garden. So did son Philip's Arbor Day elm that we planted in the fence row to shade the cow pasture. Husband David got to chopping weeds one day, and you guessed it. Long after the sob scene, the tree grew back. It is amazing what trees can survive. But cutting away a baby tree's upper half slows down the growth even more than crowding it with weeds.

Other tiny trees set hopefully in a broad expanse of lawn fell prey to the lawnmower until I learned to surround each with a wide circle of mulch. Strawy manure or wood chips serve as a security blanket for the young roots while warding off the roaring monster (the lawn mower, not my spouse). Lawn mowers and weed eaters often cause injuries to tree bark and then diseases or insects settle in the wound to cause a final blow.

Baby trees in Florida tend be more cold sensitive than they will be as they mature. If you plant a tree of marginal hardiness, put it in a protected spot, perhaps on the south side of the house or garage or where a wall or fence or another tree will cut the wind. Give it additional protection with a heavy mulch over the roots and up around the graft point if it is a grafted variety. That way if it dies back, it will come back from the grafted top rather than the root stock. I had a pink grapefruit come back as a sour orange after one hard freeze before I learned this.

I also went to great trouble to wrap up a 'Gulf Gold' plum tree through its first few winters before I learned that it needed as many chill hours as it could get. Now I keep a list of plants to protect from frost so I won't forget any or worry about any extras.

Baby trees don't need any food after early September lest they put out new growth that might be too cold tender. But make sure the soil around those roots is well-watered deep down. Like children, young trees need discipline, but with trees this comes in the form of pruning. You can also choose your tree with the final form in mind. This is especially true of trees that are going to grow large. Ironically, fruit trees in Florida, especially citrus, take much less pruning than fruit trees such as apples and peaches in the north. Here they mostly need removal of any dead, diseased, crowding, or crossing branches.

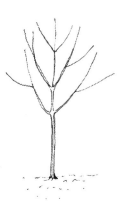

In any tree, you want to have U-shaped crotches between the limbs, especially the main limbs. V-shaped crotches are much more likely to split. But too often I found that my young trees had just such a division right in the middle of them, and if I pruned it away, I would lose half the tree. With small trees, you want to keep as much foliage as possible as those leaves are the food makers that contribute to the growth of the plant.

It took me years to figure out what to do about this dilemma. Now I select the strongest side if there is one, or if not, pick a side to be the leader. Then I cut back the other side part way. Over the next few years, as the tree grows taller, I prune the shorter side farther and farther back until only the leader is left. By that time, it has branched out higher up as it has taken advantage of the space.

As a shade tree grows, you want to cut away the lower branches so that eventually you can walk beneath it for mowing. If you let the tree form its major branches from a lower point, you will always have to duck under them. As they grow taller and taller, you cut off more lower branches to let in more light and air circulation underneath.

Fruit trees can branch out from low points because you want as much of the fruit within easy reach as possible. You should mulch under most fruit, but cultivate under citrus trees. Then you won't have to mow and you won't mind ducking under branches to pick.

I was told not to mulch citrus. Citrus trees are very susceptible to root rot. I do break this rule and mulch lightly through fall, winter, and the dry spring. But before summer rains come, I pull the mulch back to the dripline and keep the ground especially bare around the trunk. For this same reason, you want to water citrus deeply every two weeks, but give it time to dry out between waterings.

Beware of Invasive Plants

Invasive plants can fool you. The first year I was here another newcomer and I spent much of an afternoon taking photos of a fascinating vine I discovered in the vacant lot beside us. It had little yellow flowers and cute little bumpy orange yellow fruits about an inch and a half in diameter. These had opened to show bright red seeds. Soon after that I was writing an assignment for Better Homes and Gardens New Garden Book and found that vine described and named as Balsam Pear, *Momordica charantia*, a recommended annual vine that "can become weedy."

When a horticulturist first told me to pull it out because it could be a terrible weed, I didn't believe him. Since then I have pulled several thousand feet of this off of my other plantings and try never to let it go to seed.

All parts of the country have invasive plants, but I suspect Florida has the most and the most vigorous, considering that ours grow year round without pause. At first I welcomed the Virginia creeper that shaded our screened porch on the hot summer afternoons and called them my green lace curtains. They are treasured plants in the north. Now I pull them out ruthlessly, though there are some vines going up the big tree with branches bigger than my arms. Okay, I admit I am always glad that I miss a few when they turn red in winter, but if I hadn't pulled so many miles of them, they would have covered the house by now. The sleeping beauty story seemed like fiction before I moved here, but now I know it would not take anywhere near 100 years for a castle to be lost among the vines in Florida.

Many plants that are wonderful up north are invasive here. Some that are invasive in south Florida are manageable in colder parts of the state. I planted seeds of Black-eyed Susan vine, *Thunbergia alata*, and it soon grew over the top of all the azaleas and bananas. I'm still fighting it over a decade later. Still I love the ones with orange petals and black centers, but I work hard to control even them. I don't mind pulling out the ones that are all pale yellow.

Never plant four o' clocks here. I did once and they are one of my chief weeds.

FERTILIZING FRUIT TREES

-George Hoagland of Dee's Trees Nursery in Seffner, Florida, recommends these guidelines: For peach plum, nectarine, fig, persimmon, guava, banana, pomegranate, chestnut and other young trees, feed with 10-10-10 or 8-8-8 in four applications starting February 1 and bi-monthly through August.

-For citrus use 8-2-8 or any special citrus mix, four applications. My late friend and author of *Florida Fruit*, Lewis Maxwell recommends giving each tree a pint or one pound in mid February, May, and August and mature trees again in October. Increase this by a pound each year. Mature trees should be given one pound of fertilizer for each four of tree spread three times a year in February, May, and October.

-Shade trees can get by with a late-winter and a mid-summer feeding. Use one pound for every inch or trunk diameter for small trees, 2 pounds per inch for larger trees.

-To feed trees, start about 6 inches from the trunk and scatter the fertilizer over the complete area under the trees' branches.

I was in awe of the behavior of the pothos and philodendron vines that escaped from a planter and climbed the oaks while and leaves got larger and larger, split like Swiss cheese above the first branch and finally arched back toward the ground with little heart-shaped leaves again. Frosts have nipped them back a few times, but today they are starting to cross all paths and threaten to trip visitors.

One man said we should never plant a single vine in Florida and I see his point, but many of the vines are beautiful if they are controlled. I will say, plant any vine with care.

Also get on the Internet and print off the Invasive Plant Lists for Florida (http://www.fleppc.org). DO NOT plant any plant that is on the Category I list and be very careful what you plant from Category II.

Here are some invasive species that I have learned to hate:

Air potato vine (*Dioscorea bulbifera*) is on the Category 1 list. This vine grows quickly and produces little hard potatoes right on the vine. With this one it is very difficult to pull up the roots with the slender stems, and it twines so tightly it won't pull down from the trees, so I cut off huge sections between the ground and the twining. The rootless leaves don't even wilt for a week, but they stop forming potatoes. Air potato started coming over my back fence several years ago and has invaded further and more aggressively every year since, though I fight them continuously. Because so many wild places, even in the city, do not fight them at all, we have to work all the harder to keep them at bay. If you don't pull up anything else, pull these vines as soon as you see them. Don't compost them. Put these bad weeds in the trash.

Brazilian pepper (*Schinus terebinthifolius*) is worse. This shrub or small tree keeps coming up in my yard even though I haven't seen a mature plant within a mile. It is one the most invasive of the non-native plants in Florida, taking over both wet and dry habitats and really messing up the ecology. I have learned to identify the seedlings with their three to 15 finely toothed leaflets which are one to two inches long on stems already woody when they are very small. The leaves smell like turpentine when crushed. Birds spread the seeds which have a high germination and survival rate. Ignore the fact that their bunches of red berries are beautiful in the winter.

Creeping beggarweed (*Desmodium incanum*) is a perennial that has a large taproot with many branched runners, which explains why it returns every time I pull it out. The leaves have three oval shaped leaflets with smooth edges and a point on the tip. Flowers are pink to rose. The seeds cling to clothes, sometimes in rows, so tightly that even a washing won't take them off. I have picked off hundreds. The plant is a member of the Bean Family and reproduces by seeds, stolons, or broken pieces of root, so it is no wonder it finds us even more often than we find it. It hides in turf or open woods, creeps out of my father's hedge, and slinks into my ground covers. Give it no mercy.

Dog fennel (*Eupatorium capillifolium*) is another weed that looks much like a larkspur when it is young just to fool us, but unless you planted larkspur there, pull it out. It turns quickly into a tall perennial with several three to four foot hairy stems coming from a woody crown. The leaves stink when crushed. It has tiny daisy flowers and reproduces by seed from New Jersey to south Florida. More than once I nurtured it at first, thinking that it must be a flower, but I have finally learned better.

Wild grape vine is another weed that shows up on the edges of my yard on a regular basis, though it is not nearly as invasive as the Virginia creeper for me. That may be because I never gave it space. I had a huge one covering part of our barn in Ohio and could have made great jelly from it, but the fruits are so tiny it takes ages, so I never did. I've pulled it constantly but there are a few places where it comes back. If you miss it for a season, it develops thick woody stems and heads for the treetops. Pull it whenever you see it.

Persistent pests in our yards are the **seedlings of the oaks**. These also have long taproots and will come back if you don't get the whole things. Still, if you prune them off at ground level for enough years, the root will eventually die.

CHAPTER FOUR
EVOLVING YOUR NEW LANDSCAPE PLAN

Friends of ours moved to their new Florida house and put in a swimming pool in less time than it took me to put up my clothesline. They knew right where they wanted it and have never been sorry. They never found a place where it would get more sun or fewer leaves blowing in, or where it would be more convenient to the kitchen or the bathroom.

But for most people most of the time, it is a better idea to live in a new house and its surrounding grounds for at least a year before making big decisions or doing any expensive landscaping. During your first year your landscaping plan can evolve. After the first cycle of seasons, you will be ready to begin to finalize your plan: your guide to your ideal yard for indoor-outdoor living.

This evolution is even more important with such a change in climate, plant material and methods as newcomers to Florida face. And the final plan is also more important in Florida than in the North because here there is so much more opportunity for year-round enjoyment of the outdoors.

A good landscaping plan is like a road map. With it you will not waste work time or growing seasons, money, or energy in the months and years ahead. However, you will go on learning, so even the best original plan will require minor alterations from time to time.

> ### Adding or Subtracting Swimming Pools
>
> If acquiring or getting rid of a swimming pool is in your plans, be sure to to think about where you put your trees now. Leave access for the equipment that will be used to do either. You can always move a fence out of the way, but not a large tree.

DON'T WAIT FOR SHADE

Shade trees are the exception to the waiting rule. If you don't have any or enough shade, plant one or two trees as soon as possible. The size of the original plants does not matter that much. Mulch well around the new plants both to keep the lawn mower and trimmer at bay and to keep the moisture in the soil.

Don't plant trees too close to buildings, a common mistake that goes for seedlings of large trees as well. Study reference books and mature specimens and visualize that tree full grown. Put it where the canopy of branches will shade the house but not threaten it.

WHICH TREES SHOULD I PLANT?

Your local nurseryman or extension agent can recommend several kinds of trees from which to choose. Plant fruit trees in your

Consider these landscape factors:

What do you and your family want from your yard?
How much time and effort do you want to spend?
What areas are most easily seen from indoors looking out?
Where do your shadows fall, and when?
How much privacy do you want? Where is it needed?
Do you want to keep every tree and shrub?
Before you remove it, what does it do? When?
When this baby tree is mature, where will it spread?
What are the best places for gardens, patios, and paths?
Can service areas be made inconspicuous? Joined together?
Is there a nice vista to emphasize, or an eyesore to hide?
Where do you want to start? Which sections which year?

35

pentas

sunniest spots and shade trees as far from them as possible. From central Florida north, oaks are excellent and live oaks are best for they will last for hundreds of years and are more resistant to hurricanes. Many oaks are evergreen and are strong wooded although they can grow as much as five feet a year. Turkey oaks are deciduous and turn a brilliant red in the winter, giving a northern feeling. The colder it is, the more brilliant the color. But they are short lived. Almost all of the ones in our neighborhood have died in drought since we came here.

Holly trees do not spread as far but are lovely in leaf and berry. East Palatka and Savannah hollies are most often recommended. By the way, only female holly trees bear the red berries (fruits), and only if pollinated by a male tree. So plant one of each, or several females and one male. If space is tight, you can plant a male and a female in the same hole.

Slash pines can be planted in clumps for shade. Many people enjoy magnolias. Poincianas bloom yellow, red, and orange in the summer. Jacarandas are a spectacular cloud of purple in early spring in the southern half of the state. Check the chapter on trees in my *Florida Gardeners Book of Lists* for many choices of plants for various places and purposes.

Landscapers also can now move very large trees, as you will see if you watch new industrial properties, but large trees are not necessary for the average homeowner because trees grow so quickly here. Until your trees

---

STORM-RESISTANT SHADE TREES

When hurricanes come through, all kinds of trees can go down. However, trees that have been pruned regularly by professionals are the least likely to fall.

Some of the most storm resistant trees include many palms, live and sand live oak, bald cypress, southern magnolia, and red bay.

Some of the least storm resistant trees include Australian pine, laurel oak, queen palm, cherry laurel, Drake elm, sand pine, tabebuia, weeping fig, water oaks, and many flowering trees.

grow, use vines for instant shade, color, and privacy. See much more on vines, trees, and ornamentals in chapter 10.

WHAT IS THAT TREE (FLOWER, SHRUB, VINE) I SAW?

As a gardening newcomer, you'll probably ask this question frequently. You will learn many of the most common plants within the first year if you keep asking and studying. But the rest will take a lifetime, just as they did in the North. Don't stop asking questions. You will soon find out who has the answers.

Visit public gardens where trees are labeled. A season ticket to Cypress Gardens cost me less than double the price of a ticket for one day, so I went as often as I could at first. Check this with the other theme parks and arboreta as well. Look for gardens which label their plants.

There are many smaller public gardens that are much less expensive or free. The ones nearest your home are the most convenient for frequent trips and therefore the most useful, especially since hardiness and behavior of plants can vary surprisingly within a few miles. Go as often as you can with camera and notebook to see what is blooming, dormant, or promising. Write it down.

Look closely at the landscaping in your own neighborhood. What looks good? How big is it? What seems to require too much care? This will help show you what the plants are likely to do in your own yard.

Some local cemeteries also serve as arboreta. One in Tampa puts out a brochure describing the special trees you can see there. I went just to see what a monkey puzzle tree would look like at maturity before I planted my small one. It turned out that there was one right up the street and several more in my neighborhood, but I didn't know what they were until my visit. I also didn't know that a monkey puzzle drops the most painful mulch. I've been glad since that mine died young.

PRECAUTIONS WHEN BUILDING

If you are building on a new lot, it is a law in cities like Tampa that you call in the forestry department. They will help determine which trees are choice and should be saved even if you have to change your house plans, and which ones you can remove without any qualms. This is a most valuable service, and where it is not furnished by a government agency it would be well worth the cost to call in a tree expert to evaluate your trees. Otherwise you might remove something irreplaceable.

During construction, protect the trees you want to save. Keep them from contact with building machinery and from soil compaction. If you must change the grade more than four to six inches, build a well or terrace several feet away from and surrounding the trunk, and bank it with stone or railroad ties. Otherwise the smothering or scraping of the root system could slowly kill the tree. City forestry departments gladly make suggestions in such cases and often manage to save prize trees in the most difficult situations.

WHAT ABOUT WHAT I HAVE?

If feasible, ask the former owners to write down or walk around and tell you while you write down the names of all the permanent plants, or at least of the large ones, in your new yard. That will save you digging up or planting over something special.

Florida is one of the few places I've seen where some yards have too much shade. This is fine for keeping the house cool, but can be a drawback if it makes the house dark and gloomy or if you want to plant fruits and vegetables or sunloving flowers. To get more light and air circulation, and perhaps a better view, prune trees to have higher crowns and fewer low branches.

Eventually, you may want to remove less choice trees or shrubs, but don't remove anything until an expert recommends it or you live with it in every season. And even then, be very conservative. If you move in after a bad winter, some of what you see can be misleading. A tree that is usually beautiful may have skipped that year's bloom.

Start a garden notebook and record plant names, locations, and bloom times. Keep records on those in your own yard and also those of interest from other places. This will be a good base for future plans.

WHEN CAN I START PLANTING AND USING THE YARD?

The day you arrive, you can start planting if you want. Hands-on experience is the best teacher. But at first plant only annual vegetables or flowers or small plants that you can move. Experiment wisely, planting where success seems most likely. When you get a four pack of plants, put some in one location, some in another, and compare the results. Be prepared to change plantings when you are more familiar with your yard and its microclimates. If you buy larger plants, put the containers in different places and see how they look while you imagine them full grown. Move them around until you decide where they will look and grow best, but be sure to keep the containers watered during this process.

If you acquire any plants of marginal hardiness late in the year, you may want to keep them in their containers over the winter so you can move them to a warmer spot when frost threatens. Some you may want to keep in containers indefinitely. Many people do and I've kept some in containers for several years, although most do better in the ground for me.

Florida lawns, unlike those in colder states, can be started almost any time of year, as long as they receive plenty of water. For details, see chapter 6. In most of the state, soil is so sandy that mud is not a problem.

You will want to start enjoying the outdoors right after your move, for outdoor eating, visiting, sitting, and play. Young children will soon find or make their own play areas. Try to guide little ones to play areas within easy view of where you will be working or sitting, and situate swings and play equipment there, too. Grass is probably the safest and best groundcover for play areas.

Let garden paths develop naturally over the first year. A place where you find yourself and your family setting the lawn chairs is a good bet for permanent placement of a deck or patio. Make temporary paths and patios with a mulch of leaves and pine needles or small bark chips.

If you want a deck right away but are not sure where to put it, build a temporary one in sections that can be moved later if necessary, incorporated into the permanent finished deck, or used as path.

FLORIDA GARDEN FACTORS TO CONSIDER

* **Shorter days.** In Florida, during fall and winter, day length gradually decreases. You'll have around three hours less sun, and the sun is lower in the sky than in summer. Most garden plants are sensitive to this and grow faster when days are longer. Although the decrease in day length is not as pronounced as it is farther north, plants there are dormant while many of ours are still growing and blooming. Growth of flowers and vegetables in winter seems slow to gardeners from cold climates where summer days are very long and bright. However, our year round growing season more than compensates. You'll notice a definite and constant increase in both day length and in growth very soon after Christmas.

* **Sun and shade.** The amount of sun or shade a garden spot receives varies greatly with the seasons. Because of the changing angle from which the rays fall, many plots in the yard will be too shady for a fall or winter garden. The same plots may not see so much as a shadow all summer. This came home to me very clearly when my son moved down in the spring and put a dog pen in the yard. The dogs nearly perished from the heat. When the pen was moved by fall and I thought to plant vegetables in the hot spot, I found, to my surprise, that there was not enough sun.

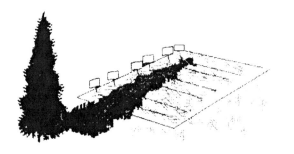

Because trees grow much more quickly in Florida, shade soon closes in beneath them. The corner plot where we grew vegetables for our first few years was very soon too shady and has long since become a shade garden.

Also keep in mind that many plants such as petunias, nasturtiums, snapdragons, and winter vegetables need all the sun they can get to grow well in fall and winter, but some shade will keep the same plants growing a few weeks farther into the summer. This can be accomplished by careful use of deciduous trees or shrubs or moving of some of those larger container plants into some shade for the spring and summer.

* **Feeding** is a must. In Iowa I grew many crops with no fertilizer at all. Only weeds and the deepest rooted native trees will grow without feeding here. Along with organic matter, spread all-purpose fertilizer like 6-6-6 with trace elements included, just before you plant. Then feed all seedlings again when they are about two inches tall and again when they bloom. Follow package directions. Often, this means about five pounds of fertilizer to a 50 foot row, or 50 square feet.

It is easier to bring home and spread time-release or slow-release fertilizer for it is lighter, lasts longer and it does not burn the plants or pollute the environment so much because almost all of it is used and does not leach away. It is more expensive, but less so in larger quantities. A single application of time-release fertilizer often carries vegetables or annuals through the growing season.

Organic fertilizers are also slow release and encourage the microbes and earthworms in the soil. While I use hardly any chemical pesticides, I do use some non organic fertilizers and can attest that my earthworms still thrive. If they didn't, I would switch.

* **Water**, so abundant in the summer, must be supplied by some type of irrigation the rest of the year. Most of the vegetable growing and much of the flower growing is done in the dry season. An automatic irrigation system can be ideal if it is well maintained and adjusted to

the season. In many cases they are not and are responsible for great water waste. Your garden needs least water in December, when it is growing slowly, and the most in April and May when growth is lush and fast, days are long and hot, and summer rains have not yet started.

The first year here I laid out a drip irrigation system with paperlike tubes. The project was neither difficult nor expensive, and worked very well without wasting any water. Unfortunately, the fragile system perished during replanting. Even the least expensive systems are much sturdier now. Permanent drip irrigation systems are highly recommended for all areas.

One friend bought a house that came with automatic sprinklers for the front lawn but none in the back where she did most of her gardening. "If I were to install sprinklers, it would be in the opposite order," she said.

I agreed at the time, but have since realized that I water much more in the front because that is where I put my choice plants so I, my family, and passersby can enjoy them. Meanwhile I get along all right with plenty of hoses to reach all areas, some soaker hoses for special spots, rain barrels, and portable sprinklers. Of the latter, the longest lasting and most effective so far have been the ones that spray with a revolving circle at the top of a three-foot stem. I can easily move this from plot to plot. Until I find something better for me and my budget, I am planting flower and vegetable beds where the water falls from each move of the sprinkler.

* **Salt tolerance** is of little concern to inland homeowners, but is top-of-the list for people who live on the coast or on coastal waterways. Many plants, like sea grape, oleander, Jerusalem thorn trees (*Parkinsonia*), magnolia, jasmine, gaillardia, palms, live oaks, yucca, and natal plum tolerate salt spray very well. Others, like citrus and bottlebrush, have fair tolerance. Bamboo, gardenia, and croton have poor tolerance. And bird-of-paradise, dracaena, caladium, orchids, spathiphyllum, banana, ginger, hibiscus, and figs have none. If you live on or close to the seaside, ask your nurseryman or extension agent or check one of

the books such as *Florida Gardens by the Sea* by Mary Jane McSwain or *Gardens by the Sea* by the Garden Club of Palm Beach. Some of Florida's loveliest yards are on the water, and it is not impossible or difficult to garden there.

Most waterfront property, especially on or near the coast, is largely man-made soil that tends to be quite alkaline. Bette Smith, who has one of these delightful yards on the edge of Treasure Island, uses chipped sulfur in a whirlybird thrower to keep the pH down to a workable level. Two treatments a week apart can last for years, she says.

* **Insects** are never frozen, seldom even chilled here, so bug patrol is very important. If you don't find the tomato hornworm soon after it appears, the tomato leaves disappear. Some say a whole privet hedge can disappear but I haven't seen that. On the other hand, when I see the striped larvae of the swallowtail or monarch butterfly eating away at the butterfly weed, I welcome them. They almost always progress to their next stage and fly away before all the plants are denuded, and their pruning is beneficial.

* **Snakes** exist in Florida and a few of them are dangerous. But I'll be darned if I let that keep me from gardening. I often announce my presence: "Okay, snakes, get out of here. It's my turn in the garden." Actually, pounding the ground with a hoe or even your foot will send out vibrations that will send them away quicker.

If I lift a log or other logical snake hideaway, I stand back with a hoe handy. But I get rid of likely hiding places and don't worry about snakes. We seldom see any and only once or twice saw a poisonous coral snake. The old saying is, "Red on black, a friend of Jack, red on yellow, kill the fellow." We have always had an outdoor cat or two who seemed to patrol the area and make me feel protected. I just learned that geese will keep snakes away, but I have been bitten by a goose but never by a snake.

One friend of mine refused to even go for a walk for fear of snakes, but we are much safer working in the garden than driving on the roads, and we take that in stride.

* **Bees** can be scarce in Florida. Although there are hives nearby, there is so much blooming that the bees do not need to fly the two miles they did in Iowa. I had to hand pollinate the squash and plant the bees' favorite plants (butterfly weed, bottlebrush bush, lavender, etc.) for two years before many came around. We have plenty now, but all the development has reduced the wild bee population. Consider having a local beekeeper keep some hives in your garden if necessary.

*Fire ants. These were new to me but we soon became intimately acquainted. They are the only creatures who have caused me frequent pain, and even that is mostly a nuisance since I am not allergic. Still I never go out in the yard without socks and shoes, watch carefully for ant hills, start stomping and scraping at the first bite, and apply water as quickly as possible to all bites as soon as I get the ants off of me. The bites itch, hurt, and swell for the first day. After that they shrink to little nubs of puss, no long painful but not pleasant, and they last for weeks and often leave scars. I get the greatest relief by coating bites with clear or tan nail polish.

I have so far found nothing that does away with fire ants. Several products will deter them temporarily, but they pop up again a few days later, especially in containers and in bags of leaves. Neem may help, and several organic fertilizer products adding a wide array of trace elements have been found to be effective by some gardeners. I just heard that pouring ginger ale into a nest produces CO_2 which suffocates the queen and kills the hive.

* **Zones of hardiness.** I always checked the USDA hardiness zones to see how much cold a plant would stand (e.g. hardy to Zone 3) before I moved to Florida. Now I look for a range of hardiness zones (e.g. hardy from Zones 6 to 10). This was missing in most books when we first came here, but is more common now.

Most of northern Florida and the western panhandle are in Zone 8. The southern quarter of the peninsula is in Zone 10 and some of the Keys in Zone 11. Tampa, where I live, is smack in the middle of Zone 9, according to the zone map. Most of the plants recommended for zone 9 and many that say they need Zone 10 do very well for me. I plant the latter in protected spots or containers and keep a list of them so that I can cover them, move them, or take cuttings when frost is predicted.

Some of the Zone 10 plants have never shown any damage, some have died out, and some have died back to the ground but came back. As plants mature, they increase in hardiness, and we have not had a terrible freeze since 1989, thank God. My shade also provides a few degrees more frost protection.

Still I find that some plants recommended for "Zones 3 to 9" will not grow here or grow only in certain seasons or with special care. Thats because our part of Zone 9 is hotter and more humid in summer than some Zone 9 western USA areas and mostly because of our summer rains. The USDA Zones are based on minimum, not maximum, temperatures. Nevertheless, those plants I really want are worth trying. If a plant is recommended only for Zones 2 to 8, it will probably resent the heat and humidity, even in Zone 8. If someone gives you a plant, try it and see what happens. Plants are unpredictable, and you might be lucky. Just remember that summer heat can be as important as winter cold. Naturally I now favor catalogs that indicate both cold and warm zonal limits.

Also note that Sunset Books use a different zoning system and Florida is considered Zones 25 in the south to Zone 28 in the north in my book *Landscaping With Tropical Plants*.

* **Translation** of all garden information becomes important. Even this book contains advice that must be adjusted to different parts of the state. When you can, choose books that give both the northern and southern zone limit for each plant or indicate N,C, or S for north, central or south Florida. Any garden book that does not talk about the effect of heat and humidity on plants will not be very helpful to Floridians. Some great ideas work anywhere. Others need a

bit of adjustment for each climate. And some ideas that you read in general garden books won't work in Florida at all.

For your first year in Florida, you may want to let most of your reading come from the list of books at the end of this book. But don't cancel any catalogs or throw away your garden reference books. At first you may feel leery of former sources, but soon you will be able to interpret them for Florida gardening. Past experience does not disappear. Don't bury it, just rearrange it to suit present needs.

* **Local conditions** take on added importance. Florida gardeners will get the most appropriate plants as well as advice from local nurserymen, Master Gardeners, extension experts, or southern sources, although some plants from California are also adaptable. Only some or certain varieties of the plants from general catalogs will do well here.

Also take new advice with a grain of common sense. One man whose terrific vegetable garden made me stop to meet him told me that I could not grow English peas here. I can and do, although we never get northern-size harvests. The secret is planting in November. A girl working at my favorite garden center told me never to use peat moss or potting soil in the ground. I can't imagine now why not. Peat moss is one of the best soil amendments here because it lasts much longer than fast-disappearing compost and retains water and nutrients so well.

But most of the advice I've gotten has proven true. I always gardened against some of the rules, planting extra late or early, or growing borderline plants. I was determined to continue this in Florida, but I found that it is much harder, often impossible, to go against the rules of timing and seasons. Here again, it is best to learn and obey the rules first. Then later you can break them with better discretion.

DRAWING UP THE ACTUAL PLAN

As you learn Florida plants and growing methods, you will automatically begin to evolve a landscaping plan, at first only in your head. Don't let it stop there. Get it down on paper, even if only in sketchy form. Use copies of any deed or lot diagrams that came with the deed to draw your plan to scale. Graph paper works well and you can let each block represent 1, 5, or 10 feet. Getting your yard on paper will open your eyes to dimensions you may never otherwise realize. If you have no diagram, measure your yard with a tape measure or by pacing off the outer borders, the distance of the house comers from the property line, the placement of trees, pool, driveway, and other permanent features.

You can then lay tracing paper over the base plan and experiment with different arrangements. Or cut out scale drawings of desired improvements like gardens, patios, paths, and such, and move them around until you have an arrangement that suits you. Some people like to cut out flowers from seed catalogs and play around with combinations of colors and textures until getting a good idea or plan.

There are now several computer programs that will help you draw your landscape plans and where the changing of ideas and viewing ahead are much easier.

butterfly ginger

DON'T FORGET THE VIEWS

Much landscaping, even in Florida, should be done from the inside looking out. Give every window a pleasant view and let most garden improvements be situated for enjoyment from the inside as well as out. Frame and preserve the pleasant views that are already there, including your neighbor's lovely tree. Be careful not to plant anything that will block your view of the flag on the mailbox, the coming school bus, or coming traffic at the end of your driveway. But plant something beautiful to cover or draw the eye away from your own or your neighbors garbage cans or compost pile or clothesline.

41

PLAN FOR COMMON SENSE MAINTENANCE, PLUS XERISCAPING

Plant only what you reasonably expect to have time to maintain. I love my large yard, but many people would hate it if they don't enjoy yard work. To me pruning, planting, even weeding are easier and much more interesting than mowing and trimming the turf we once had. Our largely woody and mulched plantings have eliminated 95 percent of the mowing and much of the watering.

With today's environmental concerns and water restrictions, it is important to plan your yard according to the principles of xeriscaping (drought-tolerant landscaping). Xeriscaping is done for beauty and success in plant growth, for lower water bills, and for commonsense care of the environment.

Besides employing soil care principles which help the soil hold water better (discussed in the next chapter), xeriscaping means grouping plants according to their water needs, with the thirstiest ones usually closest to the house, the ones that need only occasional watering once established in the next zones, and native or other plants that will survive on natural rainfall in the rest of the yard, indeed in most of the yard if you are looking mainly for low maintenance.

Another principle involves reducing turf area. Instead use large areas of mulch and/or ground cover, especially beneath trees. Use turf as a design element, not as a coverall. A lawn takes more work, worry, and water, and more fertilizer and pesticide than any other part of the yard, especially in Florida where you have to mow at least weekly all summer and less often, but still occasionally, the rest of the year.

For much more on water and work saving methods, see my book *Xeriscaping for Florida Homes* whether you are a dedicated garden or just a homeowner who wants the least yard work with the most rewards.

If you plan to undertake extensive changes, the services of a professional landscape designer or architect will be most helpful. However, take time first to familiarize yourself with Florida plant possibilities, and to make your preferences and ultimate goals regarding use of the space clear. Try to see examples of the work of several designers before making your choice.

Some nurseries will give advice and some will even draw up plans if you agree to buy a significant amount of plant material from them. Some even have crews that will do the plantings. Ask about this early in your planning stage. I spent enough on my first trip to the nursery to probably qualify, but I did not think of that at the time.

Discovery Garden, Hillsborough County Extension Office

42

CHAPTER FIVE
DIGGING INTO A NEW YARD

I started digging and planting in my yard while the rest of the family were still enjoying motel living. The work produced little plant growth, but it made me feel better. It was difficult to break the sod, but where no grass was growing, digging was as easy as in a sand pile. Our yard was pretty much a half acre sand pile. And even I had not packed compost in the van.

Getting organic matter such as compost into the soil is the first essential rule of Florida gardening. If you bring or buy plants, leave them in their containers for the time being or heel them in in a partially shaded location. Heeling In is a method of storing plants, especially bare rooted ones, in the ground when they need planting quickly but you don't have time or a place available. It involves digging a trench, then laying the plants on a slant or on their sides and then covering the roots and up to the leafy parts of the top growth with soil. Keep this watered and replant your plants in a more permanent place as soon as possible.

You can move them when you see where the light is best and rearrange your landscaping as you learn what the plants are going to do where. Unless your sanity demands instant planting. In that case, dig in.

CHOOSING GARDEN SITES

Each kind of plant has its own preference for soil type and amount of sunshine. However, few plants grow in soil as infertile as that in much of Florida, so plan on improving any site on your property.

The spots you select for fruit trees should have as much sun as possible. Vegetables and many flowers should be in full sun or partial shade. Full sun is best from September to May. Many plants that loved sun in the North will thank you for some shade during the summer months in Florida, and some will die out without summer shade, even if your seed catalog says "full sun." Finding the correct exposure involves putting the right plant in the right light.

There are plants that will grow well in Florida even in the deepest shade.

Easy access to water is vital, especially for growing plants from seed. Until they are well started, seedlings will need daily or twice-daily watering.

Gardens can be any size, but it is best to start small and then expand gradually as you evolve a definite garden plan, gain experience, multiply your plants, and improve your soil.

MAKE SOIL IMPROVEMENT A HABIT

Organic matter such as peat moss or compost adds some nutrients and much water holding capacity to Florida's sandy soil. Whether used as a mulch on top or dug into the soil, organic matter continually breaks down into humus and eventually disappears from the soil in any of the 50 states. It does so faster with Florida heat and rainfall. So make accumulation and replenishment of organic matter a constant part of your gardening.

I recently interviewed a couple who said that weeding was an every day chore at first, but since they have been bringing home hundreds of bags of leaves every winter for mulch, the weeding is now a once a month chore and the soil is continually improved. I figured years ago that mulching was easier and more effective than hoeing. And before long you can tell just by sticking a trowel into the soil how much it has improved from the humus and where more organic matter is needed.

BUYING ORGANIC MATERIAL

If you are buying organic matter, probably the best kind for lasting usefulness is Canadian sphagnum peat moss. This comes in bales of various sizes. Before you use it, cut the bale open in a big "I" shape and pour in a bucket of warm water: five gallons for a four-cubic foot bale. Then close the plastic and let it sit overnight to moisten. And if it still seems too

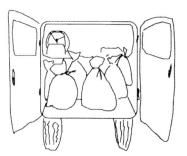

dry the next day, add more water from the hose. Peat retains from 12 to 30 times its weight in water, is sterile and weed free, and is easy to use. It provides an excellent environment for beneficial microbial growth in the soil. Its only fault is that it can crust on the top unless it is mixed with soil. Also, it does not add any

beneficial microbes or any nutrients, so use fertilizer now and begin gathering other organic matter and composting it as soon as possible, for future soil richness.

The old farmers were right: animal manure is great for the soil. When I found myself buying rabbit manure by the bagful, I decided to buy rabbits and produce it on the spot. Many horse stables or horse owners offer free manure, but all my sons with trucks were still in Iowa. Eventually I learned to visit a friend with a horse, or visit her pasture if she was busy, and bring home a bag full or so quickly shoveled from the feeding area. I mix it in one of the rain barrels, dilute to the strength of weak tea, and use it as needed. If you can get larger amounts, great. If not, get what you can.

One Christmas son Mike borrowed a truck, filled it with horse manure from a pasture—not an easy job—parked it in the church parking lot while he went to Christmas Mass, and then gave it to me for Christmas. He called all his siblings and told them, "It doesn't matter what you get her. She's going to like my gift the best." It is definitely one I'll always remember.

At any garden center you can buy black cow manure and sometimes chicken manure by the bagful. This is all fine for starting your new garden, but is not necessary to keep buying organic matter while community waste departments are spending millions to haul away what we can use so well to improve our soil.

BRINGING HOME THE LEAVES

"Please do not embarrass us by going around the neighborhood picking up grass clippings, Mom," my children used to beg. I was a little embarrassed myself until I perfected

my method. Now I wait until workers and school children leave on trash day and then set out.

Within three blocks I can gather 30 bags of leaves from about Christmas through March. Sometimes they are mixed with some grass clippings or pine needles, depending on the season. Some places put out bags of pure pine needles, a great looking mulch. Anything put out for trash collection is legal plunder and no one has questioned me in the many years now I've been doing this. My own embarrassment has all but disappeared and the trash men beg me to take more. One homeowner once helped me load his leaves and said, "There are several ladies who do this." And one fellow gardener stopped to say, "I wondered who else was smart enough to do what I do."

Tips. Do not leave these bags in the car for any length of time in Florida heat. I picked some up old grass clipping on the way to, instead of home from, a few hours work to beat the trash trucks one day and it took months to get the smell out of the car.

Also, do not leave bags of hot grass clippings where they could start a fire. It isn't likely, but it has happened. Grass clippings were blamed for a barn fire that killed 30 race horses at the fairgrounds in my hometown in Ohio.

Leaf Tips

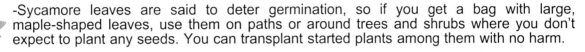

-Sycamore leaves are said to deter germination, so if you get a bag with large, maple-shaped leaves, use them on paths or around trees and shrubs where you don't expect to plant any seeds. You can transplant started plants among them with no harm.

-Only after I had spread a wonderfully light and fluffy bag that looked a bit suspicious, not containing leaves after all but some type of seeds, did I realize that I had just put down a few thousand seeds of golden rain tree. It was too late to remove them. It may help that I covered them with other leaves that may discourage germination, but I plan to be watching and pulling out many little tree seedlings in that area for years to come. In spite of that, there is much more good than bad in most of those bags.

-I use most of the leaves I collect just as they are, not shredded, and spread them either directly on the ground or over newspapers overlapped as a base to recycle the newspapers and make the leaves last longer. They don't blow about all that much, and if you are worried that they will, water them down or even spread a light sprinkling of soil over them to hold them in place.

-If you want finer mulch, pile up the leaves. (You might want to let your children jump in the piles or jump in yourself. We don't get to do that much in Florida and I always enjoyed it up north. But check for fire ants first.) After you are through playing, take your lawn mower and just move it up and down over the pile until it shreds the leaves as fine as you wish. Smaller bits of anything organic will decompose more quickly.

Do not put grass clippings in actual contact with plant parts or even close enough for a rain to wash them into contact. When combined with Florida heat, they can burn plants if they are still hot. Spread them out first and pull them well back from stems or leaves. After they dry enough to be cool, pull them closer.

Never use grass clippings from unknown sources around treasured plants. The clippings could contain herbicides, residues from someone else's lawn treatment. I have found the organic matter well worth the risk, but when in doubt I put clippings where I want to kill sod or on a spot that will not be planted for several weeks.

New laws about yard waste collection have not changed things much but mulching mowers have. Most people or their yard crews now have these and are using their own grass clipping to improve their lawns. This is good for the lawns, the people, and the planet. If you mow your own lawn, you can at least gather the grass clippings and use them on other plantings if needed. There are still plenty of leaves to gather, limited by the season.

Many Florida homeowners are neater than they need to be. One neighbor gladly sent her sons for my garden cart whenever she cut grass so she didn't have to bag it and I didn't have to unbag it. I felt compelled to tell her how the mulch would help her shrubbery. She said she knew that but preferred to buy woodchips by the truckload. This attitude will keep the rest of us supplied with leaves.

If everyone eventually uses all of their own yard waste, I will say, "I told them to," and rejoice in the advance for the environment. As mentioned near the end of chapter 2, I can always go to the landfill for compost or mulch. A friend recently called to offer me some mulch from having her tree trunk ground. Like what I've shared from the landfill, it was finely ground material, good even for mixing in potting mixes.

The pile was larger than I expected, but small enough for me to carry home in two trips. I put two garbage cans in the back of the car. Then I forked the mulch into a used 20-gallon plastic pot about the size of a bushel basket, emptied this into garbage bags saved from leaf

collection and always handy in the trunk of my car. When the load reached my 20-pound limit, I put the bags into the garbage cans, one on top of the other, until they were full. I tucked a few more loaded bags around the edges, fastened the open trunk with a bungi cord, and drove home slowly. It was easy to lift out each bag.

COMPOSTING

There are dozens of ways to make compost and you can't do it wrong, only more slowly. You can compost on the spot by letting organic mulch rot into the ground. It looks neater to cover a bucket of vegetable scraps from the kitchen with grass clippings or leaves.

On a compost pile mix layers of dry and green material and add manure, compost activator, or something with nitrogen like cottonseed meal. These steps will heat the compost pile for better destruction of harmful bacteria and weed seeds and will hurry the process. Water and air are necessary, so when you are out with the hose, remember the compost pile. Turning speeds the decomposition, but this labor is not essential. You can shovel finished compost from the bottom while you add new layers of organic matter to the top. The finished product takes a few weeks to a few months, depending on the season and the composition of the pile.

The smaller the bits of material, the quicker the decomposition of the pile, the less space it takes, and the neater it looks. I refuse to spend much time chopping garbage, but I know

people who frappe theirs in the blender. It is so easy to bring the lawn mower up and down over a pile of weeds or leaves and give them a chop. If you don't have a shredder, make a place behind a bush to pile branches and such. You can use some of them as stakes for supporting climbing or weak-stemmed plants.

COVER CROPS

In any season, as soon as possible, start to work on the soil in your proposed planting beds. Even if you are not sure where the beds will go, you can't go wrong planting cover crops to improve the soil.

With cover crops you can grow large amounts of "green manure" on the spot in just a few weeks time. When you spade or till this into the soil, you add more pounds or tons of organic matter than you'd ever care to carry from the chicken coop.

You will see plantings of sorghum and sesbania, a succulent legume, in the empty strawberry and vegetable fields in the summer. The growers plow this down, then wait two to three weeks before replanting while the soil microbes work to turn the green manure into humus. You can till your cover crop in at any time, wait for two weeks, and then plant a garden of flowers, vegetables, or shrubs, or even a new lawn, that will be headed for easy success in the greatly improved soil.

Different cover crops will do best in different seasons. If it is summer, plant black-eyed peas, crotalaria, hairy indigo, peanuts, sorghum, soybeans, or sudan grass. For fall planting, oats, amaranth, millet, soybeans, or rye grass are good. In early spring plant any kind of

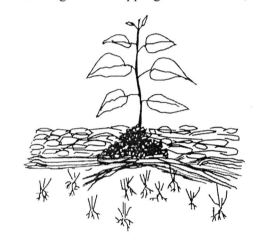

beans, more amaranth, buckwheat, millet, peanuts, or soybeans. Growing these will teach you much about Florida gardening and also about the microclimates and soil variations in your yard.

Cover crops need water and nutrients, too. Even these soil-building plants won't grow very well in unimproved soil, but by growing them you will be taking a useful step forward and improving the soil in a new garden.

For a dual purpose cover crop, use cowpeas or any kind of beans, including soybeans. Fertilize for a better crop. Sow a good edible variety and harvest whatever you can use. Then plow the rest into the soil.

If you don't have a tiller, you can mow off the cover crop, leave it as a mulch, put newspapers over the top and then add more mulch, as described to the right under *mulching instead of tilling.*

Summer is an ideal time to plant cover crops (and tropical pumpkins and cucuzzi) because other vegetables do not grow then and will not need the space. In the fall, when they do, their space will be much improved. Perennial covers or self sowers like amaranth, cowpeas, crotalaria, and indigo can be sown in groves or around fruit trees for long-term soil buildup. Mow these as often and as low as you wish for on-the-spot mulch production. Plant annual rye grass among spring corn and beans and it will loosen the soil, then die out as the days get hotter. Just leave the residue as mulch.

TILLING

You can prepare your new planting ground by tilling to break up the sod. But before you begin, call the phone company and the cable company. They will gladly send someone out to locate underground cables and prefer to do so before you cut them.

It is best to till once and then let the area sit for a few days before tilling again. The days between tillings are an ideal time to spread the ground with as much as possible of sphagnum peat, grass clippings, leaves, sawdust, manure, or whatever soil improvers you can get. You can't get too much, though it is easier to till in a

few inches at a time. If you don't have a tiller and don't wish to rent or hire one, there is another way.

You can remove sod from the area chosen for your garden without chemicals or hard labor. Just spread a heavy layer of grass clippings on it and keep it watered. In three weeks the grass sod below should be partly rotted and much easier to turn over. Dig in the clippings and the sod, too.

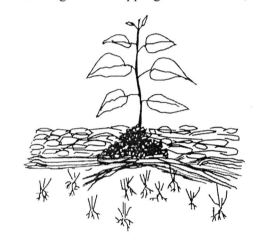

MULCHING INSTEAD OF TILLING

If you have neither tiller nor young muscles, you can carry the mulching method one step farther and never have to till the soil. Spread newspapers over the sod, where you want your garden. Overlap them so weeds can't creep in through the cracks. Over this, spread a thick layer of grass clippings and/or leaves. After watering well, you can then plant at once by pulling the mulch back to the newspapers and adding soil around the roots of individual plants or over the top of seeds as needed. Holes for large plants can be dug through the newspapers, the bits of sod removed to the top layer of mulch, and the mulch pulled back up to the trunk after planting.

This method, perfected by ECHO (Educational Concerns for Hunger Organization, in North Fort Myers) for use in third world countries, works very well for gardeners anywhere. I have used it extensively for twenty years now. The roots will penetrate the newspapers when they need to. Meanwhile, the newspaper tends to keep the moisture and nutrients at root level and slow down their

47

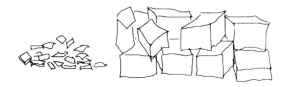

leaching through the sand. It also keeps the nematodes away from any roots formed in the mulch, blocks out weeds, and within a few months rots into the soil as humus, since paper came from trees originally.

The only problems with this method involve finding soil to add on top, the mulch sometimes smothering tiny plants, and eventual reentry of some weeds, especially grasses. For soil you can use purchased potting soil or any combination of soil, compost, peat moss, perlite, or vermiculite that you would use in containers.

This method takes less soil than is needed for container growing. Put cardboard or plastic milk cartons with bottoms cut away around small plants to mark them and protect them from shifting mulch. The weeds that enter are few compared to the number that sprout in unmulched soil.

dry crystals of water-retaining gel

moistened crystals of water-retaining gel

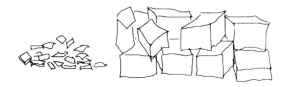

WATER-RETAINING GELS

I experimented with the addition to the soil of water-retaining polymer gels, crystals, and granules. These come under various trade names and absorb water and hold it in the root zone where it does the most good. The gels are especially effective in Florida's sandy, quick-drying soils and in containers.

They have been improved to last longer and have even more water-holding capacity, increasing 300 to 800 percent in volume. Only a minute amount should be dug in, and it should be placed **under** a planting hole. Follow label instructions. If you add too much, it will expand and push the plant right up and out of the ground. The gel also can expand back to the surface of the soil, where it looks like cubes of jello. If this happens, dig it in again right away or cover it with mulch. On the surface it quickly

breaks down. In the soil it is good now for years, some claim up to 20, certainly beyond the time it takes for permanent plants to become well established. They also reduce leaching of nutrients and loosen the soil.

In containers, especially in hanging pots, the addition of gel can reduce watering by 50 to 75 percent and make the difference between having to water twice a day or every two days. It also reduces stress on the plants and saves water. It is not a necessary additive, but it is something that you may find interesting to test in your own pots and garden.

It is also good for helping transplants and it increases seed germination and early growth of seedlings. To add it to an established plant, you can poke holes in the soil with a pencil and pour in the hydrated product. Or you can spread a thin layer under mulch to avoid ultraviolet exposure.

There is no indication that these products do any harm to the environment and they are approved by some organic gardeners. These gels are safe enough that they are used in baby diapers to absorb the moisture. Do not breathe in any product in its dry form, but that is no great danger here.

SOIL pH

The pH of soil is a measure of its alkalinity or acidity. A pH of 7.0 is neutral. Numbers below 7.0 indicate the degree of acidity; those above indicate its alkalinity. Most flowers and vegetables grow best in a slightly acid to neutral range. Trees and shrubs vary in their needs. Dogwoods, camellias, azaleas, hollies, and gardenias prefer acid soil.

Although virgin Florida soils can range from pH 3.8 (very acid) to pH 8.0 (quite alkaline), most Florida soils have a slightly acid to nearly neutral pH. If the soil is high in limestone or seashells, close to a new house, on manmade ground near the water, or in the Florida Keys, it may be quite alkaline.

Soil tests and advice are available from each county's agricultural extension office. So are the instructions for gathering samples. You can also buy a home testing kit, follow instructions, and do it yourself.

To tell the truth, I seldom test soil. Testing certainly makes for more exact feeding, higher yields, and fewer problems. It would definitely be a good idea to begin by having the soil in your new yard tested. But if your plants are growing well, the pH must be in a suitable range. If it is not, your plants will tell you with their declining attractiveness.

If the leaves of the acid loving plants turn pale, this is a sign that the roots need more acidity. Often watering with a product like Miracid ™ will make a remarkable difference in just a few days. But such treatments will need to be continued indefinitely to maintain unnatural pH levels.

Gardenias will have some yellowing leaves at bloom time no matter what, so don't worry about them.

Pine needles, oak leaves, and peat moss make an alkaline soil more acid, but it takes huge amounts to make a difference. Large amounts of organic material will bring any soil closer to neutral, correcting soil pH no matter which way it is wrong in the first place.

Chipped sulfur will make soil more acid much more quickly. A temporary home remedy for alkaline soil is to add a tablespoon or two of vinegar to each gallon of water used for irrigation. Ground limestone makes soil more alkaline. It is rarely needed in Florida except for in the northernmost sections and in manmade soils.

You can estimate a soil's pH by noticing which plants grow well in it. If your neighborhood or yard features flourishing azaleas, blueberries, strawberries, or other acid-lovers listed above, it indicates an acid soil. If these are conspicuous for their absence, alkaline soil may be the reason.

One very good plant to use for indicating soil pH is the common or "blue ball" hydrangea. Florist's hydrangeas sold as Easter plants are fine for this purpose. The flowers and bracts react to soil pH by changing colors. Oddly, the effect goes contrary to the coloration of litmus paper. Where the soil is acid enough for azaleas, the flowers will be blue. Where soil is neutral to alkaline, blooms will be pink. You can change the color of the bloom by adding aluminum sulfate to the soil to increase the acidity.

While the first hydrangeas I planted barely survived, I have since grown and seen some lovely specimens in Florida yards. They need light shade, not too much, ample water and space. Don't let other plants crowd them out or they will disappear. Note that this plant generally needs plentiful supplies of water and fertilizer, and is often potbound when sold. But mine have done well when planted in the ground and once settled in they have needed less water than I expected compared to the pampering they needed when in pots.

hydrangea

TREATING FOR NEMATODES

Nematodes are microscopic roundworms. Gardeners in northern states may hear about nematodes but never have to worry about them. In Florida, the harmful nematodes are a serious threat to many crops and ornamentals. When you pull out sickly looking beans and find swollen, knotted, gnarled roots, you are seeing a common kind of nematode damage. Beneficial nitrogen nodules on the roots of a healthy legume crop look different and will easily rub off.

There are several ways to control nematodes. They are less prevalent in soil that is rich in humus, so adding plenty of organic matter may solve or at least stave off the problem. Very susceptible plants such as figs can be mulched knee high and will do quite well. Mine have.

Nematodes are less likely to be a problem near a walk or the foundation of the house. In open ground they are most prevalent in the top 12 to 15 inches of the soil. You can plant susceptible plants in large pots filled with soil rich in humus, cut off the bottoms, and sink the pots into otherwise normal planting holes. The

49

sweet potato vine

moist two feet deep. Then simply cover the area with 2- to 6-mil clear plastic and seal the edges well with soil, rocks, or such. A plastic paint drop cloth from Wal-Mart may not be quite as good, but it will do.

Gaps or air pockets will retard the heat buildup, though they are about impossible to eliminate completely. Allow four to six weeks for treatment, longer if a cool spell comes. Afterward allow the soil to dry to workable texture.

This method was developed in Israel and has been used extensively in California. Consider it if you have soil empty now or a new plot in mind to till. In four to six weeks, soil can reach temperatures sufficient to kill many nematodes, weed seeds, and soil-borne fungi.

Solarizing the sod without tilling it is safer around buried underground cables. Solarization works on small or large plots anywhere where the summer sun is hot enough, actually in most of the country. It is safe, inexpensive, nonchemical, leaves no plant-injuring residues, and is simple to apply. It kills many soil pests and brings favorable physical and chemical changes to the soil itself.

For better or worse, it does not kill everything. It can therefore be used around trees and shrubs without doing any damage to the tree roots. In tests, soluble nutrients such as calcium, nitrogen, magnesium, and potassium proved more available for plant use after treatment. Several beneficial soil microbes either survived the treatment or recolonized the area soon after. The net result was increased plant production that lasted for several years.

sides of the pot form a mechanical barrier that prevents most nematode damage and the open bottoms let the roots spread deeply into the soil.

Some plants are not bothered, and some varieties of susceptible plants are more resistant. Marigolds, impatiens, and native plants seem resistant, and sweet potatoes seem to repel nematodes. Most other plants are affected to some degree. I was told the damage might be minimal your first year, but increase in subsequent years, but I have found the opposite to be true in my garden. Perhaps because I have used so much organic matter, I seldom have trouble with nematodes now though they seemed a major problem in the first years here.

SOLARIZATION

When I had open space, I used soil solarization during the warm months. This involves preparing the soil as if for planting, raking it smooth, and watering it so that it is

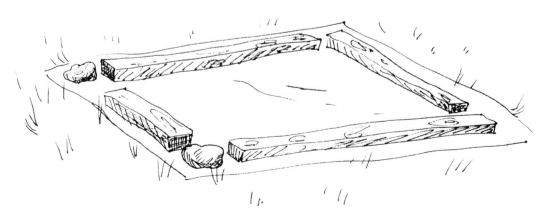

CHAPTER SIX
GREEN GRASS AND OTHER GROUNDCOVERS

The first thing you will notice about lawns in Florida is that the grasses are different. They feel different underfoot and have unfamilar growth patterns and textures. St. Augustine grass is very coarse, making for difficult walking.

Florida lawns, with proper care, can be green and lovely for most of the year, the weeks or days just after frost being the only exception. In my family, we qualified as poor lawn keepers by Florida's exacting standards, but we still came much closer to having green, green grass here for more of the year than we ever did in the North. Proper lawn care need not take a great deal of time. But it is more crucial in Florida to take the right steps when they are needed, or you could wind up with costly damage.

None of the Florida grasses will have as fine a texture, withstand as much neglect, or exhibit the comeback power that northern grasses do. Starve your turf here or let insects set in, and pretty soon you'll have patchy grass fading to none at all, with weeds coming in to fill the vacant patches. And since so many homeowners have professional lawn service, a sick stand of turf stands out in contrast.

CUT YOUR LAWN DOWN TO SIZE

There are good reasons for decreasing the size of your lawn. Turf takes more water, mowing, and care than any other type of planting. Also, there are only a few varieties of grasses that will tolerate light to moderate shade. None will grow in heavy shade. That is all right, because we treasure the shade for flowers, ferns, groundcovers, and shrubs that thrive there with a minimum of care. Many lovely groundcovers grow there rapidly. And where you don't want to grow anything, mulches of leaves, pine needles, or tanbark can be quite attractive.

It is possible to have a small and attractive yard here with no grass at all. I've seen some with white rock mulch, groundcovers, and shrubs surrounding a pool whose owners got rid of their lawnmower.

Most of us want some green lawn. But half an acre can be ridiculous. So while the neighbors were working to manicure their lawns, I was busy reducing mine to a workable size and at the same time adding some of my landscape's most desirable features.

WARM SEASON GRASSES

Unlike northern grasses that can be combined for various purposes, only one kind of warm-season grass will grow on any given area (there's a winter exception to be explained later). You must select just one, or at the most one for each section of your yard. We inherited St. Augustine grass in the front yard and bahia (pronounced ba-HAY-ah) in the back. About 80 percent of Florida lawns are comprised of one or the other of these two grasses. If you live on the coast, you'll probably have St. Augustine, for it is the most salt tolerant. If you have no automatic irrigation, you will want bahia, for it withstands drought the best.

BAHIA (*Paspalum notatum*) is probably the least expensive and least troublesome. It is the best for water conservation since the roots can go down 8 to 10 feet deep to pull up moisture. It is a coarse, pasture type of grass with an open habit that lets in weeds. It tolerates sun or partial shade, neglect, heavy traffic, dry or moist conditions, humidity, and acid or alkaline soil. It also resists pests and diseases. Though it turns brown below 30 degrees, it greens up quickly when the temperature rises. In spring and summer it grows so quickly that it is hard to control the seedheads. A friend who moved into her Florida house in July saw the lawn in full seed and thought it had been neglected for weeks, but it was only bahia grass in bloom a week after the last mowing.

You can start bahia grass from seed but it is not easy. When ours started to die out, I tried twice to overseed it. The seed takes 21 to 28 days to germinate. I didn't know that then and quit daily watering after 14 days, so germination was very poor. If I were to sow bahia seed again, I'd definitely do it during the rainy season and even then you will have to sprinkle it, perhaps twice, on any day it does not rain, so the surface where the seeds are will not dry out.

For a brand new lawn, you must prepare the ground well by weeding and raking. Add organic matter, a thin layer for over-seeding an established lawn, as much as possible for a new one. Allow 7 to 10 pounds of scarified seed to every 1000 square feet, divide this in half and sow the first half walking back and forth one way, then the second half walking back and forth in a perpendicular direction. You can also start with sod.

While we had it, bahia was plenty good enough for our backyard, though sometimes, when we were late mowing, I was glad no one could see inside the fence. Our neighbors had it in their entire yard and cared for it very well. Although ours did not look as lush as some of the more pampered St. Augustine lawns on the block, it never looked as bad as the neglected ones and was much more pleasant to walk on and to mow.

Argentine, Paraguay, and Pensacola are improved varieties, with Argentine the most popular because it has fewer seedheads, is less likely to yellow, and seems to have less mole cricket damage.

Apply a complete fertilizer three to four weeks after growth begins. Water only as needed and then with 1/2 to 3/4 inch of water twice a week or an inch once a week if restrictions are in force. But use a rain gauge and do not water if rainfall provides enough. Bahia turns brown in dry times but revives when it rains again. Feed in March and September with 16-4-8 and add iron with the March feeding to prevent yellow- ing. Use mole cricket baits during the summer. Mow to a height of three to four inches.

BERMUDA GRASS (*Cynodon dactylon*) is a lovely, dark green, fine in texture, and like a cloud to walk on, the closest to northern grasses we have here. This is what they use on the golf courses, with special varieties for the greens. It tolerates salt, drought, and pH

extremes if it gets enough trace elements, turns brown with any frosts, then green again when warm weather returns. This latter could be a definite drawback in northern counties.

There is a nearby apartment complex where it is well kept and quite attractive. But, for most homeowners, it takes too much care: mowing twice a week in summer, feeding up to eight times a year, and weeding and watering all the time. It is more resistant to pests than St. Augustine, but still needs spraying at the first sign of dollar spot fungus, and autumn treatment for army worms (sod webworms). It will not grow in shade. There are some improved varieties now that can be seeded, but they do not include FloraTex, which extension agent and author Tom MacCubbin says is the "only one variety that has good potential as a fairly carefree home lawn... It gets by on the March and September feeding the same as Bahia and has some nematode tolerance." Start it with plugs, sprigs, or sod. Mow to a height of 2 inches.

CENTIPEDE GRASS (*Eremochloa ophiuroides*), also called Poor Man's Turf, has a medium green color and texture and takes less mowing (every ten days in summer) and feeding than the others. It works well on the heavier soils of northern Florida but suffers from nematodes in the rest of the state. It is not tolerant of drought, salt, or heavy traffic, and turns brown in winter. It does best in full sun but will tolerate partial shade. You can get by with a March feeding, though another in the fall can help. If yellowing occurs—more likely in alkaline soils—in the warmer months, apply iron as needed. Start centipede grass from sprigs, plugs, or seed, and watch out for ground pearls, cousins of the mealy bug. Since it needs so much water, surround a centipede grass lawn with plants such as azaleas, camellias, and annuals that also thrive on much water. Mow to a height of 2 to 3 inches.

ST. AUGUSTINE (*Stenotaphrum secundatum*) is a coarse-textured grass with an attractive deep blue-green color year round except for a few days after any freeze. It is the most shade, salt, and cold tolerant of the warm

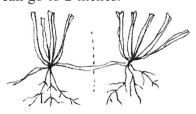

FLORIDA LAWN GRASSES AT A GLANCE

Grass type, care needed	Texture	Winter color	Shade tolerance	Problems
St. Augustine. Start from plugs or sod.	Very coarse	Green*	Light shade	Many
Bahia. Start from seed.	Medium	Green	Partial shade	Few
Bermuda. Needs most care.	Finest	Green*	None	Many
Carpet Grass. Good in wet ground	Coarse	Brown	Partial shade	Some
Centipede. Nematode problems may limit use.	Medium	Brown	Partial shade	Few
Zoysia. Slower to spread.	Fine to medium	Brown in N.	Partial shade	Few

* Can be green most of the year with proper care.

season grasses. 'Floratam' and 'Floralawn' both need full sun and should only be used away from trees and buildings that will cast shade. 'Bitter Blue', 'Delmar', 'Palmetto', and 'Seville' will take partial shade.

All need ample moisture and feeding, especially in shade but once established will go a week or more between waterings. Use a rain gauge or tuna can and be sure to apply 1/2 to 3/4 inch per watering. It will deteriorate quickly if insects and diseases are not constantly controlled. Chinch bugs are its number one enemy and can wipe out large areas if untreated. Watch during the warm months for caterpillars and brown spot and check with your extension office for the best treatment. You can start or restart a St. Augustine lawn any time of year from plugs that will spread to a dense turf in one to two growing seasons. Or lay sod on damp soil and be sure the pieces are closely abutted. Once established, mow most forms of this grass only to 3 inches. 'Seville' can go to 2 inches.

ZOYSIA (*Zoisia* species) is tolerant of salt air and partial shade and has a dense, lush, hardy growth. It will turn brown in cold, almost certainly in the winter in northern sections of the state. But new varieties show great improvements. They are faster growing than old ones and can be started any time of year.

Plugs should spread to a full lawn in one year. Sodding will give an instant, weed resistant lawn if pieces abut. *Z. japonica*, especially 'Belaire' has good cold tolerance and color and can be started from seed, but it is coarser and more open than some. Other good varieties are 'Meyer' (also sold as Z-52) 'Amazoy', 'Emerald', and 'Cashmere'. 'El Toro' shows more disease resistance and quick growth. 'Empire' is a wide-bladed kind and 'Empress' a fine bladed one from Brazil; both do well in Florida.

Zoysia should have the March and September feeding with 16-4-8 and up to four additional ones of nitrogen alone in April, June, August and October. Watch for billbugs that can cause patches of decline and require chemical control. After several years of growth, thatch can build up a layer that will prevent water penetration, harbor insects, detract from appearance and require mechanical removal. A zoysia lawn is soft for walking and can be mowed to one or two inches.

CARPET GRASS (*Axonopus affinis*) will survive in moist soil under pine trees, where it requires only spring feeding and two or three mowings a summer. It turns brown in winter, likes acid soil, produces branching flower stalks, and can be started from seed, sod, or plugs.

WINTER GRASSES, sown right over any of the perennial types mentioned, will give you a beautiful green lawn all winter long, like you dreamed of up north. Sow in October or November. Annual or perennial rye grass will both last only until May and then die out, so buy the cheapest. I rake to loosen soil and weeds in the summer lawn, then broadcast the seed and water once a day for five days until it germinates as green fuzz. Then water less often and more deeply. I've never had any trouble with germination with this, though once I sowed too early (late September) and the heat burned it out.

Temporary winter grass lawns stand out for their color and prevent weeds from getting started in the permanent grass. They also mean mowing in winter as well as summer. In my back yard, that means perhaps three times. You might have to mow a few more times in a front yard, but grass just doesn't grow as fast in winter. I have not had to use irrigation once the seedlings are established, even during dry spells. Nor have I fed the rye, as one ought, in December or January. This easy growing temporary grass satisfies my lawn yearning for another year, but I still may switch for a low groundcover since the rye is just getting started when I have my fall garden gathering and it gets considerable trampling. Usually it recovers well from this activity.

For the rye, sow five to ten pounds of Italian rye grass seed per thousand square feet. Rye is the usual choice, but you can also sow two pounds of Kentucky bluegrass, or use one pound of bent grasses for shady areas.

CALENDAR: LAWN CHORES FOR FLORIDA

January-February. Little mowing, weeding, or watering will be needed. Mowing can be as infrequent as three to five weeks apart during the short days of winter.

March-April. Feed with a high-nitrogen fertilizer like 16-4-8, cottonseed meal or manure tea. Apply according to label directions or spread about six pounds of the first two every 1,000 square feet. Treat weeds. You may want to feed a second time four to six weeks later. Be careful not to overfeed as this causes a rush of tender new grass that insects can hardly resist. Begin watching for insect damage, especially from mole crickets, chinch bugs, and sod webworms. At the first sign of any pest or disease, water with one cup liquid soap in a 20 gallon hose-end sprayer. Then get detailed material from your county agricultural extension office and treat pests accordingly.

May. Use horticultural grade diatomaceous earth, not the swimming pool type, to help control both chinch bugs and lawn fleas. This month can be very hot and dry and is the most crucial time for watering. Begin planning to make the best use of the summer rainy season by getting lawn repair work started.

June-September. These are the rainy months and grass will need mowing once a week, every week and sometimes more often. See mowing heights for your type of grass in individual descriptions. Try to never cut off more than one third of the top growth, for this will result in yellowing and sun scald. Mulching mowers cut grass clippings and leaves into small pieces for faster decomposition and will enrich the lawn as long as you don't let the grass get too tall before mowing.

For extra greening without extra growth, apply iron sulfate according to label instructions once or twice at four to six week intervals, starting in July. Check lawn mower blades for sharpness at least once a month. Continue to watch for diseases and insects and to water if

needed. Natural rainfall will usually be enough. If you have a sprinkler system, turn it on manually instead of using timers for the rainy months and you'll save water and have healthier grass.

August or September. Feed again.

October to December. Mow, water, and treat insect or disease problems as needed. Enjoy respite when not.

Any Time. Remove thatch by raking, renting a power rake for bahia or hiring a professional. Afterward, rake up the debris for the compost pile. Open and dampen a bag of sphagnum peat (see page 43) in the middle of your lawn or section of lawn. Mix with bagged cow manure or compost in little piles all over the area, then rake in to improve the soil and increase water-holding capacity.

PLUGGING FOR REPAIR OR A NEW LAWN

Any newcomer with an established lawn would do well to take care of whatever is there at first. Study the lawns you admire in the area and the different grasses displayed as plugs at local nurseries. If you eventually want to change grass types or improve or repair what you have, plugging is the least expensive and easiest way for all the runner grasses: St. Augustine, zoysia, and Bermuda.

Plugging can be done all year round for St. Augustine and Zoysia. March through September is recommended for the other grasses, but April and May will require more watering. Just before the summer rainy season is the best time to put in grass plugs because there will be ample rain most of the time and growth will be quick in the warm weather.

Plugs are sold in trays holding 18. Order ahead if you want a large quantity at once. Each tray covers 30 to 50 square feet. Another advantage of plugging is that you can do a small area at a time rather than a whole section of lawn.

While you are at the nursery, buy plug starter, a specially formulated fertilizer to put in the bottom of the holes. And rent or borrow a plugging tool. For a small job a hand plugger works nicely and lets you dig standing upright. If you are doing a large yard all at once, you can get an auger-like attachment for an electric drill. You can plug a runner-spreading grass like St. Augustine, for instance, among a seed spreading grass like bahia, weeds and all. Leave the original grass growing but mow it low, about 1.5 inches high.

You can even replace one runner-spreading grass with another, like St. Augustine with zoysia. But in this case you must first kill the old lawn with a foliar weed killer such as Roundup™. Follow the instructions on the label and wait the allotted time before replanting, usually two weeks. This will take the life out of grass and weeds without poisoning the soil. Then plug your new lawn right into the debris of the old one, which will decompose as the new grass runners cover it.

There is no quick or easy organic alternative. You can mechanically remove the old grass or suppress it with mulches. Maybe you can spray with vinegar in several applications, but vinegar does not kill the roots.

PREPARE THE SOIL WELL

For a new lawn, prepare the soil, tilling it deeply and working in peat moss, compost, and lime if needed, as you would for seeding. Add fertilizer. If using 6-6-6, apply ten pounds per 1,000 square feet. You may also want to treat for nematodes (see chapter 5).

At first the plugs will be lined up like a crop in rows. But before you know it, the empty spaces become green. Some of this will be weed growth, but don't worry. Grasses that come in plugs spread by runners and will take over with a thickness that seeded grasses seldom achieve. Depending on the kind, the season, and the care, thick coverage takes three months for most types, up to a year for zoysia.

Joe Kellerson, a retired man from New York now living in Riverview, Florida, made his St. Augustine lawn the showplace of the neighborhood, redoing it himself a little at a time. He usually bought and worked with ten plug trays each trip.

"Pick out the greenest, healthiest looking trays," he says. You can stack them up in the back of your car without any mess. One day I put in 17 trays."

The day before you work on a section of lawn, water the area well so that it is damp down a good three or four inches: about 45 minutes with most automatic sprinkler systems, up to a few hours with hose-end systems. This will soften the soil and cut your digging time and effort by as much as half and also get the plugs off to the best possible start. Watering a day in advance leaves the soil moist, but means that it is well enough drained that you do not have to work in wetness.

Kellerson recommends watering the plugs in their trays well, too. Then turn them upside down. The plugs are tough; you dont have to be gentle. Sometimes the runners have already spread enough to root into other sections. Use force to pull them apart or cut connections. If some roots on the runners are exposed, you can either cover them or not. The main root ball will sustain growth until the runners take root again.

Kellerson set his plugs about 18 inches apart in a checkerboard pattern.

"Where the ground was almost bare, I measured exactly. But where there was some lawn already, I filled in the empty spots as close to that as possible."

Zoysia grass grows more slowly, so plug it every ten to twelve inches. The closer you plant, the faster the covering.

You can remove the soil from the holes to other areas of the yard or to the compost pile. Or break it up and spread it between the holes after they are planted. The drill attachment pulverizes the soil from the hole so it is easy to spread.

Be careful about hitting tree roots with the auger. Also be sure to count plugs and fill up every hole. If you accidentally leave one empty, someone could turn an ankle.

Keep the plugs moist at all times until rooted. The first three weeks are critical. Do not sprinkle as for grass seed; but water deeply for

roots that are three inches deep. Plugs settle in as quickly as in seven to ten days. To test, tug on the top of a plug. If it does not come up, it is time to shift from daily to every-other-day watering.

When plugs have begun to take root, mowing becomes very important to encourage branching and runners instead of height. Apply lawn food every four to six weeks after installation for three applications. Continue to water and mow as needed.

LAWNMOWER CARE

Lawnmower care is the same as in the North, but you don't change for winter. Oil needs changing and mower blades need sharpening more often in Florida.

LAWN CARE COMPANIES

There are many lawn care professionals in Florida, and you may wish to employ them, especially in your first year until you become familiar with the new grasses and the problems you might expect. If you want as few poison chemicals anywhere on your property as possible, it will be more difficult to find the right company. Shop around until you find a lawn care service that will use organic products and explain why, as they do it.

LAWN ALTERNATIVES

In Florida, lawns need a lot more than just mowing, because the soils lack fertility and water holding capacity, and there is a wide array of pests and diseases. So, consider alternatives to a large lawn. Marianne Binetti, in her book, *Tips for Carefree Landscapes,* suggests that you stick your sprinkler into the middle of your lawn, turn it on high, and then keep whatever gets wet for your lawn. Around the edges, set in drought resistant groundcovers or mulch with something attractive like tan wood chips, small bark chips, pine needles, white gravel, or black chunks of coal. Binetti lives in the Pacific Northwest where it is often rainy. Her advice is that much more practical for our rainy desert in Florida.

I have seen several yards where large areas of bark mulch are part of the design, but also serve as extra parking spaces or a turn-around area. This is an excellent idea, attractive and, on busy streets where backing out is a problem, a significant safety feature. It combines low-maintenance landscaping with better access into or out of long streams of traffic.

GROUND COVERS INSTEAD

Ground covers can be perennials, low shrubs, vines or ornamental grasses that have a spreading growth habit to cover the ground densely. Once established, they are easier to maintain than a lawn. Many have flowers; some are herbs and some are edible.

Ground covers make lovely lawn substitutes that add color, texture, elegance, and ease. In Florida most are evergreen. They can be flowering, fragrant, drought-resistant, pest-free, and perfectly delightful. Some of them will take a bit of foot traffic. In the others you can put stepping stones or paths of pine needles.

While paving and light colored mulches reflect heat and can add to air conditioning costs, lawns and ground covers absorb heat, shade the ground, hold in moisture, and prevent erosion.

Ground covers take a bit of watering until established and through their first dry season. New plantings will need roughly the same weeding as a flower or vegetable garden through their first summer. This will diminish to only a bit of hand weeding as they spread and crowd out the competition. They will grow and prosper where grass will not, as in the shade. They are especially important on our few hills or berms where mowing would be difficult.

Some of them can eventually become invasive. Some only need an edging or a gardener's discipline to keep them in bounds. Since their advantage is their ability to spread and make a dense cover, it is a good idea to surround them with a foot wide border of mulch and not let them cross it. Do not let them encroach on garden paths.

As I added more and more plants to my yard, I realized a little too late that some areas of very short growth such as lawn or low ground covers, less than about eight inches tall are necessary to set off the taller plants while avoiding the jungle look. I am now working in that direction.

Look over the following list of ground covers. Then, on your first trip to a nursery, buy one or two pots of whichever ones you like, as a test. Plant them in your newly enriched ground, in sun or shade as needed, and let them start spreading. By the time you have your landscape plan settled, you'll know what will grow best and spread fastest for you and will have a good start on your planting stock. Divide or take cuttings of the original plants and plant a small area at a time for the least expense. Or buy what you need and plant it all at once. Or watch for a gardener thinning an overcrowded ground cover planting, and ask for starter plants that would otherwise be thrown away.

GROUND COVERS FOR FLORIDA

Begonias make striking edges or groundcovers for central and southern Florida gardens year round and for much of the year in the north. There it is wise to take cuttings indoors every fall.

Most types of begonias grow well in Florida and some are the brightest spots in the shade garden. They can be annual or perennial. This genus is enormously varied in shape, size, texture, and color, in the leaves as well as

RESURRECTION FERN

Resurrection fern (*Polypodium polypodioides*) is not really a ground cover since it grows on tree trunks, but it is one of Florida's most fascinating native ferns. It is often found growing up a tree trunk or out a spreading live oak branch where it does no harm to the tree. It sometimes also grows on rocks or takes root in damp, acid soil. But what makes it unique is that the fronds curl up and look quite dead during dry times but seem to magically come back to life after a rain or watering, The fronds are only six to eight inches long and it prefers light to medium shade. These plants are seldom seen in nurseries and are not easy to propagate. But, interestingly, gardener Carl Crosson of Brandon has one that stays green all the time. He keeps a fern-covered log upturned in a clay saucer of water.

flowers. Angel wings get too tall for ground covers but are great for other purposes. Only the tuberous begonias are short lived here. Too often, their tubers rot in our steamy summers.

Beware of overwatering with all begonias. Wax begonias are excellent low bedding plants but will have to be replaced periodically. The star begonias are ideal companion plants for camellias since they like the same partial shade conditions, bloom at the same time with spires of pale pink, and form another lower layer of color and interest all year round with their many colored low leaves. Most begonias root easily from cuttings and have attractive foliage when not in bloom.

Blue daze (*Evolvulus glomeratus*) is a Florida treasure that I bought right away for its lovely blue flower. It is cold tender and can be short-lived, but grows easily. Plant it in full sun for best bloom but it will tolerate partial shade. It stays about ten inches tall, spreads quickly, and is moderately drought and highly salt tolerant. It has blue flowers that open only part of the day, but open every day that is above freezing. A fertilizer low in N, high in P and K will increase bloom. The foliage is small, oval, and gray-green. My first potful spread over large areas before it died out in a freeze. The second one lasted three years and spread even farther. Blue daze can be damaged by overwatering or planting too deeply.

Bugleweed (*Ajuga reptans*) is as hardy all over Florida, in full sun or partial shade, as it is in the North, and it spreads faster. It grows only a few inches tall, but a single plant multiplies into many and will soon spread across one to three feet in area. The upright spires of flowers are usually dark blue but also come in white, pink, and purple, blooming from February through April, attracting bees. There are several available varieties with different foliage colors. The most common is a deep green that turns bronze in the winter. Ajuga has poor salt tolerance and medium drought tolerance. It is a herb in the mint family and once was used to cure coughs, rheumatism, and hangovers and to slow bleeding from wounds. Mine did well for many years but eventually was crowded out by more vigorous plants.

Ferns of many kinds do well as groundcovers in shade to partial sun throughout the state. The ones we tried and killed back in our dry, heated, northern houses will carpet the ground beneath trees and even climb the trunks of some of the palms and they show up even if you don't plant them. They will take over quickly and are Category I invasives. Don't let them run freely. I will admit I let the volunteer ferns spread in several shady areas for many years, but I have been replacing them with more choice ferns like the native swamp fern (*Blechnum serrulatum*) that grows two feet and

58

strap fern (*Polypodium phyllitidis*) that grows two feet. I love my brake fern (*Pteris* species) with its silvery foliage, and the leatherleaf (*Rumohra adiantiformis*) we used to buy for foliage in the flower shop and the many forms of maidenhair fern (*Adiantum* species) that love limy soil. There are 24 non-invasive kinds listed as good for groundcover in my *Florida Gardeners Book of Lists* and I'm sure my friends in the fern society would come up with more.

Honeysuckle, Hall's and trumpet (*Lonicera japonica* and *L. sempervirens*), will grow in northern and central Florida as vines or groundcovers. Only the first, with white flowers turning yellow, is fragrant. The pink flowers of the other have little odor. Florida soil and humidity tame these in our area. They are hardy and consistently poking through my neighbor's fence. But the cuttings I've taken have grown very slowly, much to my astonishment. In Pennsylvania we were careful not to park where this could cover our car while we were gone. Hall's honeysuckle blossoms are said to be antiviral. Gather and dry them when they are abundant and use for tea when a virus threatens.

Hottentot Fig or Ice Plant (*Carpobrotus edulis*) is a creeping succulent that is moderately drought tolerant, good for shore or open sun groundcover for central and southern Florida. Its gray-green, leaves grow six inches tall. Yellow or rose-purple daisylike flowers bloom in summer.

Ivies (*Hedera helix* and *H. canariensis*) are excellent groundcovers for all of Florida. They thrive even in the deep shade of oak trees, and will climb trunks without damaging them. Ivy has moderate salt tolerance. A gardener I met put a sad looking 15 cent plant beside a tree and in 25 years it grew to cover a large section of the yard and curtain the tree most attractively with enough extra to supply a local florist occasionally. There are hundreds of varieties of ivy with different leaf shapes, colors, sizes, and markings. Ivy requires water, and sometimes there are problems with scale or spider mites.

Jasmine. Several jasmines, though most often grown as shrubs or vines, may also be allowed to sprawl as groundcovers.

Confederate jasmine (*Trachelospermum jasminoides*) is hardy in all of Florida, likes sun for best bloom, but will tolerate deep shade. It grows slowly to climb or spread 20 feet and is covered with very fragrant white, twisty-shaped three quarter inch flowers from February to May. There is also a variety with variegated leaves. This one is quite salt tolerant and withstands medium drought as well.

Jasmine minima, small-leaf Confederate Jasmine (*Trachelospermum asiaticum*) is Brandon nurseryman Larry Kerby's all-time favorite plant. It makes an excellent groundcover for sun or shade with its small shiny green leaves. There is also a cultivar with variegated foliage, 'Bronze Beauty' with bronze new growth, some kinds that are extra compact, and a few other named varieties. Check them out at your local nursery. While in theory all plants bloom, the blooms of *Jasmine minima* are seldom seen. If you want spring flowers and fragrance, mix a little Confederate jasmine in with it. Both of these species have medium drought and salt tolerance and will form a thick mat that eliminates weeds. Larry uses his long handled hedge trimmer to cut his back a few times a year to make it grow ever thicker.

Junipers (*Juniperus* species) are hardy all over Florida and are the best of the needled, coniferous (cone-bearing) evergreen groundcovers. They prefer full sun to partial shade. Some are shrubs or trees, but many are sprawling to prostrate groundcovers growing from slowly to moderately fast, staying as low as six inches tall, and spreading from three to eight feet. One of the best groundcovers is the shore juniper with blue-green foliage and good salt tolerance. Some cultivars have foliage with decorative yellow tips. Junipers sometimes have problems with spider mites or juniper blight, but are drought tolerant. They seldom fruit in Florida.

Kalanchoe (*Kalenchoe* species) can be used as an interesting succulent groundcover for southern Florida, and in protected spots in the central area. Drought tolerant, they need full sun to light shade. There are various types, some with lovely blooms for several weeks from Christmas to spring, some with taller flowers. All are excellent for cut flowers. These are fairly salt tolerant. Take cuttings if it frosts. They will root lying on top of wet sand. I have never lost any plants but sometimes blooms get nipped by frost. These can overspread.

Lantana. Creeping lantana (*Lantana montevidensis*) grows wild and slightly woody where protected from frost in much of Florida. In the north it dies to the ground but comes back quickly in the spring. It blooms best in full sun but does well in shade also. The flowers, in colors of orange, yellow, lavender, pink, and white, are abundant in the summer but also in flushes for much of the rest of the year. Plants have excellent salt and drought tolerance and the leaves and stems have a delightful fragrance when crushed or brushed. Avoid *Lantana camara*, the taller and wilder kind. It is on the Category I list of the worst invasives that are altering our native plant communities.

Lovely lantana can be a pest. Choose the creeping type over the woody tall wild kind.

Lilyturf (*Liriope muscari*) is hardy in all sections of the state and all soils in the shade. Its grassy leaves grow 12 to 18 inches tall and crowns spread slowly to 30 inches. It blooms with lavender spikes of flowers in spring and summer, followed by black berries. It is showier than mondo grass and is widely used as an edging and a groundcover. There are improved forms and some have variegated leaves.

Some of the best cultivars include: 'Silvery Sunproof' with striped white and yellow leaf blades that withstand a good bit of sun and purple flowers, 'Monroe's White' with bright white flowers in large clusters, gets 12 inches tall, and does best in shade and 'Christmas Tree' with unusual light lavender flower spikes in the form of an evergreen tree, gets 12 to 15 inches tall, and prefers shade. Creeping lily turf (*Liriope spicata*) is ideal for a lawn replacement and spreads faster than *L. muscari*. 'Silver Dragon' has slender, variegated green and white leaves and lavender flowers 12 inches tall and is great for brightening a dark area. 'Franklin Mint' has pale lavender spikes above green leaves 12 to 15 inches tall and a bit wider. All are moderately salt tolerant and very drought tolerant.

Mondo grass (*Ophiopogon japonicus*) looks much the same as liriope, though leaves may be shorter, more slender, and darker green. It is sometimes called dwarf lily turf. Mondo grass is hardy and adaptive, growing in sun to full shade. It has lilac flowers in summer, though they are often hidden in the foliage. It has high salt tolerance. Both mondo grass and lily turf are fine groundcovers in the shade, often used for edging. The loveliest planting of this I've seen was a broad expanse of dark green in front of a stately white house with accents of the whitest of the caladiums.

Ornamental peanut (*Arachis glabrata*) is a tropical perennial groundcover for full sun to partial shade. It is especially good for holding soil on berms or banks. Untrimmed, it gets little taller higher than 6" and it can be kept to an inch and a half by mowing it every two to four weeks through the summer, less in the winter. Mowing does promote more flowering. The leaves are a light green, small and oval. Bright yellow flowers begin in the spring and continue until September. Unlike the related edible peanut, these flowers do not bury their heads in the soil but remains upright.

The plants are drought resistant and easy to maintain. The only problem could be that if you change your mind, the underground rhizomes are difficult to eradicate once established. None of the references I've found mention foot traffic, but I have this covering some of my paths in the front yard and have seen no damage from my feet or even after the many visitors when the garden was open.

I've been taking cuttings and moving them to my small area of turf in the back yard where they are spreading slowly. I'm sure I could cover the whole area in a single summer if I bought enough plants to place them every six to nine inches. In the front where I started with larger plants already with many runners, they spread very quickly. I must admit that some of my cuttings have died. Other growers report that the tops may die back after a frost but the plants come back from the roots even when temperatures dip to the low twenties.

Ornamental sweet potatoes (*Ipomoea batatas*) make a lovely groundcover or do well cascading over hanging baskets or the edges of large containers. There are several different varieties, including 'Blackie' with deeply cut leaves of darkest burgundy, 'Marguerite' with heart-shaped leaves of bright chartreuse, 'Vardaman' with plum colored heart-shaped leaves, and 'Pink Frost' which is tricolored with green, pink, and cream. The latter is less vigorous, as all variegated plants tend to be. The foliage has the deepest color in full sun but it also does well in partial shade. Cuttings root so easily you can root them in water. Now and then there are a few little pink flowers, but not often.

If you dig around them, you will find some tubers underneath which are edible. The one serious problem this plant can have is its attraction for slugs and snails. I find watering with soapy water fairly often will help immensely, but even in the best gardens there are some holey leaves. It sometimes helps to cut them back to the base and let them start over. They can overspread if not controlled and can look a bit peaked in cold weather.

Peacock gingers or peacock lilies (*Kaempferia* species) are fascinating perennials with attractive foliage somewhat like the hostas, more like the prayer plants we had indoors in the north. They grow throughout the state in light to full shade with low rosettes, six to eight inches high. They go dormant in my yard toward the end of November and pop up from the ground with unrolling leaves as late as April or May. The simple four-petalled flowers are small, lavender, pink, white, or white and violet, never terribly showy, but constant from spring to fall. They have low salt and medium drought tolerance, though I seldom water mine. Sowing alyssum seeds around them over the winter will give a pleasant year round combination.

Periwinkle. Madagascar periwinkle, often referred to as vinca, is now officially *Catharanthus roseus*. This drought and salt-tolerant plant is hardy in the central and southern sections of the state, in sun to partial shade. It is grown as an annual in northern Florida, and in states farther north. Plants from cuttings or seeds spread quickly and grow up to two feet tall and wide. It blooms prolifically all

summer and much of the rest of the year with white, pink, or lilac flowers on shiny, dark green foliage. Some varieties stay shorter. Pinch back when small for bushiness.

Silver licorice (*Helichrysum petiolare)* has small silver fuzzy leaves crowded along silver stems and branching to eight inches high and 18 long. It maintains a bushy appearance without any pinching and is excellent for hanging baskets and containers as well as groundcovers in full sun to light shade.

Although it is grown and sold by herb growers, it is not a true licorice. If this one has any herbal qualities, I have yet to discover them. It is actually a cousin of both the curry plant and the strawflower, but I find it longer lasting than either. I babied my first plant in a container lest it melt in the summer rains as most silver-leaved plants do. It did not. I still have that plant, in a much larger container, many years later and it has survived without any extra help through winters and summers. The blooms either haven't come yet or are so inconspicuous that I haven't noticed them.

Mine has rooted by natural ground layers where it grows over the pot and touches the ground, but I have not had good luck with cuttings. One grower, however, reports his cuttings root easily. It can also be grown from seed, but since it is available in most nurseries, I'd recommend getting a started plant. There is a lovely chartreuse variety called 'Limelight'.

A grower from New Jersey said his helichrysums were eaten by caterpillars that turned into Painted Lady butterflies and that the plant leafed out again very quickly. I have never seen caterpillars on mine.

Society garlic (*Tulbaghia violacea*) is similar to liriope and mondo grass, but with lilac flowers in sprays atop long stems rather than on spikes. It tolerates either sun or shade, but salt only slightly. The whole plant is edible and may be used like chives. It is not as commonly used, but leaves have a garlic fragrance and flavor when crushed.

Wandering Jew (*Zebrina pendula*) grows only four to ten inches tall. It is hardy in the central and southern areas, and requires shade and moist soil. Leaves have various stripes of purple, green, or white. To propagate it, cut off the trailers and drop them on the ground. Or root pieces in a glass of water on the windowsill.

*

Many other plants do well as groundcovers here, including daylilies, dichondra, coontie, and creeping figs, in all parts of the state. Aloe, bromeliads, beach morning glory, and wedelia grow in central and southern zones. Be careful of wedelia. It can be invasive. So can northern houseplants like Chinese evergreen, pothos, and philodendron. Creeping charlie, partridgeberry and winter creeper grow in northern zones. Artillery plant grows well in southern Florida.

CHAPTER SEVEN
FLOWERS IN FLORIDA

Florida gets its name from its abundance of flowers. Hundreds of species, both natives and new arrivals, thrive here and richly color the seasons. Some will be familiar to you. Many will be new.

You can still grow most of your old favorites, but may need to plant them at different times of year than you did in the North. Some flowers, especially hardy perennials, will not do well here because of the hot, wet summers, and you'll be glad to know in advance that it is not your fault! Others will thrive without too much care. Right away, you will start learning the names and needs of the intriguing new flowers you see around you. Some old favorites will grow at new times and have new requirements for water, fertilization, and soil improvement as explained in the former chapters. But you will soon adjust to these and find it is very easy here to have flowers every day of the year.

abutilon, flowering maple

HANDS-ON EXPERIENCE

Seedlings of old favorites like salvia and nasturtium sat in my first flowerbeds that whole first summer and sulked. Looking back, I wonder that they survived. I had no idea then that, come winter, those same seedlings would take off, grow, and bloom abundantly. As with vegetables, timing is all-important (use the chart of planting times on page 00 as a guide).

On the other hand, the moonflowers that I had tried for years to grow in Iowa, with the most limited success, now grew and lit up the night. These cousins of the morning glory have larger blooms of a delicate white, open in the evening, and fill the air with their heavenly perfume. They are natives of Florida swamps, and the best way to raise them is to move to Florida. Many other exotic "wish book" flowers are equally suited to growing conditions here.

Right from the beginning, I was learning from my mistakes. Nothing makes more of an impression or helps a person learn more quickly than hands-on experience. Luckily, with flowers, experience is not expensive. Of course, seed is cheap. You can also start with bedding plants and have an instant garden. And you are sure to have some successes right from the start. I've never had such globe amaranths as I grew that first summer.

ASK OTHER GARDENERS

One of the houses near our new home was set in a paradise of trees, shrubs, and blooming flowers. When I called and asked if I could have a garden tour, the owner, Mrs. Georgia, agreed readily. Most gardeners are flattered by such requests. I am.

Among the many things I learned from her were that impatiens will continue to bloom from year to year in central and southern Florida unless there is a severe freeze. In that case, plants come back readily from seed where the ground is kept moist enough. Or you can easily start them from seed or cuttings. The same is true of coleus. And she told me that caladiums need not be dug up in the winters except in the coldest parts of northern Florida. In central and southern regions, they die down in winter and come back reliably in spring.

Here is a hint I pass along, in the same spirit as the advice: "too much money can be a problem." Often the plants that people are glad to share are invasive growers, so be careful about such garden gifts and don't let anything overrun your space. Mrs. Georgia gave me a start of false roselle that has dark red leaves and darker red hibiscus-like flowers. All parts are edible and useful for making drinks or mixing in salads. I like it, but the plant goes crazy. Fortunately it dies back in the slightest freeze, but a million seedlings come up to replace it. Now I've learned to hoe out seedlings and prune branches mercilessly to keep it in its place, and warn anyone to whom I give starts.

Mrs. Georgia also gave me names of and directions to her favorite nurseries. Look for the same information from an experienced gardener who lives near your Florida home.

NURSERIES AND GARDEN CENTERS

Before we moved, I bought a few plants every spring and a few supplies throughout the year. The people at the local garden center knew me because I asked so many questions and wrote columns about the answers. Since coming to Florida, the people at the nurseries are less likely to know me but likely to make more profit from my visits. I figured that I had left many plants behind, and anything I buy here is an investment in learning as well as landscaping. I am now too old to be frugal and learn slowly.

I always found nurseries to be great places. When we first came here, most of them featured plants labeled with the botanical and common name, whether to plant in sun or shade, and how tall the plant will grow. Don't hesitate to walk around with a notebook writing all this down so you can remember it.

Since then there seem to be many fewer nurseries, I am sorry to say, but some are so large that they are almost like parks. Their displays give good ideas for plant combinations, especially in containers, and you can learn much by noticing what is set out in full sun and what in shade. Many people go there just to enjoy the flowers, sit on the benches, and savor the scents. Everyone knows me now at our nearest nursery and I often take a camera, still ask questions and make notes, and especially enjoy visits to their butterfly house.

When I mention that I am going on a trip, people tell me of nurseries in other parts of the state that I just have to see, and I do. I often bring home a new plant for my garden.

Most reliable nurseries will sell the bedding plants appropriate for the season. If everything in my yard freezes, I go shopping the next day and at least get plants to add color by the front walk. Be aware that the garden departments in discount stores with nationwide franchises may not be so true to the climate. I especially notice them selling bulbs that won't grow here and books with methods that won't work here. This is not true of all. Some have excellent garden departments and employees that can give great advice.

gardenia

READ ALL YOU CAN

I mentioned the county agricultural extension service in chapter 1, and recommend visiting the extension office often. Local newspapers are also good sources of timely information, but be careful to look for the work of Florida writers. Some papers take articles from wire services that are not oriented to Florida. Some of their tips are relevant and some are ridiculous, but a newcomer does not know the difference at first.

The internet is not essential to gathering gardening information, but if you have it you will enjoy the ways you can use it to find plant information and photographs, local and distant suppliers, and even online driving directions to botanical gardens and garden centers. In the back matter of this book, you will find addresses of many garden oriented websites, including my own.

It took me a long time to get comfortable with the internet. I still use books first. But there is a limit to how many books a person can cram into a house and there are always so many new varieties along with plenty of information. I especially enjoy checking comments of how certain plants are doing for people in various

Quick Tips on Propagation from Cuttings

Take a piece of a stem. Stick it into water or a sterile medium, and it will form new roots and a new plant. Taking such cuttings is both very handy and very amazing. You can get a start of a plant without doing any harm to the parent plant as long it is strong, healthy, and has enough stems that a few cuttings won't be missed. In fact, taking cuttings often improves the shape and encourages more compact growth. Take the cutting from where you would prune the plant.

Not all plants can be rooted from cuttings. Ferns, many gingers, and plants whose stems come from the ground such as Bird of Paradise cannot be propagated from stem cuttings. Coleus and pentas root easily. It is best to take cuttings from stems without blooms if you have a choice.

Cuttings usually make larger plants more quickly than seeds. Also, cuttings will have the same characteristics as the parent—same color flowers, fragrance, flavor of fruit, etc—while seeds, which have two parents, can vary greatly from the parent.

So, here is how to do it:

1. Use clean pots or flats with drainage holes. I put holes in old dishpans or styrofoam coolers. Fill these with sterile medium. I like vermiculite. Other choices are perlite, a mixture of perlite and peat moss, sterile sand, or potting soil. You want a medium that will hold water and air, stay wet for a long time and yet not get soggy. Dampen it well and pack it down with your hands.

2. The best time to take cuttings is early in the day when the plants are full of moisture. With a sharp knife or scissors, snip a five inch long piece, choosing a vigorous young tip or side shoot. Green stems root more quickly than woody ones. Cut just above a node so you won't leave a stub. Remove and discard any flowers, buds, or lateral shoots. Make a slanting cut just below the lowest node and discard that lower piece of stem because new roots will form at the node on most cuttings. Remove leaves from the lower two inches of the cutting. If a plant has large leaves, trim away most of them, leaving only a small area. Leave the small new leaves at the tip unless you are trying to ppromote side branches.

3. You can dip the stem ends in liquid or powdered rooting hormone such as Rootone™. Shake off the excess. I don't unless I've had trouble with that plant. Stick the stem ends into the planting medium about two inches deep and two inches apart. Firm the medium around the stem, water with a fine spray, and label.

4. Keep the cuttings in shade, the medium wet but not soggy, and mist often to keep humidity high. Also, remove any dead leaves from the surface to prevent disease. Cuttings may wilt a bit at first. Misting once a day or so with a spray bottle will help.

5. After one to five weeks you can gently pull a cutting to test for roots. If it resists, there are roots. Use a trowel or large spoon to lift roots intact and pot up or plant the cutting in the ground. Shield it from sudden sun for a few days until it becomes acclimated. If the cutting comes up unrooted, just put it back, firm the medium around it, and wait a little longer.

---

parts of the state and the country. Okay, I was not the first person to enthuse about the web but I couldn't do without it now!

I have always believed that gardening can be a spectator sport for people who so desire. You don't have to actually do it to enjoy reading about it or looking at great plants. And even for us who do enjoy it, a pleasant and practical way to rest is to do some garden research online.

But in 1987 books got me started in Florida. Before I had been here many weeks, I got a surprise present in the mail from someone I had never met. Betty Mackey, who heard from a magazine editor with whom we both worked

that I had moved, sent me a copy of her book, *A Cutting Garden for Florida*. It was small and specific, and helped me in growing cut flowers, and everything else, too. Betty moved North from Longwood, Florida just after I moved South, so when she wanted to expand the book a few years later, she asked me to be her coauthor. My garden bloomed with new and old favorite flowers while I researched that book, and continues to bloom because of it.

For anyone interested primarily in growing flowers, reading that book, now in this third and expanded edition, is the logical next step after this one. The books listed in the back matter of this one would be next.

LEARN AS YOU GROW

That first summer I had only the slightest inkling of all the factors of Florida growing mentioned in the third chapter. If you read or reread them now, they will save you many problems. But one of the most important parts of adjusting is to make some mistakes and learn from them. Don't let them discourage you. You will overcome most of that unsettled, unrooted feeling by the end of the first year (but you can still use it as an excuse for at least five years). Relax and enjoy your garden. Here are some suggestions for flowers to grow in all seasons, and tips to make them bloom abundantly.

AUTUMN

Experienced Florida gardeners think of fall as the start of the garden season, but you can stretch this notion from August to October. Before September, when the rains stop, it is still very easy to root cuttings, so propagate any of those bedding plants you bought. When the rains stop, remember to sprinkle or mist the cuttings as needed, as often as every day. Prepare your soil while you are waiting for the season to change. One morning you will wake up and go out to feel wonderful coolness again. Then you can turn off the air conditioning, open the doors and windows, and intensify your gardening efforts. Seedlings thrive in the cooler weather and in autumn sunlight that is not too intense for them. Mature plants spring out of the doldrums into new leaf and bloom.

In southern Florida, you can continue to grow summer annuals all fall and winter. Here in central Florida, I still take a chance on any I want. The weather varies considerably from year to year, and during many winters we have lost very little to cold. In northern and central Florida, you can enjoy chrysanthemums, which can be transplanted at any time of year. Most bloom both in fall and in spring.

You'll see petunias, dianthus, and pansies for sale in the fall, and these will bloom through most or all of the winter. Pansies are the sturdiest choice because they are most impervious to frost. The other two will lose flowers but not leaves to light frost unless protected from it.

chrysanthemum

In the northwestern counties of Florida, only the pansies have a chance of blooming all through the winter; the others will freeze very late in fall. As if in exchange, gardeners here have a climate cool enough for dafodils and lilies and other hardy perennial flowers we loved farther north but cannot grow in central and southern Florida.

In all parts of Florida, fall is a good time to sow seeds of biennials, perennials, and hardy annuals. In northern Florida, plant in September. Possibilities are violas, *Phlox drummondii*, alyssum, Ammi or bishops flower, poppies, stocks, cornflowers, rudbeckia, larkspur, love-in-a-mist, babys breath, snapdragon, and sweet peas.

In central and southern Florida, sow seeds after the weather turns milder, in October or even November. Plant those flowers listed above plus nasturtiums, silene, jewels of Opar, sunflowers, clarkia, and California poppies.

The seeds grow slowly. A few plants will bloom in fall and winter, others not much until February or March, but then they start growing rapidly and will be large and vigorous plants that will give you flowers by the bunch.

WINTER

In a good year, we hardly notice that winter has come in central and southern Florida, except for the changes in day length and sun and shade patterns. Fall tends to melt into spring. Northern Florida has a more definite winter, but it is a fairly mild one, especially in contrast to states farther north.

Some of the trees, the sycamore, liquidambar (sweet gum), northern fruits, and shrubs like crape myrtle, will lose their leaves and let in more sunlight. January is the closest we come to the dormancy of a northern winter, so if you have to move any woody or perennial

66

Favorite Plants That Were New To Me In Florida

Bishops Flower. This is one to plant for white clouds of bloom in spring. I ordered Queen Anne's lace, but the seed company sent me this, *Ammi majus*, instead. I was disappointed until it started to bloom. Wow! Seeds planted in fall grow slowly until spring, then take off. The plants have shiny, compound leaves which are less coarse, feathery, or carrot scented than Queen Anne's lace. The flowers are similar, but there is no dark floret in the center, and there are many more flower clusters per plant for quite a show from early April until late May. Some of the plants grew six feet tall and needed staking. It is best to pinch them back at least once. Ammi is excellent for cutting, and now the pros are raising it for florist flowers. Sometimes it is said to be perennial, but mine are biennial. The plants bloom themselves to death and do not reseed, so I start a new batch every fall.

Jewels of Opar, Fame Flower, and Waterleaf are some of the common names for *Talinum paniculatum* or other *Talinum* species. This is very easy to grow, and new information about it has me very excited. It has been growing in my garden from seeds planted over ten years ago and it reseeds and naturalizes easily without being a pest. It seems to prefer sun but tolerates light shade and loves to grow in flower pots, though it grows well in the ground as well. I first planted it as a cut flower. The blooms that shoot up about two feet provide large, airy decorative panicles which are masses of buds, little pink or lavender flowers, and tiny, shiny, round red seedpods smaller than peppercorns. When I found a cultivar with variegated leaves and yellow fruits, I begged a cuttings and now have that, too. Both withstand heat, drought, and neglect.

A few years ago an older gardening friend told me of someone who had gone to the doctor and was given one of these plants and told to eat a leaf a day for the rest of her life. My friend had taken up the practice, and I came home and ate quite a few leaves myself. Then another young gardener told me that her grandmother had similar advice, telling her that the leaves were rich in iron and good for anemia. My husband and I have taken to eating a leaf a day and are feeling less stiff, and we survived two winters without colds or flu though we got no flu shots.

 You can find seeds in the catalogs of J.L. Hudson, who also mentions that the leaves are edible both raw and parboiled, and of Thompson and Morgan. I suspect that the green variety would be best for leaf eating and it is also the quickest growing. When I started digging up plants for my friends, I found that they have tuberous roots, some even in clumps like dahlias, though not as large. They are members of the Purslane family, whose other members are sometimes used as vegetables.

plants, do it then. In southern Florida, it is the best time of year to plant bulbs, tubers and corms of flowers such as gladiolus, caladium, dahlia, amaryllis, crinum, and rain lily. Wait a few weeks longer in central Florida. In northern Florida, wait until late winter when the danger of frost passes.

Be sure to decrease the amount and frequency of watering and fertilizing during the short days of winter because the plants just won't be growing as much so they won't need as much. Too much water can cause rot and too much fertilizer at this time can cause new growth before it is safe from frost. Once the days grow longer, you will notice a definite increase in growth that will continue through the spring. With this you can increase the water gradually as needed and then add fertilizer when new growth will be safe from frosts.

In all regions, prune flowering shrubs before new growth starts. Until you have lived here long enough to know when that is, prune when you are in the mood or when you see swelling buds or new growth just starting. Or do it when you see your neighbors, the ones whose yards you admire, do theirs.

In northern Florida, bring in the plants you want to save from frost. They will need protection for a few weeks, at least, usually from mid-December to February or March. Start your seedlings on the windowsill, in a sunroom, in a coldframe, or under lights indoors, or in pots or right in the ground outdoors.

In much of the state, you can sow seeds all winter and only bring in plants if it gets cold enough to threaten frost. On the other hand, many plants that lived through winter in the North may die out here in frost simply because

it is so sudden and the plant has not prepared for cold by sending sap safely to the roots.

SPRING

The main difference between spring here and farther north is that Florida's spring is the glorious end for many plants, rather than the beginning. So it is even more important to make the most of it. Starting plants in the fall and winter helps here. Then they are ready to bloom with the first warmth. In South Florida, that can be January as days start to lengthen. Almost any annual flower will bloom and grow in Florida's spring, and a few of them are heat lovers that will continue into or through summer.

Many plants bloom themselves to death here, without winter weather to finish them off. Some, like pentas, impatiens, coleus, vinca, and butterfly weed, just keep on blooming and always look good. Cutting bunches for the house encourages more growth. Prune plants as needed or as you pick them for bouquets.

Geraniums, if they have some summer shade, will continue to bloom nicely, but never with the vigorous growth and intensity of color they had in the North.

Others like zinnias, marigolds, cosmos, and begonias will bloom for several weeks and then start to look seedy. Shearing back will help some but you will have to be hard hearted now.

Yank out fading plants and replace them with something else. Cosmos will drop seeds and renew the planting automatically, but only after a period of adjustment that may be fine in the cutting garden, but not neat or colorful enough for the front door planting. Professionals in places like Busch Gardens and Disney renew beds of most annuals with fresh plants every five or six weeks.

Ageratum, alyssum, petunias, pansies, and nasturtium will continue to bloom until they die of their own accord when the weather no longer suits them.

SALVIAS I NEVER SAW BEFORE

The demonstration garden at the Extension Office yielded my first cutting of Mexican sage, *Salvia leucantha,* and it has grown in my garden ever since. It has many white stems with long, narrow, textured, gray-green leaves that can grow as tall as four feet. Each stem starts opening a showy spire of white flowers surrounded by vivid lavender calyces. These last indefinitely and can be hung to dry. Cut stems back after flowering and a new bunch will come up from the crown. These root easily from softwood cuttings. Give Mexican sage full sun, enriched soil, and room to spread. It looks good with pentas. Plants are fairly carefree, but need water and flower fertilizer occasionally.

Many other perennial tropical sages thrive in Florida gardens. These include:

Salvia farinacea, blue or mealy-cup sage. Though it is grown as an annual in the North, it is a perennial here. Plants can be removed and replaced after their first flush of blooms if you wish. Indigo Spires is a hybrid with dark blue blooms.

Salvia uliginosa, or bog salvia, grows in a large clump four to five feet tall with lovely, ice blue spires in early summer.

Salvia elegans, pineapple sage, has deep red, edible flowers and fragrant foliage. This often proved short lived for me until author Tom Hewitt wrote in *Florida Gardening Magazine* that he treats his as a cool season annual that he plants in October and pulls out in May. A slightly leggier native form, *Salvia coccinea,* grows wild in my yard and throughout Florida. It is more orange-red than the blue-red of pineapple sage, does not have much scent, and blooms from frost to frost with little care, only occasional pruning. One of my friends from Ireland says this one reminds her of the fuchsias there. I now also have other salvias, one with yellow spires called forsythia sage or *Salvia madrensis* and two different forms of dark blue. I have seen lovely pinks, too. I recommend trying any salvia in your Florida garden.

68

Perennials For Sun

A few of these will be shorter lived than others. Some will go dormant. More will be evergreen, even everblooming, and can become shrubs, especially in central and south Florida.

Air plant (*Kalanchoe* species) CS

Blue daze (*Evolvulus glomeratus*) NCS

Cacti and succulents, many, NCS

Calliopsis (*Calliopsis grandiflora*)

Canna (*Canna* x *generalis*) NCS

Century plant (*Agave americana*) NCS

Chrysanthemum (*Chrysanthemum* sp.) NCS

Copper Canyon daisy (*Tagetes limonii*) NCS

Coreopsis (*Coreopsis* species) NC

Daylily (*Hemerocallis* species) NCS

False dragonhead (*Physostegia virginiana*) NC

Gaura (*Gaura lindheimeri*) NC

Gerbera daisy (*Gerbera jamesonii*) NCS

Lavender (*Lavandula* species) NCS

Paper-white narcissus (*Narcissus tazetta*) NCS

Pentas (*Pentas lanceolata*) NCS

Pinecone ginger (*Zingiber zerumbet*) NCS

Purple coneflower (*Echinacea purpurea*) NCS

Rudbeckia (*Rudbeckia maxima*) NCS

Rain lily (*Zephyranthes atamasco*) NCS

Sages and Salvias, many, NCS

Society garlic (*Tulbaghia violacea*) NCS

Stokes aster (*Stokesia laevis*) NCS

Verbena (*Verbeba* sp. and hybrids) NCS

impatiens

Popular Annuals Elsewhere that May Be Perennials in Central and South Florida

One of the most wonderful surprises for transplanted northern gardeners is the fact that cannas, glads, and some other bulbs that we once dug every winter can stay in the ground in our Florida gardens indefinitely. Impatiens bloom for years in frost free areas. Some of these plants will be annuals in north Florida, perennials in south Florida, and vary greatly in the middle depending on the location and the yearly variations of the weather. Others such as flowering maple and pentas can become shrubs.

Amaryllis (*Amaryllis* spp.) bulb

Amazon Lily (*Eucharis grandiflora*) bulb

Angel trumpet (*Datura* spp.)

Blue daze (*Evolvulus glomeratus*)

Caladium (*Caladium* spp.) bulb

Canna (*Canna* x *generalis*) bulb

Castor bean (*Ricinus communis*)

Coleus (*Coleus* hybrids) bulb

Dusty miller (*Senecio cineraria*)

Flowering maple (*Abutilon pictum*)

Freesia (*Freesia* hybrids) bulb

Geranium (*Pelargonium* spp.) bulb

Gerbera daisy (*Gerbera jamesonii*)

Gladiolus (*Gladiolus* hybrids)

Glorisosa Lily (*Gloriosa rothschildiana*)

Impatiens (*Impatiens wallerana*)

Jacobinia (*Justicia carnea*)

Lantana (*Lantana camara*)

Lily of the Nile (*Agapanthus africanus*) bulb

Moonflower (*Ipomea alba*)

Pentas (*Pentas lanceolata*)

Periwinkle, vinca (*Catharanthus rosea*)

Poinsettia (*Euphorbia pulcherrima*)

Wax begonia (*Begonia* x *semperflorens-cultorum*)

Perennials for Shade

Angelonia (*Angelonia angustifolia*) CS

Begonias, many species and hybrids NCS

Bromeliads, many species and hybrids CS

Caladiums (*Caladium* species and hybrids) CS

Cardinal flowers (*Lobelia cardinalis*) NCS

Cat whiskers (*Orthosiphon stamineus*) CS

Chinese ground orchid (*Bletilla striata*) CS

Crinum lily (*Crinum* species and hybrids) NCS

Crossandra (*Crossandra infundibuliformis*) CS

Eucharis lily (*Eucharis amazonica*) CS

Ferns, many species and hybrids NCS

Gingers, species and hybrids NCS

Lily-of-the-Nile (*Agapanthus africanus*) NCS

Nun's orchid (*Phaius tankervilliae*) CS

Salvia (*Salvia guaranitica, S. madrensis, S. vanhouttii*) NCS

Snake plant (*Sansevieria* species) CS

Shrimp plant (*Justicia* species) NCS

Walking iris (*Neomerica* species) CS

Violet (*Viola odorata*) NCS

Salt-tolerant Perennials

Adam's needle (*Yucca filamentosa*) NCS

Blanket flower (*Gaillardia pulchella*) NCS

Cacti and succulents, many, NCS

Century plant (*Agave americana*) NCS

Daylily (*Hemerocallis* species) NCS

Lantanas (*Lantana* species) NCS

Sages and Salvias, many, NCS

Society garlic (*Tulbaghia violacea*) NCS

Snake plant (*Sansevieria* species) CS

Flowering Perennials to Treat As Annuals

The heat, humidity, and pounding rains of Florida summers cause some plants that are perennial in cooler climates to be annuals in Florida. Soil conditions, unusual weather, or expert gardening skills may give two years on rare occasions, but for the most part, figure on planting the following over again in the fall, at least in central and south Florida. Those marked with as asterisk do often grow as perennials in north Florida.

Calla lilies (*Zantedeschia aethiopica*)*

Delphinium (*Delphinium* spp)

Easter Lily (*Lilium longiflorum*)*

Gayfeather, blazing Star (*Liatris spicata*)

Hollyhocks (*Alcea rosea*)

Lavender (*Lavandula* species) NCS

Paper whites (*Narcissus tazetta*)*

Wandflower (*Sparaxis* spp.)

Yarrow (*Achillea* spp.)

Flowers for Wet Places

Blue flag iris (*Iris hexagona*) NCS

Daylily (*Hemerocallis* species) NCS

Calla lily (*Zantedeschia* species) NC

Cardinal flower (*Lobelia cardinalis*) NCS

Crinum lily (*Crinum* sp. and hybrids) NCS

Louisiana iris (*Iris* species) NCS

Pentas (*Pentas lanceolata*) NCS

Pickerel weed (*Pontederia cordata*) NCS

Rain lily (*Zephyranthes atamasco*) NC

Rose mallow (*Hibiscus moscheutos*) NCS

Spider lily (*Hymenocallis crassifolia*) CS

Yellow flag iris (*Iris pseudacorus*) NC

PLANTING GUIDE FOR ANNUALS AND BIENNIALS (MOST

Name Of Plant	Best Planting Time N. FL -- C. FL -- S. FL			Main Bloom	Ease	Exposure	Cold Toler.
alyssum (seed)	Mar, Aug	Sep-Feb	Oct-Feb	most of year	1	sun or ps	hardy
ageratum (seed)	Mar	Feb-Mar	Nov-Feb	frost to frost	2	sun	tender
ammi (seed)	Feb-Mar	Nov-Feb	Nov-Feb	Apr-Jul	2	sun	tender
aster, China (seed)	Mar	Feb	Feb	May-Jun	2	sun or ps	tender
baby's breath (seed)	Apr	Feb, Nov	Nov-Jan	spring	2	sun or ps	hardy
balsam (seed)	Apr-May	Mar-Apr	Feb-Apr	Apr-Nov	1	sun or ps	tender
begonia (plants)	Apr-May	Mar-Apr	Feb-Apr	frost to frost	-	sun or ps	tender
browallia (plants)	Apr-May	Mar-Apr	Feb-Apr	frost to frost	-	sun or ps	tender
calendula (seed)	Aug-Sep	Sep-Nov	Oct-Dec	winter-spring	1	sun	hardy
calif. poppy (seed)	Sep-Feb	Nov-Feb	Nov-Feb	Apr-Jun	2	sun	hardy
candytuft (seed)	Sep-Feb	Nov-Feb	Nov-Feb	Apr-Jun	2	sun	hardy
celosia (seed)	Apr-May	Mar	Feb	May-Nov	2	sun	tender
cleome (seed)	Feb-Mar	Feb-Mar	Jan-Feb	Apr-Aug	1	sun	semi-hardy
coleus (plants)	Apr-May	Mar-Jun	any time	-	-	ps, shade	tender
cornflower (seed)	Sep	Oct-Nov	Nov-Dec	Feb-June	1	sun	hardy
cosmos (seed)	Apr	Mar	Nov-Feb	Apr-Aug	1	sun	tender
dianthus (seed)	Sep	Oct	all year	all year	2	sun	hardy
didiscus (seed)	Apr	Mar	Jan-Feb	Apr-Aug	2	sun	tender
dusty miller (plants)	Apr	Mar	Nov-Feb	-	-	sun or ps	hardy
gaillardia (seed)	Mar	Oct-Dec	Nov-Jan	until frost	1	sun or ps	hardy
gazania (seed)	Sep	Oct-Jan	Nov-Jan	Apr-Sep	4	sun or ps	semi-hardy
globe amaranth (seed)	Apr	Mar	Feb-Mar	May-Sep	2	sun	tender
hollyhock (seed)	Sep	Oct-Nov	Apr	Apr	3	sun or ps	hardy
larkspur (seed)	Sep	Oct-Nov	Nov-Dec	Apr-May	3	sun or ps	hardy
lobelia (plants)	Apr	Mar-Apr	Dec-Feb	spring, fall	-	sun or ps	tender
marigold (seed)	Apr-Aug	Mar-Sep	all year	until frost	2	sun	tender
morning glory (seed)	Apr	Mar	Dec-Feb	Apr-frost	3	sun or ps	tender
nasturtium (seed)	Apr	Mar	Dec-Feb	Mar-Jun	1	sun or ps	tender
nicotiana (plants)	Apr	Mar	Jan-Mar	spr-summer	-	sun or ps	tender
phlox (seed)	Sep-Mar	Oct-Nov	Nov-Jan	spr-summer	2	sun	hardy
poppy, shirley (seed)	Sep-Feb	Nov-Feb	Dec-Feb	spring to frost	3	sun or ps	hardy
portulaca (seed)	Mar-Apr	Mar-Apr	Dec-Mar	spring to frost	1	sun	tender
salvia (seed)	Apr	Mar	Dec-Mar	most of year	2	sun or ps	tender
snapdragon (seed)	Sep	Oct-Mar	Nov-Feb	spr-frost	4	sun or ps	hardy
statice (seed)	Sep	Oct-Nov	Nov-Dec	Mar-May	2	sun	hardy
sunflower (seed)	Apr	Mar	Nov-Feb	spr-summer	1	sun	tender
tithonia (seed)	Apr	Mar	Nov-Feb	until frost	2	sun	tender
torenia (plants)	Apr	Mar	any time	until frost	-	part shade	tender
zinnia (seed)	Apr-May	Mar-Apr	Oct-Apr	until frost	2	sun	tender

Ease: 1 and 2, easy, 3 and 4, harder   ps=partial shade s=shade toler.=tolerance
If you buy plants not seeds, most garden stores supply them when it is time to plant them.

Summer

Let trees and shrubs like hibiscus, crape myrtle, and oleander provide much of your color during the summer. But along with them, plant and enjoy summer flowering bulbs like canna, caladium, Aztec lily, butterfly lily, crinum, clivia, society garlic, spider lily, agapanthus, and gladiolus. Perennials that keep blooming constantly include blue daze, lantana, pentas, many salvias, butterfly weed, and impatiens. Various kinds of daylilies will bloom and often bloom a second time at their appointed seasons.

The annuals that bloom all summer include pink or white periwinkle, deep blue torenia (Florida pansy), pink or purple globe amaranth, and portulaca and purslane in their many sunshiny shades. Marigolds, zinnias, tithonia, and cosmos will bloom for a time and then need replacing. Use plenty of coleus, impatiens, torenia, and bromeliads in the shade.

GROWING ANNUALS AND BIENNIALS

* Buying plants is quicker, easier, and more certain than starting seeds, but some types are not available.

* Start delicate seeds in the clear plastic containers that come from the deli or bakery. Put holes in the bottom. Open and close as needed like a tiny greenhouse.

* Watch plants closely after planting out. Water often but do not drown them. Protect plants from slugs and insects.

* Set out plants when they are available in bloom at nurseries. Follow the chart on the next page for starting your own plants from seed.

GROWING PERENNIALS

Don't be surprised if you hear conflicting reports about which perennials are reliably hardy in which parts of Florida. Sun, shade, soil type, moisture, and temperature all come into play and it varies from garden to garden. Some perennials are grown like biennials here and will not last through summer. All are best planted during moist, mild weather.

amaryllis

GROWING BULBS

Flowers from bulbs, corms, tubers, and rhizomes use these underground structures to help them survive inhospitable times of the year. For some, it is a double challenge of surviving frost damage from winter cold and rot damage from steamy summer heat. Some types of bulbs will survive in the ground, unassisted, while others should be dug and stored, then replanted. Keep storage time at a minimum, never longer than nine months. Digging may be for either dry summer storage or for winter warmth. Many bulbs can stay in the ground for several years, until clumps need dividing. In northern Florida, more types should be dug for winter warmth, or else mulched deeply to protect them from frost.

Oxalis comes in many well behaved varieties, but the common roadside weeds with green cloverlike leaves and pink or yellow flowers should never be let loose in a garden. The one with white flowers is fine and I have some lovely ones with dark maroon leaves and pink flowers.

72

Calla lily

Bulbs to Replace Yearly
anemone
iris, Dutch
ranunculus

Bulbs and Roots to Dig and Store
achimenes
alstroemeria
anemone
calla, dig in north
dahlia
gladiolus, dig in north
gloriosa lily, dig in north
eucharis, dig in north
lily, true
polianthes
sparaxis
tritonia

Bulbs to Leave in the Ground
amaryllis (but mulch or dig in north)
Amazon lily, eucharis lily
agapanthus
allium
alstroemeria
blood lily, *Haemanthus*
caladium
calla, in central and southern zones
crinum lily
eucharis in central and southern zones
freesia
gladiolus
gloriosa lily
leucojum
lily, in well drained soil
lycoris
narcissus,
oxalis
polianthes, only if in well-drained soil
sparaxis
spider lily, *Hymenocallis*
Tritonia
Zephyranthes, rain lily

Blood lily, *Haemanthus*

BULB PLANTING GUIDE FOR FLORIDA

NAME OF PLANT	*PL. DEPTH	SPACING	BEST PLANTING TIMES		
			N. Florida	C. Florida	S. Florida
Achimines	.5 inches	2 inches	Mar-Apr	Mar	Jan
Agapanthus	cover	18 inches	Mar	Feb	Jan
Allium	varies	varies	Nov-Jan	Nov	Nov
Alstroemeria	6 inches	24 inches	Mar	Feb	Jan
Anemone	2 inches	12 inches	Nov-Dec	Nov	Nov
Caladium	2 inches	24-36 inches	Mar-May	Feb-Apr	Dec
Canna	3 inches	varies	Mar-Apr	Feb-Apr	Nov-Apr
Crinum	varies	varies	Nov-Dec	Feb-Apr	Nov-Mar
Dahlia	cover	12 inches	Mar	Feb-Mar	Nov-Jan
Eucharis	cover	12-24 inches	Apr	Mar	Jan-Feb
Eucomis	3 inches	6 inches	any time	any time	any time
Freesia	4 inches	4 inches	Oct	Nov	Nov
Gladiolus, standard	5 inches	6 inches	Mar-May	Feb-Jun	any time
Gladiolus, miniature	4 inches	4 inches	Mar-Jun	Feb-Jun	any time
Gloriosa Lily	just cover	18 inches	Mar-Apr	Feb-Mar	Dec-Feb
Hippeastrum (Amaryllis)	just cover	12 inches	Feb-Mar	Nov-Feb	Nov-Feb
Iris, Dutch	4 inches	6 inches	Nov	Nov	Nov
Ixia	3 inches	3 inches	Mar	Feb	Jan
Leucojum	3 inches	6 inches	Nov	Nov	do not plant
Lilium	varies	varies	Nov	Nov	Nov
Lycoris	3 inches	4-6 inches	Nov-Mar	Nov-Jan	Nov
Narcissus, paperwhite types	6 inches	6 inches	Nov	Nov	Nov
Oxalis	2 inches	4 inches	Feb-Mar	Feb	Nov-Feb
Polianthes	2 inches	8 inches	May	Feb	Nov
Scadoxus, blood lily	3 inches	8-10 inches	any time	any time	any time
Sparaxis	3 inches	4 inches	Nov	Nov	Nov
Tritonia	3 inches	3 inches	Mar-May	Feb-Jun	all
Zantedeschia	just cover	12-24 inches	Feb-Mar	Nov-Feb	Nov
Zephyranthes	1 inch	3 inches	Nov	Nov	Nov

*PL. DEPTH: Planting depth means cover with this much soil.

CHAPTER EIGHT
GROWING VEGETABLES IN FLORIDA

"It is harder to grow vegetables in the subtropics than almost anyplace else." I read that in the late Marian Van Atta's newsletter *Living Off the Land* shortly after arriving here and set out to prove it wrong. After all, I had been growing mainly vegetables for forty years and I knew that many of the vegetables grown commercially for the country are grown in Florida. How hard could it be?

Well, Marian was right, and it was in the vegetable garden that I had my greatest setbacks. But it was also in the vegetable garden that I was most determined to succeed. And I have, to a pleasant extent. I still don't often have the abundance I had in the North, but that is a fact I can live with.

CULTURE SHOCK

At first it was appalling to me that we saw very few vegetable gardens in Florida, compared to the northern states. This may be because many people tried the old ways, failed, and quit before they learned the necessary methods for Florida success.

There still seems to be a different attitude here in Florida, though, a greater distance from the basic, down to-earth values that made a vegetable garden part of life for so many of us, no matter where we lived. Coming from Iowa to Tampa involved a great deal of culture shock for me. Seeing so few gardens was one indication. This did turn out to be a trend of the times as well. Twenty years later I am appalled at how few people grow their own vegetables anywhere. They don't know the excitement and good taste they are missing, not to mention the health benefits.

"Why would you want to grow your own?" one man asked me. "You can go out to the fields and buy everything cheap." Sure you can, on certain few days of the year. But time on

the road is not the same as a pleasant walk in the garden to pick something for supper.

I prefer to go out into my own yard daily and pick fresh vegetables. If you enjoy the entertainment, exercise, fresh air, and therapy of watching things grow, you can do that, for one crop or another, almost all year in all of Florida, though it will mean learning about new crops.

There are, as I realized after a while, some vegetable gardens hidden behind fences. Also, people plant their vegetables inconspicuously among the flowers and shrubs.

I like that gardens in Florida produce smaller amounts over longer times, so less canning and fewer large harvests are necessary. I don't miss the work of canning, but I still miss that feeling of accomplishment that comes from bountiful production.

Many years into Florida living, I know that the difficulties of growing vegetables here are real. Nevertheless I manage to grow a good amount, though nothing like I grew in Iowa. I have written articles about professional growers who seem able to grow almost anything. They are usually willing to use more poisons than most home gardeners are (or should be). Even so, we can emulate their strict adherence to timing, which is the most important ingredient of vegetable growing success in Florida.

THE UPSIDE DOWN YEAR

Florida vegetable gardens, like school, start in the fall when you can plant the cool season crops like arugula, carrots, lettuce, radishes, celery, beets, cabbage, cauliflower, broccoli, herbs, collards, kale, kohlrabi, mustard, spinach, onions, and turnips. All of these tolerate a touch of frost.

How far north or south you live and the vagaries of each year will dictate whether you start planting these in August or October. In the panhandle and the northern section of the state, plant early because there is a definite, though short, winter when some of these hardy vegetables might perish.

Here in the Tampa area, they often grow all winter, though an occasional hard freeze means we have to start over again, especially with beans and tomatoes. If we wait until November and the season is kind, we can grow some English peas, but only for a treat, not for filling the freezer. I eventually gave up on corn because it takes more room than it is worth for me, but I've had much more success with fall-planted green beans, although they will also be killed by the first hard freeze. Farther south, such crops are less of a gamble. The pros grow tomatoes and if they freeze, they just start over. I keep one or two tomato plants in large pots that can be covered or moved into the garage if necessary.

Spring is the main vegetable gardening season. At that time of year, almost anything grows, but you have to make the most of it because almost everything burns out sometime in June. After that the only crops to grow are heat lovers: calabaza pumpkins, cucuzzi, eggplant, black-eyed peas, cherry tomatoes, sweet potatoes, and okra.

There are vegetables to grow in Florida that I had never heard of. Now our diet includes chayote in the winter, cucuzzi and Seminole pumpkins through summer, green papayas almost all year, and tampala and Malabar spinach for summer greens, and Okinawa spinach and Dawn Dewa all year long. I enjoy the lovely blue flowers and the edible root of the jicama.

Since I found James Stephens' book *Manual of Minor Vegetables* I now know how to grow and cook the chaya that I grow for butterflies and the pokeweed that comes up whether we want it or not. Both of these can be toxic if not used according to directions. And I have many more of the minor vegetables to try. Even in Iowa I liked to try something new every year just to keep things interesting, and I won't outlive the list for Florida if I keep going, as my father has, to be one hundred.

I've also learned to make the most of the edible flowers and foliage of many ornamental crops to add color, interest, and nutrition to salads. In warmer months when we must buy lettuce, I can stretch a single head or bunch to two weeks of salads by adding rose petals, nasturtium flowers, leaves, and seeds, hibiscus flowers and the deep maroon leaves of the cranberry hibiscus and bits of various herbs. A niece who was a caterer assures me that these cost dearly in that business but added greatly to their reputation. For those of us who add flowers for our family, each plant also adds different nutrients, so the more variety we use, the better for our health. Just be sure that the flowers you use have not been treated with poison sprays—not a problem in my garden.

EDIBLE FLOWER FAVORITES

anise hyssop
bean
beebalm (monarda)
borage
calendula
carnation
chamomile
chive
citrus blossoms
cucumber
dandelion
daylily
dianthus
elderberry blossoms
geranium
hibiscus
honeysuckle
marigold
mint
nasturtium
pansy
pineapple sage
purslane
rose
squash and pumpkin
sunflower petals
violas
yucca

THINGS TO SEND FOR:

ECHO SEEDLIST. Educational Concerns for Hunger Organization, 17430 Durrance Road, North Fort Myers, FL 33917. This is an amazing organization. If you come to the area, go on one of the tours of their small but mighty global farm, where they develop methods and train Peace Corps workers and missionaries of all faiths in order to help 150 Third World countries fight hunger. The tour will make you feel like you can do and grow anything. Their domestic seed catalog is $4.00 (including postage) and they welcome requests for the catalog by mail or phone (**239-543-3246**). It will give you a source of the more unusual vegetables. You can also order seeds on their website: www.echonet.org.

FLORIDA MARKET BULLETIN. To receive this free biweekly newsletter, write to MARKET BULLETIN, Mayo Building, 407 Calhoun Street, Tallahassee, FL 32304 or go to the website at www.florida-agriculture.com. This includes articles on Florida agriculture and recipes. There are free ads about plants, seeds, and bulbs available, and U-pick farms, too. If you do not find the plants and seeds you need, you can put an ad in the wanted section.

OTHER FACTORS affect vegetable growth and production. Our veggies are growing when the days are shorter and the sun is lower in the sky, so the plants grow more slowly than they did in the long days of northern summers. This requires patience from newcomers. Be sure there are at least seven hours of full sun a day for vegetables. Some places too dark for a fall garden will do just fine for a spring one.

Soil needs enriching. Watering and feeding are necessities. See chapter 4 for more information. I also found that stored seed does not keep its vitality as long as it did in the north, so I store all my seeds in the freezer when not in use to keep them viable longer.

* Varieties are different here. Get the *Vegetable Gardening Guide*, Circular 1 04-0, from the Extension Service and use it or your local seedsman's suggestions for varieties. This may mean abandoning some old favorites and working with unfamiliar varieties, but that is best at the beginning. After you gain more experience, try a few of your old favorite varieties just to see whether they will work here or not.

When we first came, there were at least three places in the area that sold bulk seeds which seemed to me to be fresher and definitely were less expensive. Then there were two, then only one, and now I know of none. When we want larger quantities than we can find on the seed rack, we get them from the internet.

* Crops will vary as you learn what grows well for you here and what doesn't. We never ate chayote before, but it grows well for me and we like it very much now. Green papayas replace or accompany squash in all recipes for much of the year. Corn is a special and infrequent treat, but we eat more pumpkin now because I have that from June through November. I never grew arugula before, but we have it all winter now. We also grow and eat more fruit here than we ever did before. The list of vegetable crops starting on page 79 includes regular and subtropical crops. Some of them may be completely new to you.

* Depth of planting is different. In the North, we planted seed deeper in hot weather to prevent its drying out, so I did that here at first, also. But Barney Yelton, the owner of one of the lushest vegetable gardens I have seen in Florida, planted his seeds no deeper than their longest side, much more shallowly than I had done. Following his guideline seems to work better. Sprinkling often until germination is necessary except in the rainy season, during which time a slightly deeper planting might prevent seeds from washing out.

* Pests and diseases are perhaps more of a problem than in the North. Nematodes can be a serious problem. See chapter 2. Lewis Maxwell's book, *Florida Vegetables*, recommends spraying most crops each week

Growing Neem and Using it for Garden Pests and Diseases

-Neem trees grow well in Florida sun, in the ground where they have frost protection, and in containers farther north. They grow quickly even in sandy soil, more quickly the more humus and mulch used.

-Spread dried leaves around the house, outdoors or inside as strewing herbs to control insects.

-Keep some neem leaves on the potting table when working there, also dropped near your feet when mosquitos are thick. For walking, put a neem leaf or two in a hat band, a pocket, a shoe or sock. Or wad up a big leaf and scrub it over the skin of feet and lower legs.

-Put neem oil with some soap and water in a hose end garden sprayer and do the whole yard every few months.

-Neem oil chases off fire ants. If you have some on your hands and feet, ants climb up and go right back down. (Make sure it's the all-natural version, not the kind that's been formulated for spraying.) Neem oil is also a potent anti-inflammatory agent and makes the itch from fire ant, wasp, or mosquito bites go away.

-If your trees are good size, cut back the branches and use them as a mulch around plants that end up with bugs, particularly veggies. The branches will break down and become a systemic pesticide, plus you get the water-saving benefits of the mulch. No need to break them up. Just lay them flat where you want them and then use the larger pieces for vertical vines once the leaves have all fallen off.

-The general recommendation is to mix a pound of neem leaves in a blender with a little bit of hot water. Strain it through the leg of old pantyhose and then hang it in a bucket with two or three gallons of water overnight. In the morning, mix a little bit of soap in the water and spray plants. Be sure to use the ground-up leftover neem as mulch on an extra-sensitive plant.

Much of the above information comes from Patti McGauley of Organic Edibles Nurseries in Lakeland and from Vicki Parsons of www.neemtreefarms.com.

---

with a combination insecticide and fungicide. I don't and I won't, for I'd rather not chance the effects of eating pesticides. Maybe that is why I have not been wildly successful, but there is still plenty of great produce growing here! I keep pesticide use to a bare minimum, even though I am not strictly an organic grower. I don't mind sharing, but if bugs take more than their share, I fight back. Advocates of spraying say such action comes too late, but I can live with that.

For disease control, plant the most disease resistant varieties. And mulch well. This keeps the rain from splashing soil borne disease spores back up onto the leaves. In his book, *Vegetable Gardening in Florida*, James M. Stephens advocates Integrated Pest Management (IPM) which offers several more natural, less poisonous methods for dealing with insects. The

first involves keeping a close watch, at least twice a week, checking under the leaves and in the bud whorls for eggs and excrement and then deciding whether these indicate harmful or beneficial insects. His pest chapter has excellent photos for identification.

It is especially important to keep a sharp eye out. Last night I found the telltale damage of a hornworm on a tomato. If I do not find and squash the worm today, it will eat the whole plant. Squash it even if you hate to. I had not seen horn worm damage since we left Ohio nearly 20 years before, but recognized it at once. Nothing else eats the whole thing and leaves behind only stubby stems like that.

Spraying the leaves of many plants with a forceful stream of water from the hose on a daily or frequent basis will wash off many pests and disease spores and keep plants in good health. But do it early enough in the day so that the foliage can dry before nightfall. Insecticidal soap controls many pests but until you get that, use a dish soap solution, one teaspoon soap per gallon of water, which may be strong enough. *Bacillus thuringiensis* (Bt) controls worms in all stages safely. The are other new and more natural pesticides available today. Rotenone and pyrethrum are from plants, and biodegrade quickly after use. But they kill bees and other beneficial insects along with the pests.

Choose your own method of pest control. If you use pesticides, start with the safest and use stronger ones only if needed. Always read labels and follow directions carefully. Wear protective clothing during application, then wash it and take a shower immediately.

HOW TO GROW AND USE FLORIDA VEGETABLES

* **Arugula** or roquette has long, slender, dark green and deeply lobed leaves. Seeds planted in fall will come up in only two days with cabbage-like seedlings, and then grow slowly. But even before Thanksgiving you can add a few leaves to a tossed salad for a peppery pickup. Surprisingly, they are not too strong for a delicious and pretty salad composed of arugula leaves, oranges and/or ripe papayas, and nuts, tossed with a celery seed dressing (or Colonial Salad Dressing from Bob Evans.) By starting a few seeds in the spring, you can have some arugula all summer, but it only grows abundantly in the cooler months. Another great thing about arugula is that the flowers are also edible and the leaves never get that strong taste that lettuce leaves get after they bolt.

* **Asparagus** is possible though difficult to grow in central Florida, a little easier in northern Florida. Plant at almost any time, the same way you would in the North, either roots or seeds. Plants do not have to go two feet deep, the way people used to do it. A depth of six inches is enough, with 12 to 18 inches between plants. Harvest takes two years from plants, three from seeds. Keep plants moist and well

fed. Mulch well to discourage nematodes. If plants don't go dormant on their own, mow them down in early February. Harvest new spears in March and April. The trouble is that it can be quite warm then, and the spears grow quickly and more spindly than one would prefer.

* **Beans** planted in early fall will make a treat for Thanksgiving dinner from central Florida southward, but frost often takes them before they finish bearing. Replant soon after the New Year (how soon depending on where you live) for a spring crop. Fertilize them well, protect from light frost, and replant every few weeks for continuous crops. If leaves are pale despite feeding, add lime and water well. Beans have more diseases here. Never touch wet plants. Rotate crops to clean soil. Rust-resistant varieties like 'Harvester' have fewer problems. But none of the beans I've grown have had the continuous crops that we had in the north, so I plant a new section every few weeks within the time frame recommended.

It was only after we began growing them here that we discovered the Romas, large and flat beans with excellent flavor, that fill the kettle in such record time that we wish we had known about them up north, too. My son Mike, who has full sun and muckier soil, can grow enough green beans to fill a five gallon bucket. As my sunny spots shrink, I am happy with smaller amounts.

Many growers do well with lima beans, but I have had beautiful vines that never yielded a single bean. Too much nitrogen and not enough phosphorus and potassium in the fertilizer, no doubt. Limas like warm weather and can be planted from March through August in northern Florida, March through June and again in September in central, and in all but May through July in the south.

* **Beets** grow fairly well in their own very limited season of September (in northern Florida) or October through February or March in the rest of the state. They must have fertile soil and adequate moisture. Cover during frosts.

These are tricky here at best for me, though James Stephens says they are easily grown. He lives farther north in the state.

* **Broccoli** has done well for me almost from the beginning. Plant seeds or plants or both from August to October and right through January or February. Watch for the same bugs you had up North, aphids and cabbage worms. Feed lightly every two to three weeks, water well, and harvest as ready. After you cut the center cluster, side shoots will continue to develop until the weather gets too hot. If any get away from you and begin to bloom, snap them off at once to promote new growth. Or enjoy the blooms if you have picked enough.

* **Brussels sprouts** grow much the same way and need the same care as cabbage. Plant only in the fall or early winter. This plant does not always do well in Florida, for it needs a longer cool season. Remove bottom leaves to encourage bud development. Or cut the center of the top out of the plant when it is tall enough. Insects can be a problem and warm weather may result in puffy rather than solid little heads.

* **Cabbage** has always done well for me here as long as I grow it in cool weather. The red ones are especially attractive in the garden, in salad, and even in bouquets. Sow from September through January or February. Cabbage is a heavy feeder, so fertilize often. It is a cabbageworm's delight, but no more difficult in Florida during the winter than elsewhere in summer. It will survive light freezes. One neighbor remarked with surprise that my cabbage looked "real, just like in the grocery store." Usually insects are not too pesky, but be ready with *Bt* if the worms attack. Ornamental cabbage or kale also thrives here and is edible as well.

* **Carrots** are grown much the same as beets, but are a little easier. I've had fairly decent carrots from the first. Again, grow them only during the cooler months and be sure to harvest before summer, or some pest will do it for you. An easy way to grow carrots that need no thinning is to make a wide row and sprinkle a few seeds together at one-foot intervals along the row. The little clumps have room to spread out because of the spaces between them.

* **Celery** does remarkably well here. A dozen plants or less, planted six inches apart in a little plot of well-enriched soil near the hose or the rain barrel, will produce plenty for a family.  Plant in fall or earliest spring because it likes cool weather. I harvest side stalks as needed until summer comes. Then I harvest the whole plant before the summer heat. Blend the leaves with a little water, freeze in ice cube trays, and package in bags for adding to soups or stews. Or dry them. Chop and freeze the stems for cooked dishes. Keep celery for weeks in the hydrator drawer of the refrigerator for eating fresh.

Homegrown celery is greener and thinner, but more nutritious and flavorful than the blanched product in the grocery. You can blanch your homegrown celery by hilling up with soil or surrounding with tarpaper rings to keep out the light, but it seems to me more trouble than it is worth. You may wish to store some celery seed in the freezer (for good germination) because it is not always possible to find plants or seeds when you want them.

* **Chinese cabbage** grows easily during the cool weather. Harvest while young and tender and before the heat turns it bitter.

* **Collards** need the same care as cabbage and do very well in Florida's cool months. Sow from August through April.

* **Cauliflower** has done well for me from the first winter. Treat like cabbage, but pin up

the leaves with snap clothespins to cover the developing heads and keep them white. Check the seed catalogs for interesting new types. The 'Snowball' Strains, 'Snow Crown,' and 'Snowdrift' do well here and are the best kind of snow for our Florida winters.

* **Chayote (*Sechium edule*)** is an edible member of the cucumber family that is native to Guatemala and grows as a tender perennial in Florida. We had such a bountiful crop of chayotes this winter than we could not eat them fast enough, even though I served them in strips with dip to family visitors at my father's 100th birthday party. Some said they taste like peas, others like jicama. Only one granddaughter said she thought they were raw potatoes. None of these are related.

The whole fruit can be planted on its side or at an angle with the stem end either slightly exposed or barely covered. They have large fuzzy green leaves all year round but only bear fruit in the shorter days of winter. I once had a vine in full sun and the leaves wilted at midday all summer no matter how much rain we had. They perked up by late afternoon but were depressing to see. And for several years they froze before or just as they started to fruit. Some years ago I planted these in the bright light beneath a tree and let them climb to get the sun or shade they needed. They have not frozen out since and just drop the fruits as they ripen. They can be baked, creamed, buttered, pickled, or cooked any way you would cook a squash or eaten raw.

Though their season is too short for my liking, they need hardly any care and are both edible and interesting. If you can reach them pick when they are not much bigger than a fist and they will keep in a cool place for several weeks. A single plant can produce three bushels of fruit and each can weigh up to three pounds.

* **Corn** needs well-enriched soil, plenty of sun, heavy feeding, and lots of water. It can endure only a little water stress. Plant it in blocks of four rows for best pollination. Corn can be transplanted, even purchased in market packs here, and these do well. Feed every two to three weeks. Do not crowd. My late friend, writer Lewis Maxwell, planted on his birthday in late July for a fall crop. Most of the market growers plant only in the spring. There is nothing I like better than seeing the tiny shoots piercing the ground. Much of mine came to little more, but occasionally I got a crop of almost northern quality. I kept trying until my sunny spots were too few.

Now I buy ripe corn from the markets during the season and enjoy it for the few weeks it is available. 'Silver Queen' is a favored crop here, but we think yellow corn like 'Bonanza' tastes better. Be aware that what is sold in the markets in the summer was probably grown in your northern home state and shipped. Market people have told me proudly on a Saturday, "That is real fresh. It just came in on Thursday." I was shocked at the time since we considered any corn picked before we started the water boiling in Iowa too old. Thank goodness, the new extra sweet varieties stay sweeter longer and that some of our demands of life mellow a bit as we age.

* **Cranberry hibiscus** or *Hibiscus acetosella*, is a decorative but invasive plant with burgundy leaves and darker flowers that are both edible and add eye appeal to a salad. You may as well eat it because you'll have to keep pruning to control it. If you know anyone who has it, they will be glad to share.

* **Cucumbers** are supposed to be easy and often grow by the fieldful, but I have had trouble with them. Plant suggested varieties such as 'Poinsett,' 'Sprint,' 'Spacemaster', 'Galaxy', or 'SMR 18.' These are most resistant to mildew and other diseases. Our shortage of bees can reduce pollination. Planting some of two varieties, one with male flowers, will help. Keep vines mulched and well watered, and watch carefully for caterpillars, pickleworms, angular leaf spot, and down mildew. *Bt* will control the first two. Planting disease-resistant varieties is the best help for the latter.

* **Eggplant** likes hot weather and does very well here. But somehow my first success, the best eggplant production of my life, took a few years to repeat. Some people get plants to thrive and produce for several years, without frost killing them. The Japanese varieties that produce small, oblong fruit seem to get less bitter than standard types. Also try white, egg-shaped 'Albino' and 'White Beauty.' I've seen 'Neon' doing very well with bright lavender fruits of nice size. All of these have a sweet, mild flavor and are ornamental besides. Both Renee's Seeds and Thompson & Morgan offer packets of mixed varieties. This is my favorite way of finding new varieties that do well. Feed every two to three weeks until plants begin to bloom, every three or four weeks after that. Pick and eat the fruit while it is still shiny.

* **Herbs** do very well here. In fact, we can grow more of them, including some of the spices, than we could in the north. But they also take different timing and different methods. So I wrote the book *Herbs and Spices for Florida Gardens*. The herbs I planted during my first fall did so well all winter that I was elated. Then summer came and wiped a few of the most popular ones out.

Herbs that will live over summer in central Florida include anise-hyssop, aloe, ajuga, basil, butterfly weed, chicory, comfrey, dandelion, elderberry, eucalyptus, fennel, ginger, goldenrod, lemon grass, some mints, moneywort, passion flower, periwinkle, rosemary, certain sages, and a Cuban oregano (a coleus variety that tastes like oregano), and many others.

Nasturtiums, chives, and lemon balm survive the heat if moved into deep shade, and perhaps several more species will do this as well. Others like parsley, savory, leek, coriander, borage, cress, dill, and marjoram are best restarted from seeds or new plants in the fall.

The dandelions I brought down, among guffaws from my northern friends, from a spring trip to Ohio, grow just fine but tend to be too bitter to eat most of the time. The blooms come and go so quickly in the heat that they are seldom seen, but I like to see a few for old time's sake. The comfrey does not grow as tall or lush, and only blooms rarely. I have to replant it occasionally, as I never did in the North. I am still experimenting, but many herbs grow well in poor soil or in containers and are as or more rewarding here as they were elsewhere. We just have to work around summer for those herbs that can't take heat and humidity, protect tender types like basil from winter freezes, and sometimes be satisfied with less vigorous growth.

Nasturtiums that cover the fence and bloom abundantly from Thanksgiving to June weigh nicely in the balance and we enjoy them in colorful, tasty salads.

* **The horseradish tree, *Moringa oleifera*,** grows up to a foot a month in central and southern Florida if it has full sun and will eventually reach 25 feet and give light shade. It does well in our poor soil and is drought resistant. Start it easily from seeds or cuttings or buy small plants. Moringa trees begin to bloom with fragrant white flowers in loose clusters as early as eight months after planting and bloom year round.

All parts are edible: the root has a strong horseradish flavor. The tender young leaves and stem ends can be used like spinach, including raw in salads. India's tradition of ayurveda says the leaves prevent 300 diseases. Ounce for ounce, they have seven times the vitamin C in oranges, seven times the vitamin A in carrots, three times the potassium in bananas, 4 times the calcium and two times the protein in milk. Older leaves can be fed to livestock. In theory, moringa leaves could practically wipe out malnutrition on our planet.

The pods are said to taste much like asparagus. The largest pods can still be tender at 12 to 15 inches in length. The seeds within can be shelled out and cooked like green peas. Seeds can be purchased from ECHO Farms.

* **Hyacinth bean, *Dolichos lablab*,** is one of 70 some different kinds of beans in the *Manual of Minor Vegetables* book. I first saw this growing in Iowa as an ornamental vine and only later learned that the fat, flat pods and seeds are good food. There are two kinds, one with green pods and white flowers that is not so showy, and the other with pink and white flowers and dark maroon pods that is quite striking. The first come from a tan seed with a white seed scar, the showy one from a darker seed with the same scar. Once you have these, they come back either from perennial roots or self seeds forever and we find them quite tasty, especially in the summer when we have fewer other vegetables. The vines can be very aggressive and, of course, they need full sun.

* **Lemon grass, *Cymbopogon citratus*,** is also an ornamental and culinary herb that is rather the opposite of hot peppers. Lemon grass is soothing and sweet and lemon grass tea might be just the thing to drink if the peppers light your mouth on fire. This easy-to-grow tropical perennial loves Florida's hot summers and takes well too much moisture although it also has moderate drought tolerance. In very dry climates the leaves turn brown and the plant goes dormant until the rains return. It then forms a 3 to 5 foot tall clump of green flat blades about 3/4 inches wide.

The inner, lower, white portion of the stem is tender and is the part most often used in cooking. To make tea, put a quart jar of water in the microwave to boil. Go out and pick 6 to 8 stems and cut away the leaves. Put the stem bases down in the boiling water, let steep, and serve hot or cold.

The green blades are tough, but you can still lay them on chicken or fish as it cooks to give it flavor and then remove the leaves afterwards and put them in the container that you take to the compost pile. Lemon grass is a

natural repellent for flies, fleas, and mosquitoes and it also destroys many types of bacteria, fungi, and odors. It grows best in sun but will survive in partial shade.

* **Lettuce** does moderately well from early fall to mid-spring. It thrives in mid-winter where and when the frosts are light. Leaf and Bibb types do best but head lettuces are possible for the skilled or determined. For the warmer part of the year, forget lettuce and **plant other greens** like tampala or Malabar spinach, Okinawa spinach and Dawn Dewa, both Gynura species. These like the summer and can be harvested, with the right growing conditions, in only five or six weeks.

* **Kale and kohlrabi** grow easily in cool weather, much the same as cabbage but with a somewhat shorter season.

* **Melons** (cantaloupe, watermelon, honeydew, and others) are grown commercially in Florida in the spring and are possible in home gardens with a little extra care if you have the room in the sun. Plant from February to April, after danger of frost passes, and again in August and September for southern Florida only. Mulch and treat weekly with *Bt* or Sevin to control pickleworms. Check fragrance and color for ripeness. Stems do not slip as easily in Florida, so don't depend on that to indicate ripeness for you. For the best flavor, melons need sun and enough but not too much water. If you don't have space to grow your own, buy local melons from fruit stands in May and June. I've gotten delicious big cantaloupes for only a dollar.

* **Mustard or mustard spinach** is a natural for Florida gardens, for it has a long season of weather tolerance. Sow these greens from September right through March in all sections of the state. Mustard seed can germinate almost overnight. Speed of growth depends on the season. Keep it cut back by harvesting often, to within two inches of the ground. Feed every two or three weeks. Keep moist, and cover during all but light frosts.

83

HOMEMADE EGG NOODLES, GREEN OR OTHERWISE

When I was first married, my husband was shocked to be fed "store bought" noodles. Luckily, I soon learned how easy they are to make.

- Just break as many eggs as you want into a large mixing bowl. To make green noodles, put the eggs in the blender and add washed greens of any kind. Liquefy, then turn this mixture into the bowl.

-Then simply add enough flour, white or whole wheat, and stir with a spoon to make the dough as near to manageable as possible.

-Turn the dough onto a pastry cloth and knead in enough more flour to be able to roll it out. For three eggs, one pastry cloth is enough. I use seven eggs and two cloths which I keep in the freezer between uses. I cut my dough in half and roll it thin to cover each well-floured pastry cloth.

-Allow to dry for a few hours or until the edges just begin to lift from the cloth. Then cut it in lengthwise strips as wide as you want your noodles long, about four inches. Dust the top surface with flour. Stack these strips and cut across them to make noodles of any width. .

-Stir them about and leave to dry further. I put the bags of noodles in the freezer. Now that our family is small, we get several meals from a batch.

Over the years when I threatened divorce, my husband was unmoved, but when I threatened to give him store-bought noodles again, he paid attention.

Cook it like spinach or use it in stir-fries. There was a time when my family would not touch it even in salads, but they loved it in green noodles. Wash and blend the mustard with eggs for noodle recipes, with milk or tomato juice for meat loaf, or with as little water as possible and freeze it like celery leaves for seasoning, or for other recipes that call for spinach.

* Okinawa spinach, *Gynura crepioides,* is a fine but little known perennial ground cover that we now use and enjoy in salads year round. I found this at a herb sale. I have several plants of it growing around my yard in sun to partial shade because it roots easily from cuttings. The leaves are about two inches long and one inch wide, dark green on top, maroon underneath. The plants grow about 18 inches tall and 24 inches wide.

* Okra also likes summer, but needs continuous supplies of water and fertilizer to thrive. It is particularly susceptible to nematodes so mulch it well. You can grow varieties that range in size from three to 15 feet and choose pod colors of green, white, or red. I especially like the red, which turns green as it is cooked. If you grow okra, pick it daily to keep the pods from developing past the small and tender stage.

Cut crosswise slices and add them raw to salads for a delightful flavor and texture.

Let a few pods escape at the end of the season to use in dried arrangements or wreaths, but constant picking is necessary to keep the plants producing. Wash and slice the pods crosswise, toss them in a bowl with cornmeal, and pan-fry in butter for an easy and delicious introduction to a favorite Southern vegetable. Some people like steamed or pickled okra, and almost everyone likes okra in gumbo.

* Onions grow large and lush at the ends of the rows in strawberry fields when the berries ripen, a hint of their growing time. Onions are fairly easy, but not quite the carefree crop they were up north. Without plenty of water and feeding, they will come to nothing. With it, they will grow as large as baseballs and as sweet as Georgia's Vidalias, because of the climate. Plant seeds or transplants of Florida varieties from September to November in southern and central Florida, and from September to December in northern Florida. Sets will produce good scallions, not large bulbs. Feed every three or four weeks. Onions and their relatives tolerate light freezes.

Gary Staley of Brandon, Florida grows thriving rows of Texas Granex red and white onions that looked very large even the year he only planted them from plants in January. "The best time to plant onions is when you plant strawberries," he says. "In Florida you must plant short day onions. The long day kinds, including onions from sets and all kinds of garlic, will never form bulbs here."

* **Peanuts** should be sown in early spring only in central and north Florida and make a fascinating garden project for children. The little yellow flowers bloom and then bury themselves in the soil to form the nut. Be sure the pH of your soil is slightly acid. Plant shelled seeds with the brown covering intact if possible any time between March 15 and May 15. Feed well with low-nitrogen fertilizer and add calcium and gypsum when flowering begins. Dig the vines when pods seem mature. Boiled peanuts make a favorite dish here. Roadside stands have large kettles boiling away, but I haven't adjusted to a soft vegetable that is more pea than nut. Boil them as soon as you dig them. Allow peanuts for roasting to dry out in the sun first.

* **Peas** of the English and sugar snap type (*Pisum sativum*) are not at home in Florida, but you can grow them during cooler months with careful timing. Sow in October through February in central and southern Florida, January through March in northern Florida. Plants but not blossoms will tolerate light freezes. Because there will be no large pea harvests like the 50 quarts a year we used to freeze, the sugar snaps (eat the whole pod) are the most practical.

On the other hand, Southern peas (*Vigna unguiculata*, black-eyed, conch or crowder peas) thrive through summer and are an excellent cover crop even if you don't eat them. But frequent harvests are necessary if you want continuous production. These are very good. I favor the 'Zipper Cream' variety because it is easy to shell.

* **Peppers,** both the sweet bell types and the many hot types, will grow and sometimes live for several years if protected from frost. They do well either in pots, or in the garden. Hot peppers are ornamental in flower beds and I like to grow a few. Chile and exotic peppers do well because of the long growing season. More and more kinds are available. Ancho chilies are moderately hot, and great for stuffing. There are Pepper Festivals around the state that draw huge crowds, have hot sauce contests, and give out samples of everything from stuffed peppers to hot pepper ice cream. The latter tasted good to me even though I seldom eat hot peppers intentionally. Yellow, orange, red, and brown bell peppers have time to ripen here to their full coloration and the colored ones have more nutrition than the green.

The Amazing Earthbox

The EarthBox™ was developed in 1991 by Blake Whisenant, a man with farming in his background and in his blood, in Parish, Florida, which is just south of us off of Route I75. You can usually meet the man himself at his Earthbox Research Center and shop at 1023 Ellenton-Gillette Road, Ellenton, Florida. Check the website: for the schedule (http://www.earthboxresearch.com) and go to one of his free classes on using the EarthBox, a 30" x15" x 12" innovation that can produce an average of 30 to 40 pounds of tomatoes in each crop. These boxes have a water reservoir in the bottom and 2 cups of dry fertilizer are added to the potting mix in a trench down the center for each crop. The top is covered with the mulch kit or with a plastic garbage bag once you have worn out the original and this keeps down the weeds, evaporation, and rain damage. The plants can take in as much water and fertilizer as they need and this is where I plant both flowers and vegetables that I can't seem to grow elsewhere. This concept has spread worldwide and allows users to have maximum production and quality with minimum water and work, even on a sunny porch or patio.

85

Vegetable Varieties at Sweetwater Organic Community Farm

These are varieties currently grown at Sweetwater Organic Community Farm, a fabulous place in Tampa where people join to work and learn and get organic vegetables, or join and not work and buy a bagful of whatever is in season at a slightly higher price. The website is **www.sweetwater-organic.org.** These "picks" may work well for you, too.

Arugula
Bean, 'Golden Wax'
Beans, Winged
Beans, Bush, 'Green Potted'
Beans, Lima
Beets 'Round Red Ace'
Broccoli 'Genji'
Brussels Sprouts 'Oliver'
Cabbage 'Regal Red'
Cabbage, Chinese 'Napa Rubicon'
Cantaloupe 'Edisto' and 'Musketeer'
Carrots 'Nelson'
Cauliflower 'Snow Crown'
Celery 'Tender Crisp and 'Ventura'
Cilantro 'Santo'
Collards 'Champion'
Eggplant 'Black Bell' and 'Neon'
Fennel 'Zefafino'
Kale 'Toscano'
Kale, 'Winter Bor Green Curled'
Kohlrabi, 'Purple Kolibri' and 'White Winner'
Leeks

Lettuce 'Endive', 'Ermosa', 'Galactic', 'Green Forest', 'Integrata Red', 'Kalura', 'Loma' 'Magenta', 'Nancy', 'Nevada', 'New Red Fire', 'Pirat','Red Oak Leaf', 'Red Sails', 'Redina', and 'Rosalita'
Onions, red, white, and yellow
Pac Choi 'Joi Choi' and 'Mei Choi'
Parsley, 'Curley Leaf' and 'Italian Dark Green'
Peas, Pigeon
Peas, snap green 'Sugar Ann'
Pepper 'Antohi Romanian' and 'Red Night'
Potato, 'Cranberry' and 'Rose Gold'
Radicchio
Radishes, black, white, and tricolor Rutabaga
Sorrel
Spinach 'Avon' and 'Savoy Leaf'
Swiss Chard 'Bright Lights' and 'Ruby Red'
Tamarindo
Tomatillo
Tomato, cherry, 'Sungold'
Turnip 'Purple Top White Globe'

Feed plants every three weeks and stake them if necessary. Mulch and keep soil moist. Peppers produce three to four crops a year rather than continuously, so freeze the extras.

For homemade pest repellant, put a few of the hot little peppers into the blender with a quart of water, and a garlic clove for extra pungency. A spoonful of salad oil helps the concoction stick. Blend, let sit, then strain and spray the liquid on garden plants. Few insects or squirrels like the taste.

* **Potatoes,** regular (white or red) can be grown in Florida, but they do better the farther north you live in the state. Plant them in January, February, or March in northern Florida. January and February are best in central Florida, September to December in southern Florida. Feed well or they will be the size of marbles.

Sweet potatoes and yams like the heat and humidity and are perennial in Florida. They will make quite a good groundcover. Start them by planting tubers or pieces that have begun to sprout. Those from the grocery have been treated to prevent their sprouting, but you can rough up their outer coating with a little soap and water and steel wool and get them to grow for you anyway. Or buy starter plants of named varieties at the garden store. If your soil is too rich in nitrogen, sweet potatoes can be all leaf and no root. Mulch well to prevent nematodes and hill up with soil for more production. And beware: they can take over your whole garden.

* **Pumpkins** are a fine example of the necessity for planting the right variety. Get Seminole pumpkins or calabaza squash from ECHO Farms. I planted them once and had big squashes to give away for five months of the summer. And since then, new plants volunteer every year. Let them take over the garden in the summer when little else will grow and learn from the Cubans the many ways to cook them. Some will turn a fine tan and we make our Jack-o-lanterns from these. I cook and freeze whole ones and have a constant supply for pumpkin bread, muffins, or cake. Cook and serve them almost any way you would sweet potatoes. You can also cook the vine tips and young leaves like spinach or in stir-fry. And roast the seeds with butter and salt for a delicious snack.

* **Radishes** have a short season, but at last I had almost a ground cover of them with big sweet bulbs from sowings among the peas in November. They withstand light freezes and can be sown at frequent intervals from September to March in northern Florida, from October or November to March in central and southern Florida. Winter radishes don't necessarily need winter. Sow them in September in northern Florida, October through December in central and southern Florida. Feed lightly every three or four weeks.

* **Spinach** is possible, like beets, for a short season in the winter when and where conditions cooperate. It is easiest in northern Florida, where a September sowing is best. Here in central Florida, I saw a garden with one wide row of spinach that would make any northern gardener proud, but I never had any luck myself though market gardeners in Ruskin, Florida, grow it for the grocery stores. Then my friend Della Sarsfield brought me several bags that we ate in great salads before I realized she had grown them herself. So I tried again. My first two plantings came up well and promptly died. The third one I planted in pure compost in the front yard where I would remember to water it frequently, and at last I got a great spinach crop. Plant in October to January. Other greens like collards and kale have a longer season. Use them in the same recipes and don't mention the difference.

* **Squash** is variable crop here. Most of the northern ones can be grown if you employ pinpoint timing. Among them, the scallop 'Patty Pan' has done best for me. Cucuzzi is a delicious, dependable substitute for zucchini in the summer; give it the water, fertilizer, and support it needs. But pick it quickly or it gets to be as large and hard as a baseball bat. For much of the year, we use green papayas and chayotes in squash recipes. Our favorite is a scalloped casserole with herbed bread crumbs, cream of chicken soup, and sour cream or cream cheese mixed with the cooked squash and then baked.

* **Swiss chard,** especially rhubarb chard, was one of my favorite crops up north, though I used it mostly as an ornamental and in flower arranging. It did not do well for me, though I saw it doing well in one garden I visited. Now I plant it in my EarthBox™ and get enough to add color and nutrition to our salads. Again the secret is with rich soil and a constant supply of moisture.

* **Tomatoes** grow nicely here until frost or summer kills the plants. Some of the cherry types will survive most of the summer. However, a horde of pests may arrive to eat them before you do. I pick them as soon as they start to turn color and let them finish ripening indoors or on the screened porch. Best success has been with heritage varieties.

Marian Van Atta recommended the ring method of growing, with a circle of concrete reinforcing wire about four feet in diameter and also in height. Make the ring a compost pile with leaves and grass clippings. Put four or five tomato plants around the edge and train them up through the wires. My own best tomatoes have been those grown in pots, almost hydroponically considering the soil, with tomato rings for support. Lots of feeding and watering is needed for these. With the plants up off the ground, the bugs have a harder time finding them. When the sun moves, so do the plants. In case of frost, several can come into the garage. Half a dozen potted tomato plants can supply a family.

* **Turnips** and other root crops are not difficult if you plant them in the fall or early spring. Most will tolerate frost and light freezes. Prepare soil well, add fertilizer before planting, and feed again every two to three weeks. Eat the tops of turnips as well. Rutabagas need cool temperatures to grow large. *Bt* will keep cutworms from making your seedlings disappear. Harvest turnips when mature and refrigerate in a plastic bag. Insects move into them if they stay in the ground too long.

Planting Times for Florida Vegetables

VEGETABLE *	JAN	FEB	MAR	APR	MAY	JUN	JUL	AUG	SEP	OCT	NOV	DEC
asparagus	NC	NC	NC	NC	NC	NC	NC	NC	NC	NC	NC	NC
bean, lima	S	S	NCS	NCS	NC	NC	N	NS	CS	S	S	S
bean, snap	S	S	NCS	NCS	C	-	-	N	NCS	CS	S	S
beets	NCS	NCS	NC	-	-	-	-	-	N	NCS	NCS	NCS
broccoli	NCS	N	-	-	-	-	-	NC	NCS	NCS	NCS	NCS
Brussels sprouts*	-	-	-	-	-	-	-	-	N	NC	NCS	NCS
cabbage*	NCS	N	-	-	-	-	-	-	NCS	NCS	NCS	NCS
cab.,Chinese	NCS	-	-	N	-	-	NCS	NCS	NCS	NCS	NCS	NCS
cantaloupe	-	S	NCS	NC	-	-	-	S	S	-	-	-
carrots	NCS	NCS	NC	-	-	-	-	-	N	NCS	NCS	NCS
cauliflower*	NCS	N	-	-	-	-	-	N	N	NCS	CS	CS
celery*	NCS	NC	N	-	-	-	-	-	C	C	CS	CS
collards	CS	NCS	NC	C	-	-	-	N	NCS	NCS	NCS	NCS
corn, sweet	S	CS	NCS	N	-	-	N	NCS	CS	S	S	S
cucumbers	S	NCS	NCS	N	-	-	-	NC	NCS	S	S	S
eggplant	S	NCS	NC	N	N	N	N	CS	CS	S	-	S
endive	CS	NC	N	-	-	-	-	-	NCS	S	S	S
kale	NCS	NC	-	-	-	-	-	-	-	NC	NCSS	NCS
kohlrabi	S	CS	NC	N	-	-	-	-	-	NC	NCS	CS
lettuce	CS	CS	NC	N	-	-	-	-	NCS	CS	CS	CS
mustard	NCS	NCS	NCS	-	-	-	-	-	NCS	NCS	NCS	NCS
okra	-	S	NCS	NCS	NCS	NC	NC	CS	S	-	-	-
onions	-	-	-	-	-	-	-	-	NCS	NCS	NCS	NC
parsley	CS	N	N	-	-	-	-	-	S	CS	CS	CS
peanuts	-	S	NCS	NC	N	-	-	-	-	-	-	-
peas, English	NCS	NCS	N	-	-	-	-	-	-	CS	CS	CS
peas, Southern	S	S	NCS	NCS	NC	NC	NC	NCS	CS	S	S	S
peppers*	S	S	NCS	NCS	-	-	N	NCS	CS	S	S	S
potatoes, regular	NS	NC	N	-	-	-	-	-	CS	CS	S	S
potatoes, sweet		S	NCS	NCS	NCS	NCS	CS	-	-	-	-	-
pumpkin	S	S	NC	NC	-	-	NCS	NCS	S	-	-	-
radishes	NCS	NCS	NCS	-	-	-	-	-	N	NC	NCS	NCS
rhubarb	N	N	N	N	N	N	N	NCS	NCS	NCS	N	N
spinach	S	-	-	-	-	-	-	-	-	NCS	NCS	CS
spinach, Malabar	-	S	CS	NCS	NCS	NCS	NCS	NCS	CS	-	-	-
squash, summer	S	S	NCS	N	-	-	-	NC	NCS	S	-	-
squash, winter	S	S	NC	-	-	-	-	C	-	-	-	-
strawberries*	-	-	-	-	-	-	-	-	NCS	NCS	S	-
Swiss chard	NCS	NCS	NCS	-	-	-	-	-	NCS	NCS	NCS	NCS
tampala	-	S	CS	NCS	NCS	NCS	NCS	NCS	CS	-	-	-
tomatoes	S	S	NCS	N	-	-	-	NCS	CS	S	S	S
turnips	NCS	NCS	NC	N	-	-	-	N	NC	NCS	CS	S
watermelon	S	CS	NCS	N	-	-	N	NCS	S	-	-	-

* = plants not seeds   N = northern, C = central, S = southern Florida

CHAPTER NINE
WONDERFUL FLORIDA FRUITS

Growing fruit in Florida is as easy and natural as it is fun and rewarding, and there are many kinds from which you can choose. The wide range of possibilities includes both familiar and exotic varieties. If you ever wished you could have as much fruit as vegetable production from your yard, that wish can soon come true.

Different parts of the state have different climates, and there are also annual fluctuations. This variability is an advantage as well as a disadvantage. If it is cold, certain fruits like apples, peaches, pears, and plums do better, for they like chilling in winter. If the winter is warm, citrus and tropical fruits will bear abundantly. Plant fruit from each group, and you will always have something, no matter what kind of weather you get.

FIRST LESSONS

Here is information on growing fruit that I wish I had known when I first arrived in Florida:

* Growing trees here does not require the investment in years that it did in the North. Trees grow quickly and some produce even within the first year. Therefore, if a tree freezes out every several years and has to be replaced, it may still be well worth the effort and expense of planting and replanting. We have not had any serious cold damage since the 1989 Christmas freeze almost 20 years ago. There was one time in the late 1800's when almost all the citrus trees in the state were destroyed by a big freeze. It can happen. We go on the premise that it won't.

* Most fruit trees in Florida are natural dwarfs or can be pruned to grow that way. The dwarf varieties that were so important and more expensive in the North are seldom needed here.

Depending on the root stock, some citrus will stay naturally smaller than others. A 'Flying Dragon' rootstock can keep a tree down to 10 feet for people with limited space and for easy picking. It is very slow growing and therefore more expensive and takes a bit longer to produce a crop. 'Swingle' keeps the tree smaller than some but not quite that dwarf. 'Kinkoji' rootstocks make a big tree.

There are varieties of mango that will stay dwarf. 'Julie' gets only eight feet tall and is a true dwarf. 'Cogshall' is a semi-dwarf mango tree that can grow up to 12 ft. high over 20 years and it produces more mangos than 'Julie'.

* Florida growers can use only a few of the fruit selections from general mail order catalogs that are sent all over the country. It is best to buy from local nurseries or Florida-based specialists who will have the varieties that are hardy here. Tree and plant sales sponsored by the Rare Fruit Council International (RFCI) are great for buying fruit trees of all kinds. At RFCI meetings, where we have "more fun than God ought to allow," guests are usually welcome, and you'll also find recipes, information, and fellowship with other fruit growers. I have enjoyed my membership in this group tremendously. There are chapters in various areas or the state. Check for their very informative websites or call your county extension office for the nearest group.

* Many fruit trees, especially citrus, are so ornamental that edible landscaping is easy. In fact, you may want to save your sunniest spots for fruit trees and let trees like mangos, avocados or loquats give you your shade. But keep in mind the possible results of frosts. I plant all clumps of bananas in the back yard, out of direct view from any window, because they look bad during almost any winter and terrible after a frost. However, they come back from the roots or from much higher on the stalk and are a

Mmm, ponkan mandarins.

lovely, lush, tropical accent from April until cold weather the next winter. So I keep one clump close enough to the living room windows to cast delightful shadows and give me the music of their large leaves rustling in the breeze.

* Citrus are among the easiest of fruits to grow in Florida. Except for the frost worry, they have few problems as dooryard trees. Choose kinds and varieties that are hardy for your area. Given ample water and fertilizer, they will soon bear plenty of fruit. The blossoms perfume the air for an entire month in spring.

There are stringent and ever-changing laws to protect the citrus industry. Various diseases threaten from time to time. Citrus canker led to the destruction of many trees in the state since the last edition of this book. Citrus canker can now be eradicated within two hours and no more trees are in danger. But for a time no homegrown citrus fruit could be shipped out of the state. That rule has changed, but could change again because of disease or pest problems for the industry.

Citrus greening is now threatening both commercial and dooryard citrus. I recently interviewed Paul Harris, a nurseryman from Lithia, Florida, who buds, grows, and sells both wholesale and retail some 105 different varieties of citrus. He feels that this problem, too, will be solved, and that the citrus industry in Florida definitely will survive.

In the meantime, I have some 15 different citrus trees in my yard that have been thriving for nearly 20 years with no spraying, little pruning, and ample feeding. I get delicious harvests. My favorite navel is dying from deadly decline, but Paul Harris says that is because it was grafted on a sour orange rootstock that they haven't used since the early 90s.

When we bought our first a citrus trees, we had to register that fact, and inspectors came to our garden a few times to check the citrus plants for pests and diseases. They have done neither for years.

"Don't mulch citrus trees," my fruit growing friends told me, so I hardly ever did except when the grass got very threatening. It took me years to learn why we shouldn't mulch

them: the trees are susceptible to root rot and need free air circulation and good water drainage around the root area, especially near the trunk. Cultivate carefully, but do not mulch, as a rule. If it is a choice between mulch or weeds, mulch is better, but keep it away from the trunk and pull it back as soon as it kills the weeds or as soon as the summer rains begin each year.

Once your citrus trees are established, water them deeply every two weeks if rain is not sufficient. Do not overwater. They need to dry out between waterings.

As a grower, you can have amazing fruits that never appear in the grocery and seldom even in the produce markets. My favorites include any kind of pommelo, the ancestor of the grapefruit with its many and huge fruits that are sweeter, dryer and less acid than the grapefruit. We make our own orange juice from November to June, adding tangerines early in the season, and blood oranges that turn the juice red to purple in the later months. Our 'Valencia' makes the most juice. 'Page' has small fruits but they are sweet and juicy. The ponkans are so sweet and easy to peel that we eat them out of

hand, every last one. I've also tasted 'Satsumas' that are almost as good and will grow as far north as Georgia.

WILL MY FAMILY LIKE GRUMI-CHAMA? OR WHATEVER?

Of course, plant your favorite fruits first and buy varieties recommended by a friend or a book. The RFCI in Tampa has a Citrus Celebration every year on a Sunday at the State Fair where you can taste many different kinds of citrus. You can also buy and taste exotic kinds of fruit from the grocery to see whether you should plant them. Don't let this prejudice you. The first carambolas I bought, at a surprisingly high price, did not taste all that good. But when I got tree-ripened ones, they were delicious.

I learned that carambolas, mangoes, papayas, and many other Florida fruits vary in taste from plant to plant and even from the same plant at different times. Ripeness and freshness affect flavor, too, as with any fruit. Try exotic new fruits along with your favorites. Whatever you plant, your family will like it at once or learn to like it soon, for you will be harvesting each kind at its peak.

HOW SHOULD I START?

The county agricultural extensive service is a great help with both bulletins and advice. To start, ask which days the volunteers are there if you'd rather talk to them than bother the experts. On your first trip to the library or book store, get Lewis Maxwell's small book, *Florida Fruit*, or Marian Van Atta's *Growing and using Exotic Foods*. You will use either one for years. I use both. There is also an extensive chapter on

Edible Landscaping in my *Florida Gardener's Book of Lists*, a reference for growing almost any kind of plant in Florida. More recent books include Charles R. Boning's *Florida's Best Fruiting Plants* and Jackson and Davies' *Citrus Growing in Florida*.

As your interest grows or time permits, join the nearest chapter of Rare Fruit Council International. I went to their annual tree sale back when I was too green to know which questions to ask or plants to buy. And the last thing I thought I wanted was to join any group. Months later, I got out their flyer to look at the list of plants one can grow in our area. Then I saw that, at the next plant sale, members would get a discount that would more than cover my dues. The meeting date and place happened to be convenient, but many members never go to the meetings, instead reading the newsletter's encapsulation of each speaker's talk.

Our Tampa group has friendly people, a free seed and sometimes a free plant exchange, a delicious spread of food where you can taste fruit and gather recipes, and a plant auction and raffle from which many of my own trees have come. At first much of the talk at meetings went over my head, but soon I began to understand more of it. I always come home feeling like I can do anything. My "fruit friends" are some of my favorite people.

Mostly, you will learn by growing and have so much fun doing it that the time will fly. Whatever you grow will help you learn more about growing everything else, and eventually everything you learned before coming to Florida will stand you in good stead as well. You are really not starting from scratch, just taking a sharp bend in the road.

SHOULD I BUY A SEEDLING TREE OR A GRAFTED ONE?

If you win a tree at a fruit meeting, or are given one, accept either a seedling or grafted tree happily. If your space is limited, leave the seedling in the pot until you check on bearing time in *Florida Fruit* or a similar book.

Some trees, like carambola, have been known to bear in as little as 24 months from seed. Others, like avocado and mango, will take up to ten years to bloom from seed, but only a year or two from grafted stock. All seedlings are surprises. Grafted fruit will have the same flavor, fruiting time, and such as the parent plant. So for most purposes, grafted is better, but sometimes it does not matter. Eventually you may want to learn to graft (the RFCI will teach you) so you can try many varieties on a few trees. Then you can keep the ones that are superior and discard the others.

HOW BIG A TREE SHOULD I BUY?

How big a tree can you transport home? If you don't have an orange tree yet, what price would you put on getting a crop next year instead of three years from now?

The difference in price between a larger and a smaller tree can seem less important if you consider how much you'll enjoy getting ripe oranges right away. I wished, after I'd bought the gallon pot size, that I'd invested in the three gallon pot size for at least one of the orange trees and one of the grapefruits when we first started planting. Kumquats and calamondins bear on smaller, younger trees or shrubs. Those already large enough to bear these fruits are not expensive. After a few years, it was a convenience to me to buy second varieties in small sizes so that I could afford more, get more in the car, dig smaller holes, and cover the plants more easily during frosty nights. But first I wanted to have some trees that were large enough to produce fruit.

After 20 years, I have 40 some different kinds of fruit, most of them now bearing fruit. For the first time in my life and for many years now since I've been growing in Florida, I have had some fruit to pick and eat almost every day all year. Some of the people in our RFCI have as many as 200 different kinds. You can plant potted trees and shrubs at any season of the year, so you can start your fruit growing before you finish unpacking. A trip to a reputable nursery is a good morale booster during your settling in time. Once you get your new plants home, you don't necessarily have to hurry to plant them. You will find a new way of growing them in containers here that will far surpass all your initial prejudices.

SOME FRUIT FAVORITES

Grumichama, *Eugenia dombeyi* or *brasiliensis*, grows to be a small, compact tree, about 15 ft. tall and 10 ft. wide. It has beautiful glossy evergreen opposite leaves 3 to 4 in. long. I won two small plants from the RFCI raffle years ago and planted them around our above ground pool because the tops will freeze at 27 degrees. The pool is now long gone and the trees have never frozen, but for many year they had only a sample of fruit. That sample was delicious, so I tried to treat them better, but it was only when the neighboring avocado went into decline and gave them more sun that we began to have wonderful crops. I noticed a great many small white flowers in March. But I forgot to check in time. Now I know that it takes only a month from flower to fruit.

The dark black/red cherrylike fruits have a tiny tuft of sepals that stays on the blossom end and one or two seeds, easily removed, inside each one. They look and taste much like the sweet Bing cherries that come from Pennsylvania Dutch country in the summer, but they have just a slight spicy taste that identifies them as a cousin to the Surinam cherry. We ate most of them right out of hand, but I did freeze some seeded and soaked in their own juice. They are also good in jelly or stewed. Superior types are grafted. Mine probably took so long to fruit because they were seedlings.

They like sun or partial shade, have fair salt tolerance, and supposedly have low drought tolerance, though I seldom watered mine and they have never shown any signs of wilt. Now I make sure to water them well from bloom time to harvest, to harvest them every day, and to feed them an acid soil mix with minor elements in late winter.

A row of **pineapple plants** (*Ananas comosus*) in a neighbor's backyard yielded 25 fruits in one year. Pineapples are easy to grow and take little care. In the mid 1800's, they were a big Florida industry along the St. John's River and in the Keys. By 1900 there were over 5000 acres in pineapple cultivation with production of a million crates a year. In 1910 Cuban pineapples glutted the market and the industry declined after that with freezes, droughts, and nematode troubles. But Florida gardeners have continued to grow them in their yards and you can't get one even in Hawaii that tastes better.

You can start them from the tops of purchased fruits. Cut or twist off the top, perhaps with a bit of flesh attached, but not necessarily. Peel away the lower leaves and root it like a cuttings, either in water or in well prepared, humusy garden soil. Keep them moist until well rooted. It takes from 15 months to three years to get fruit. Each stem produces only one, but suckers will continue to produce others.

I saw **elderberries** blooming almost all year in the wild. I had tried a few cuttings and failed when I finally recognized a few of the "weeds" in my yard as elderberries, my old friends from the ditches of Ohio. I now have several bushes growing, blooming, and fruiting. I use both the bloom and the unripe berries in flower arranging, the ripe berries for pies and wine, and the flowers for herbal cosmetics and teas. I find the large shrubs quite attractive, but if you don't, you can tuck them into the back corners. Or you can seek out the ornamental cultivar with white and green variegated leaves or the purple-leaved form with pink flowers.

Elderberries love water and will grow in low places. You often see them as ten-foot shrubs along the roadside, bearing huge, flat umbels of white flowers or of dark purple berries.

Rhubarb may be grown in Florida, but it must be grown like an annual. It will never match what you had farther north, but half a dozen pampered plants will produce a few pies and batches of jelly before they perish in the summer heat.

I have successfully dug and frozen roots over the summer and replanted them in fall, but soon I gave up this favorite as a Florida homegrown. Instead, every time anyone in the family visits the children and grands still living in Iowa, they are encouraged to bring me a bag of rhubarb stems that my friend Carolyn Browne happily supplies. I've carried it in a bag on the plane or in a cooler in the car on a two day trip. I cut it up and put it in the freezer as soon as possible after arriving home and turn it into pies and jelly later on, a jar of it for everyone at Christmas if I have enough.

Strawberries also grow like annuals in Florida. Whether to get everbearers or June bearers is not a consideration here. Florida varieties bear from December into June if well fed, watered, and protected from frost. And even the frost will kill only the blossoms, not the plant. Plants will begin to bear again in about six weeks. It is fun to have a few in the garden or in containers to watch and use to perk up fruit salads. If you want to fill your freezer, hit the fields in the spring as soon as the ads for three or four quarts for a dollar, pick-them-yourself, appear in the classified ad section. They don't take long to pick. I just wash, hull, and freeze, and then use them all year long.

One of my favorite trees for a long time was my yellow 'Gulf Gold' **plum**. It was very hardy and would bloom all winter if the weather

93

was mild. At first I lost most of the fruit to insects as it ripened. But then I learned to pick a bowlful every day of the ripest or just-dropped plums. Whatever we did not eat was cut up, seeded and frozen before the next picking. These are good in winter desserts. After many years of harvest, that tree died and I have recently replaced it with a 'Gulf Red' that has not borne fruit yet. I can't wait to once again have fresh, sweet plums as delicious as any in the North, and have them for weeks in May and June. Figs and other fruits also must be picked daily, so put them near the house or along your daily path.

GROWING FRUIT IN CONTAINERS

In Florida, growing plants in containers outdoors is not at all like growing houseplants indoors in the North. There the atmosphere was completely unnatural. Outdoors here there is plenty of light and humidity. You still have to add water and fertilizer, but you have to do that for in-ground plants as well. Outdoors you can water with a hose instead of worrying about dripping on the furniture.

The insects that were uncontrollable in a heated house are not nearly as difficult outdoors. You have natural predators to help. The plants are far enough off the ground to discourage some pests. You can easily wash insects and disease spores off with water from the hose, with or without using a hose-end sprayer filled with a mix of detergent and water.

The only disadvantage to container growing is the eventual size of pot you will need to accommodate the ever-growing plants, and the necessity of shifting them into larger pots. However, it will take some time before they grow large enough to need extremely large pots. In the months ahead, you can figure out whether to continue growing the plants in pots or to plant them in the ground.

But in the meantime, you can grow more plants in less space in containers. You can take better care of them if they are together. You can move them from shade or partial shade to more sun as you become increasingly aware of the changing shadow patterns with the different seasons. You can put your calamondin orange tree by the door where you'll catch its fragrance while it blooms, and its color when it is bearing. And when something else you have looks better, you can interchange the two.

Even if it is too large to move indoors, you can turn a large, container-grown tree on its side and cover it with a blanket to protect it from frost. It is much easier to protect if it is not vertical. Later, when immediate danger of frost is past, set it back up. If it is small enough you can bring a container into the house or garage if a frost comes and save a plant you might have lost in the ground.

Many of my "fruit friends" grow some trees in containers permanently because they would not survive our frosts here otherwise. One man planted two fruit trees of the same size and species, one in the ground and one in a container. The one in the container bore fruit first.

The containers themselves can be expensive. Save any large pots you empty or see left out for trash pickup. Some garden centers will let you have their used pots either free or for a small sum: they cannot afford the time it would take to wash them.

One RFCI member came to the rescue by selling recycled plastic barrels he had gotten from work. He had cut them in half, put drainage holes in the bottom, and handle holes in the top. Mine are 21 inches across the top and 16 inches deep, large enough to keep a small tree happy well into its fruit-producing days. He sold them at a price that was a real bargain for us and a profit for him. They are heavy to move and they gobble up the soil, though.

Another advantage to growing fruit in containers is that you can fill them with plenty of good soil, making a friendlier environment for the roots than they would find in the ground.

One excellent fruit grower, who picked an amazing variety of fresh fruit from a fairly small yard in Tampa every day of the year, planted his trees in the ground by digging a large hole to which he added one 40-pound bag of treated manure and two 40 pound bags of

topsoil. I do not treat my in ground plants quite that well, but that much amending can almost fill a large container.

To make the containers lighter when filled, and the medium more water-retentive, use up to one third good organic matter. Sphagnum peat moss is one of the best choices because it does not break down and disappear as quickly as compost. It is also sterile. But it does not add any nutrients, so feel free to use as much compost or well-rotted manure as you have. Some experts find that using perlite for up to a third of the organic third is helpful for aeration. Perlite and vermiculite have virtually no weight themselves; they are only as heavy as the water they hold. Most garden stores sell them by the small bagful, but if you ask, you can order the four cubic-foot size, which is much more economical. You can also put plastic peanuts recycled from packages in the bottom few inches of the container and use lighter, even soilless mixes if you want.

Placing mulch on the top of your containers will hold in the moisture and improve appearance. You can also grow flowers, herbs, or salad vegetables around the base of the large fruit tree, in its large pot or in smaller pots set on top of the soil surface in the larger pot.

To make the best use of limited space, you can put half of your fruit in containers, the rest in the ground. Sit plants in containers among and between the younger trees until they spread

and need more room. The containers dry out quickly, and will force you to get around with the hose every few days, so none of the plants, in ground or in containers, get too dry. You'll have better control during frosts and grow and fruit some plants, like black sapote (chocolate pudding fruit) that would never survive in the ground in my area. A small garden can be landscaped largely with deliciously productive edible plants, and be quite unique.

There was not much grass area left in the garden of my late friend Armando Mendez, none on the sides or in back. But when asked which took more time and work, the grass or the fruit, he answered without hesitation, "The grass."

PROTECTING FRUIT FROM FROSTS

Frosts are a fact of Florida life in almost all areas. All of Florida is too warm for most of the fruits we grew up North, though there are some varieties of apples, peaches, nectarines, blueberries, and grapes, the ones that need the fewest chilling hours to bloom and fruit, that will grow here. On the other hand, we are too far north to grow truly tropical fruits without extra help during those occasional frosts. So most of us fruit growers plant some trees for a tropical and some for a temperate climate, so we are sure to have something to harvest even in an abnormally cold or warm year. But without advice, it would be all too easy for a newcomer to conclude that nothing will grow here!

Concentrate on planting types of fruit that will grow with no frost protection in your area. Because our climate is so variable, most fruit growers can't resist the challenge of trying borderline plants. "I can grow anything along the south side of my house," says one fruit grower. "The trouble is, I've run out of south side."

Check for cold hardiness before you buy or plant any fruit trees, and plant them accordingly. Plant the ones that are hardy anywhere there is enough sun, ones that are borderline in protected spots or where you can cover them easily, and tender ones in containers so you can move them inside as needed.

For a time I planted my marginal trees around the perimeter of our above-ground pool, hoping that the water would hold in some warmth. It was great fun to take my evening swim while I counted the first dozen avocados and watched them ripen. Now the pool is gone but the trees remain, a jaboticaba that is finally bearing fruit, two grumichamas that taste somewhat like sweet cherries and the avocado, which seemed to be dying, then dead, and which then sent out new growth and is returning.

A few fruit growers have greenhouses, very tall ones so small trees can go inside. One friend in Spring Hill, Florida, had a framework of PVC pipe over his grapefruit tree and covered that with a secondhand parachute during frosts. He bought the parachute at an army surplus store for $75 and used it for years. He also put a heater under the branches. After the Christmas freeze of 1989, he lost some leaves, but still picked 18 bushels of grapefruit. Most trees bear half that at best.

Fruit trees tend to grow more hardy as they mature, so it is often possible to cover them during frosts for the first several winters and have them survive on their own after that.

Many fruits grow and bear well for several years, are killed back by a severe frost, and come back from the roots to bear again in a few months for bananas, or in a few years for citrus. But if they are grafted plants and come back from the roots below the graft you could have a very different fruit. That is why it pays to hill tender plants with soil to above the graft point before frost. You often see this done in commercial groves.

I finally learned that when the bananas are frozen back, it is best to leave the sad looking corpses just as they are to protect the heart until all danger of frost is past. Then cut them back, not to the ground, but as high up as you can reach. Cut the outer rim, going lower and lower if necessary, until you find green growth at the center. Let the plant restart from there and you will get blooms much sooner.

My first papayas hung green for months, and I did not know to take them in, green or not, before that 1989 Christmas freeze. They were pulp by the next morning. Now I pick and use the green papayas all year long, and before a freeze I pick from a boxful to the entire crop, according to the forecast.

WHAT IF I GET TOO MUCH?

You will be amazed at the amount of fruit your family can use if they pick and eat it fresh.

My banana plants froze to the ground for the first two winters, but a Plant City grower assured me that his nearly always froze, yet always came back and produced bananas. The winter of 1990-91 was a mild one, and the banana bloom that opened on Christmas day ripened in mid-May. That year we had 12 bunches of bananas, probably between 150 and 200 pounds altogether, and not more than one pound went to waste. In fact, not more than ten pounds made it to the freezer. They were so delicious, sweeter and tastier than any we had ever bought, that we just ate them up.

One friend with 45 persimmon trees in his yard says simply, "We have plenty of friends who will be glad to eat the ones we can't."

Should you ever get to the wonderful point of overabundance, you could easily sell the extra. Or if you want to give them away, just take them to your place of work or worship and put on a "Help Yourself" sign. It is amazing how few people take advantage of the climate to grow citrus trees.

It is easy to make preserves, fruit leather, and special treats with all the fruit. Marian Van Atta's book, *Growing and Using Exotic Foods*, is filled with growing instructions and recipes, including a basic wine recipe Marian and Jack

Van Atta used with great success with most fruits. Only their sea grape batch turned to vinegar—which Marian then used in chutney.

RECIPES

Here are recipes my family loves:

Fruit slush (for any fruit). After our first spring of picking many quarts from the strawberry farms, friends were singing the praises of strawberry daiquiris. I found the strawberry slush so delicious that adding spirits seemed a waste. Soon I learned to love a liquid breakfast of fruit slush. At first I used apple juice for a base, with a bit of orange juice for the tang. Into the blender with a cup of juice went one banana, fresh or frozen, and a handful of strawberries. If necessary, I add enough water to make the slush swirl. As new fruits ripen in the garden, I freeze the extras and experiment. I find a very little of grapefruit or papaya can be plenty. A bit of mint, lemon balm, or pineapple sage adds a nice touch. Try your own combi- nations. You can use almost any fruit this way with very little work. The drink is better than chocolate and much more nutritious. It is also a great way to start or stay on a diet or to use fruit without eating all the sugar of jams and pies.

Fruit leather. There were years when our single small plum tree outdid itself. We picked about two dozen plums every day from early May until the end of June. When I had frozen all I figured we would eat in the off season, I made fruit leather. It involves blending a mix just a little thicker that the slush described above, and you can use any fruit. Try some after your first strawberry picking.

First cut up a blenderful of plums or other main fruit. Puree, then add one banana for sweetening, a few strawberries for color, half a cup of sugar or 1/4 cup of honey if desired (plums can take on a certain bitterness once past their fresh stage), half a tablespoon of lemon juice, and half a teaspoon of cinnamon. Blend all this together and taste to see if you want to add anything else.

Then spray a large, edged cookie sheet or two 13 by 9 inch baking dishes with a non-stick coating or line with waxed paper. Pour in a thin layer of puree, up to 1/4 inches thick. Put it into your food dryer, if you have one, or the oven set on the lowest setting for 12 to 30 hours. Leave the door open two or three inches.

The puree dries to a thin, flexible sheet that you can cut into squares with knife or shears. Store in a tightly covered container. Thanks to the popularity of fruit roll-ups sold in the stores at a hefty price, even the neighbor kids gobble these up instead of candy. Experiment with whatever fruits you have in abundance. Add mint, lemon balm, or pineapple sage if you wish.

THE FRUIT GROWERS CHOICES

The more you learn about growing fruit in Florida, the more you appreciate the incredible range of choices. Look on the next page for a chart of the main fruits and how and where they grow in different parts of the state.

Frost protection and, for some, chilling time in winter are deciding factors in your selections. Often you can grow borderline ones if you are ready for the challenge of protecting them in winter. And sometimes you lose the "safe" ones. After a deep freeze, our Rare Fruit Council International newsletter comes out with a black border, but we just try again.

passion flower

FRUITFUL CHOICES

name	type	Northern FL	Central FL	Southern FL	comments
apple	tree	best	fair	do not plant	Plant two kinds. Spray for disease.
annonas	tree	In tubs	in tubs	in ground	Deciduous. Delicious.
avocado	tree	In tubs	tubs, ground	in ground	Feed like citrus.
banana	tree	fair	good	best	Feed and water well.
Barbados cherry	tree	In tubs	protect	good	Acerola, high in vitamin C.
blackberry	shrub	good	good	good	Can be rampant. Mulch plants. Acid soil.
blueberry	shrub	best	good	poor	Plant two or more pollinating kinds.
calamondin orange	tree	In tubs	*protect	good	Ripens October through January.
canistel	tree	In tubs	*protect	good	Fruit like dry egg yolk.
carambola	tree	In tubs	*protect	good	Protect from wind and cold.
Cherry of Rio Grande	shrub	In tubs	protect	good	Dark red fruit from April through June.
Chinese chestnut	tree	best	good	do not plant	Deciduous trees bear prickly burrs.
elderberry	shrub	good	good	good	Blooms and bears from frost to frost.
fig	shrub	good	good	good	Starts easily from cuttings.
grape	vine	good	good	good	Muscadines and Florida varieties.
grapefruit	tree	in tubs	*protect	good	Pink or white, seedless available.
grumichama	shrub	in tubs	*protect	good	Shrub with cherrylike fruit.
guava	shrub	In tubs	*protect	good	Landscape shrub or small tree.
jaboticaba	shrub	In tubs	*protect	good	Delicious fruit right on wood.
jambolan	tree	do not plant	protect	good	Rampant tree, can take over.
jujube	tree	good	good	good	Small reddish brown fruit in fall.
kumquat	tree	protect	good	good	Hardy, salt-tolerant, 'Meiwa' is sweet.
lemon	tree	in tubs	*protect	good	Evergreen. 'Meyer' is hardiest.
lime	tree	in tubs	*protect	good	Key lime has good salt tolerance.
limequat	tree	in tubs	*protect	good	Cross between lime and kumquat.
longan	tree	do not plant	tubs, in ground	good	Easier to grow than lychee, hardier.
loquat	tree	good	good	good	Handsome tree, fruit like apricots.
lychee	tree	do not plant	tubs, in ground	good	Protect from wind, mulch well.
macadamia nut	tree	in tubs	protect	good	Delicious nut from Australia.
mango	tree	poor	tubs, in ground	good	Flavor varies. Buy grafted plants.
mulberry	tree	good	good	good	Delicious fresh, ripens January to February.
natal plum	shrub	in tubs	protect	good	Easy ornamental. Fragrant flowers
nectarine	tree	best	good	poor	Select grafted varieties.
orange	tree	protect	protect	good	Different varieties give long harvest.
papaya	tree	in tubs	protect	good	Most need male and female plants for fruit.
passion fruit	vine	in tubs	good	good	Lovely flowers, hand pollinate most kinds.
pawpaw	tree	best	good	do not plant	Hard to establish.
peach	tree	good	good	good	Select appropriate varieties for your region.
pear	tree	good	good	good	Subject to fire blight.
persimmon	tree	good	good	fair	Some Japanese cultivars are not astringent.
pineapple	peren.	in tubs	protect	good	Pick just before fully ripe for best flavor.
plantain	tree	in tubs	protect	good	Treat like bananas. Can eat green, cooked.
plum	tree	good	good	poor	Most like cold weather. Easy care.
pomegranate	shrub	best	good	fair	Fruits best after cold winter.
pommelo	tree	poor	*protect	good	Large as grapefruit, more cold tender.
prickly pear cactus	shrub	good	good	good	Tasty, eat fresh or in jams or juice.
raspberry	shrub	good	good	good	Plant only 'Dorma Red' and 'Mysore' cvs.
rhubarb	peren.	best	good	poor	Plant seeds or plants in fall as annuals.
rose apple	shrub	do not plant	in tubs	good	Attractive plant with new leaves that are red.
sapote	tree	poor	in tubs	good	Sapodilla, black and white kinds available.
sea grape	shrub	do not plant	protect	good	Huge round leaves, seaside garden plant.
strawberry	peren.	good, protect	good, protect	good	Grow as annuals. Pick December thru June.
Surinam cherry	shrub	in tubs	good	good	Attractive shrub, spicy fruit.
tangelo, tangerine	tree	in tubs	*protect	good	Easy-to-peel fruit.
tree tomato	shrub	in tubs	protect	good	Large leaves, colorful fruit.

*Protect in youth if necessary. Often sturdier and more resilient in maturity.

CHAPTER TEN
OUTSTANDING WOODY ORNAMENTALS

At all times of year, there are outstanding ornamental plants throughout Florida. Drive a short way in any neighborhood and you will see a colorful array of exotic palms, shrubs, and trees. Especially if you've prided yourself on knowing landscape plants in the North, you'll be eager to acquire information about these southern beauties. Even familiar plants like oaks and sycamores may behave differently in this climate. The oak leaves of most species have different shapes, are evergreen, and fall slowly all winter until a hard freeze brings all the rest down, or the new leaves push off the old ones some time in March.

A frustrating aspect of being new to Florida is not knowing the names and behaviors of all the new plants. And during the time you are getting to know them, it is likely that you will buy a few you will later regret, or allow less desirable types to grow on your property.

After doing just that, I have formulated for myself and pass on to you this rule: Don't let any tree grow too large for you to cut down yourself before you find out what it is and what it does. At the same time, do not be too quick to cut down a tree you inherit unless you are sure of what it is and what it does. With our variable weather, you could have a treasure that will miss a year or even two of bloom and then be the star of the neighborhood.

Or you could have what you thought was a treasure but it proves not to be. On my bike route one winter I was amazed to find a fairly large tree covered with pink flowers. When I went to the door to ask what it was, the homeowner not only did not know, but she did not even realize it was blooming. I found out later it was a Tabebuia which is marginal for our region. I watch it now and that tree blooms only briefly once every several years. Others in the area, perhaps other species, do very well.

Don't worry about the small plants. You still have some time to change your mind about them. One friend said of her garden, "My plants have to learn to live on the shovel."

When we first came to Florida, we had three cold winters in a row. My new trees and shrubs were young and therefore less hardy, and I didn't always know which ones to cover or how to cover them.

But Florida is a great place for starting over because recovery is very quick. Shrubs often freeze back, sometimes with great advantage. They also come back from the roots if we let them, grow very quickly if we nurture them, and maybe die out if we don't.

If you drive more than a few miles in any direction, but especially north or south, you will find different plant species growing, and the same ones showing various traits. A short distance can bring out amazing disparities. St. Petersburg has more tropical plants than does nearby Tampa. Nearer the water they get frozen less often and bloom earlier. One year the jacarandas bloomed in April in St. Pete, but not until almost June in Tampa where they are never quite as impressive. One the other hand, Tampa has many more large oaks.

Here are recommended woody plants that you may see and want. If you used to garden in a state farther north, and your new residence is in northern Florida, you will find trees that you already know. In southern Florida, there will be few of these, but more of the wonderful tropical trees will grow and bloom without special protection. You'll learn names and habits of those that do best in your neighborhood as you visit nearby gardens and nurseries. Additional rare and unusual plants for your garden will become familiar as time goes on.

99

One of the most wonderful aspects of gardening in Florida is finding new plants I had never heard of even after 20 years here, and knowing that there is time to try them because everything grows so quickly here.

SEMI-TROPICAL TREES

Acacia (*Acacia auriculiformis*) thrives in Zones 9 to 11. Other species are recommended only for Zones 10 to 11, but I have learned over the years that many plants recommended for Zones 10A and 10B do very well in our central Florida Zone 9, especially in protected pockets. I had one of the native acacias for a while, and it wasn't the cold but the lack of sun that finally did it in. Acacias have flattened branchlets instead of leaves and fountains of small yellow flowers that vary with different species from insignificant to showy and fragrant. There are few problems. You may find several other acacias at nurseries. All have yellow flowers.

Araucaria **species** in southern Florida will probably be the Norfolk Island pine (*A. heterophylla*), unique in its dark green color and tiers of very horizontal branches. Since we have had quite a few warmer winters, there are now some large Norfolk Island pines in the Tampa area. In central Florida you can find another handsome araucaria that is called the monkey puzzle tree, *A. araucana*.

I could hardly wait to get one of these because my friend from Ireland loved them. There they are picturesque, very sparse trees, but here they are dense and as prickly as a tree can get. Mine died in the Christmas freeze of '89. Like many plants, this one becomes hardier as it grows older. Many large monkey puzzle trees in my neighborhood survived the same freeze. I did not replace mine because because these trees have sharply needled leaves that bite any hand or foot that touches them.

It took me even longer to learn that fruits are fairly rare and found only on female trees of a certain age. Then they are so far up and hidden in the foliage that it is hard to see them until they fall with a crash. These fruits, weighing up to 7 pounds or more, could seriously hurt anyone standing beneath them.

They could also dent a car or break a windshield. The conelike fruits are almost as bristly as the monkey puzzle foliage. After they age a bit, they break apart into sections. The many seeds are edible. Boiled, they taste somewhat like chestnuts. Most of these trees are dioecious—that is, with male and female flowers on separate trees. Some trees are male and therefore fruitless.

Bottlebrush trees (*Callistemon* species) grow 20 feet tall in central and southern Florida. They bloom in spring or summer with red-orange flowers that look just like their name. This is an excellent tree for color, as well as for luring bees to your yard to help with the pollination of vegetables and fruits. Large specimens do not transplant as well as smaller ones and they need a sunny spot. There are both erect and weeping species, with the latter more interesting to most of us.

Citrus trees are as lovely as they are fruitful. There are hardier kinds like kumquats that grow anywhere in the state. Some types of citrus fruit ripens in fall, some in winter and spring, and few into the summer. Check with your county agent for recommended varieties for your local climate, or buy from a trusted local nursery. See more on Citrus in chapter 9.

Floss silk trees (*Chorisia speciosa*) are planted to such spectacular effect at Cypress Gardens that you want to fill your sky with them. David got me one and it soon became a large tree. There are a few around us in Tampa and it seems that every year they bloom more beautifully, not sparsely and unreliably as I once thought. But the bloom time varies from early summer to November depending on both the year and the tree.

They have poor salt tolerance. The flowers are three to five inches wide, with five long petals in watercolor shades of off-white, rose, or lavender. Trees reach 40 or 50 feet in height and produce a silky seed floss used for stuffing pillows. They are fairly weak wooded. Ours lost several limbs in the storms of 2004 and one is still hanging there. The only other drawback to this tree is that the trunks are covered with frightful looking thick thorns. It is definitely not a climbing tree for no tree trimmer is going up there, and it would take a crane to get it out if it died.

Jacaranda acutifolia (one of my absolute favorites) grows 25 to 40 feet tall only in the central and southern counties, for it has little tolerance of frost. It has lilac-like but larger flowers that start as dark purple buds on a bare tree, and then make a profuse cloud of lavender blooms, and finish with a few lavender flowers among foliage in August. Like other spectacularly flowering trees, the jacaranda drops petals and is somewhat messy, also short lived. The graceful, feathery leaves are deciduous and compound, and make light shade in summer. The silhouette is bare in winter. I now have one that is crowded by the oaks and therefore blooms very high. Both this and the floss silk carpet the ground beneath them with lovely dropped flowers that made grandson Mike say, when he was four, "Wow. It looks like a wedding." The flowers become mulch in the garden, but would be slippery on a driveway or patio.

Oaks (*Quercus* species) are the biggest trees in our neighborhood, spreading and producing acorns as in the North, but very different in leaf. Live oaks are the longest lived, strongest, and most beautiful. I have seen one that spreads its almost horizontal limbs over a very large yard with a spread of at least 200 feet. Myrtle oaks grow in every county of Florida. Laurel oaks and sand live oaks grow down to the everglades. Chestnut oaks and dwarf post oaks grow mostly in the southern counties, extending into the central region. Oaks are often planted in groups, though a single tree makes an excellent shade and specimen tree very quickly.

cassia

SMALL TREES
(under 25 feet tall, nice for small yards)
Acacia
Bauhinia (orchid tree)
Callistemon (bottlebrush)
Cercis (redbud)
Citrus
Cornus (dogwood)
Eriobotrya (loquat)
Eugenia dombeya
   (Grumichama)
Ilex (holly)
Pandanus (screw pine)
Tabebuia
Vitex (chaste tree)

TREES WITH FRAGRANT LEAVES
Myrica species
   (Bayberry)
Eucalyptus
Ficus (fig)
Pines

TREES WITH SHOWY FLOWERS
Acacia
Bauhinia (orchid tree)
Cassia
Citrus
Cornus
Chorisia (floss silk tree)
Jacaranda
Koelreuteria (golden rain
   tree)
Magnolia
Tabebuia

TREES WITH FRAGRANT FLOWERS
Acacia
Cananga (Ylang-ylang)
Chionanthus (Fringe tree)
Citrus
Magnolia
Plumeria

They can grow five feet taller and wider every year. Most are evergreen, though the turkey oaks have lovely winter color.

Orchid tree (*Bauhinia* species) is one of the showiest flowering trees in central and southern Florida. It grows to 20 or 25 feet with moderate speed and needs annual shaping for best umbrella form. Leaves are round but with twin lobes. Various kinds bloom at different seasons of the year with orchidlike flowers of white, lavender, or reddish purple, some up to six inches across. The Hong Kong orchid tree is quite fragrant in bloom. Propagate by grafting or air-layering. Salt tolerance is fair, drought tolerance good.

LARGE SHRUBS OVER 15 FEET
Callistemon (bottlebrush)
Camellia
Coccoloba (sea grape)
Lagerstroemia (crape myrtle
Ligustrum (privet)
Malpighia punicifolia
    (Barbados cherry)
Oleander
Pittosporum, some cvs.
Podocarpus

SMALL SHRUBS I TO 2 FEET
Harland boxwood
Japanese holly
Kurume azalea
Pyracantha (dwarf)
Yaupon (dwarf)
Zamia (coontie)

MEDIUM SHRUBS 5 TO 10 FEET
Acalypha (copper leaf)
Azalea
Burford holly
Carissa macrocarpa (Natal
    plum)
Croton
Dwarf natal plum
Gardenia
Hibiscus
Ixora

Japanese boxwood
Lantana
Nandina
Plumbago
Raphiolepsis (Indian
    hawthorn)
Rose
Roselle
Surinam cherry

Pines (*Pinus* species) grow throughout Florida. The species differ from those of northern states, but are similar in needle and cone bearing, not in overall shape. Traveling through northern Florida you may see vast forests of pine. Their trunks are the source of those long logs you see on trucks on the way to the sawmill.

In the northern and central part of the state you find pond, sand, longleaf, and loblolly pines. Slash pine grows from southern Florida as far north as Tampa. Pines are often planted in groups in Florida yards. They eventually tower above most of the other trees and give light or dappled shade. The needles make excellent mulch. So do the heaps of pine cone chips the squirrels leave behind after savoring the edible pine nuts.

Tabebuia. Silver trumpet, pink trumpet, and others of the many *Tabebuia* species grow quickly into small trees, 25 to 40 ft. tall, with leaves in whorls of three to seven and trumpet shaped flowers in clusters, followed by cylindrical pods. The hardiest, known as silver trumpet, tree of gold, or yellow poui, has an interesting irregular shape, silver-gray foliage and bark with golden yellow blooms in late winter followed by long brown beanlike pods. They are easy to start from seeds or seedlings growing under the tree and begin to bloom when quite small. Mine was a seedling gift and has grown quickly. They need full sun. Others bloom in shades of pink, rose, or white with colored veins, some with mild fragrance, all in late winter or early spring, much too briefly.

Some species have fair salt tolerance. All have excellent drought tolerance. They thrive in poor soil though they prefer it more fertile, and do well in sun or shade. They have few problems other than frost.

PALMS

Palms are often referred to as trees though they are actually more closely related to grasses. They are variously decorative and some have edible fruits. To most people they are a symbol of everlasting summer. The great majority are easy to move, even when large, and are fairly easy to grow.

Palms in many sizes and kinds grow throughout Florida. They are variously hardy, and there is a wide selection on the coast and in the south. Northern Florida has only a handful of choices.

Most palms will grow in full sun to partial shade, are fairly salt tolerant, and are easily transplanted since they are shallow rooted. All bear fruit, some of which is good for eating fresh or using for jelly. Everyone knows the edible date, for instance, which comes from date palms. Below Miami you find roadside stands selling "coco frio," cold coconuts from local palms. They are opened with a machete and served with a straw inserted for drinking the coconut milk.

Palms need watering during the dry months, feeding, and considerable trimming of older fronds. Apply one pound of palm or regular fertilizer per inch of trunk diameter yearly, in February, June, and October in the south, in late winter and midsummer in the north. Also apply half a pound of manganese and magnesium, up to five pounds yearly to minimize yellowing or frizzling of fronds.

TALL PALMS

David loved all palms, especially those with tall, unique shapes. So I was thrilled when someone at church was selling small queen palms for only three dollars. I bought him five and we already had one growing close to the house, too close. Like all trees in Florida, they grew very quickly. I prefer a tree with either fruit or bloom or both, but I didn't mind the palms, even though they needed lots of pruning and shed all sorts of stiff stemmed fronds and fruit, until they grew too tall for me to prune them.

I made the mistake of running over a pile of palm debris one day when our driveway was crowded. One of those fronds caught under my car and did hundreds of dollars worth of damage. Never run over a palm stem.

After the hurricane scare in 2004, we paid dearly to have all but one of the queen palms removed. That was the year the tree trimmers took out nine tons of woody debris from what had been, in 1987, a very open yard. So now I only have the problem of those hundreds of palm seeds still sprouting. I pull them out or cut them back on a regular basis.

My new rule for palms is that I will never again plant one that grows taller than I can reach. But if you don't mind trimming them annually, consider the following types.

Gru-gru (*Acrocomia totai*). Central and southern Florida. 45 ft. tall. Black spines on its trunk can be vicious.

King Palm (*Archontophoenix* species). Uneven ringed trunk, graceful, young plants very cold tender.

Sabal or Cabbage Palm (*Sabal palmetto*). Northern, central, and southern Florida. 60 ft. tall. This native is the state tree and grows wild throughout Florida. It is salt and cold tolerant and has fragrant flowers.

Canary Island Date Palm (*Phoenix canariensis*). Northern, central, and southern Florida. 50 ft. tall. The trunk has a diamond pattern, like pineapple. Highly ornamental. Check with your county extension office about the fruiting and harvest times of date palms in your area. They grow well in the Tampa area but bear their fruit in the rainy season when it often rots before it ripens.

Queen Palm (*Arecastrum romanzoffianum*). Central and southern Florida. 40 ft. tall. Straight, ringed trunk. Needs full sun and is not very salt or wind tolerant.

Washington Palm (*Washingtonia robusta*). Northern, central, and southern Florida. 60 ft. tall. Excellent for avenues but too large for small yards. Old fronds hang like a skirt. Needs full sun and has good salt tolerance.

MIDSIZE PALMS

Areca or Cane Palm (*Chrysalidocarpus lutescens*). Central and southern Florida. Grows 20 feet tall in bamboolike clumps. Needs a frost-free climate and salt-free soil. This can be grown in tubs.

Bismark Palm (*Bismarkia nobilis*) is one of the most striking and beautiful of the fan palms with its bluish green foliage. It grows slowly to 30 ft and needs full to partial sun.

Very drought tolerant, it will also withstand light frost but not seaside salt.

Chinese Fan Palm (*Livistona chinensis*). Central and southern Florida. 20 to 30 ft. tall. Grown for its large, fan-shaped, palmate leaves. The trunk is vaguely ringed. White flowers have an unpleasant odor.

European Fan Palm (*Chamaerops humilis*). Northern, central, and southern Florida. 10 to 15 ft. tall. This grows slowly in clumps and is good as a specimen or in small groups. It is the most cold-hardy palm.

Fishtail or Tufted Palm (*Caryota mitis, C. ureus*). Central and. southern Florida, 20 to over 40 ft. tall. Notched leaflets on fronds give it its name. This is one of my favorites to see, but I have not grown one. It grows quickly and does well in containers. It is not salt or cold tolerant and only moderately drought tolerant.

Pindo or Jelly Palm (*Butia capitata*). Northern, central, and southern Florida. 15 to 20 ft. tall. Grows slowly, has excellent salt tolerance and edible fruit, and gracefully curving, blue-green fronds. Needs room. I have a nice one, but it is more of a lawn tree than a garden tree. Palms are good in lawns where you can mow out any seedlings that are not wanted. These seedlings get to be a problem in shrubbery areas and groundcovers.

SMALL PALMS

Cycads. These are not true palms but ancient, leathery-leaved plants that resemble them. In the plant order, they are between ferns and pines. They grow very slowly, prefer shade, and have male and female flowers on separate plants. Sago palms, up to six ft. tall, are the hardiest cycads and grow in all parts of the state, but these have suffered from Oriental cycad scale since we have been here and many of them are being replaced with less difficult alternatives such as coonties.

Coontie (*Zamia floridana*). Also a cycad, this plant has no aerial trunk but makes a low clump of fernlike fronds. It likes shade but tolerates sun and drought.

Lady Palm (*Rhapis* species). Northern, central, and southern Florida. Species range from five to 15 ft. tall. This is a moderate grower with poor salt tolerance. It grows in a clump, often with leaves to the ground. It prefers shade and is a good container plant.

Date Palms (*Phoenix* species). Northern, central, and southern Florida. Height ranges from dwarfs under 2 ft. to specimens 100 ft. tall. Date palms are hardy from Jacksonville south, but seldom ripen fruit here, though some I heard of in Clearwater produced six pounds of dates one year. Pygmy date is useful in the landscape for its feathery foliage. It prefers shade and fertile soil. The Senegal date grows slowly in clumps, reaching 20 feet, and has good salt tolerance, but is hardy only in central and southern Florida.

SMALL PALMS AND PALMLIKE SHRUBS

These palms and shrubs stay small rather than growing tall, so you may include them in your shrub plantings. They are the easiest of the palms to keep trimmed. NCS indicates whether they will grow in North, Central, or South Florida.

Ceratozamia (Ceratozamia mexicana) CS
Coonties (Zamia spp.) NCS
Dioon (Dioon spp.) CS
Fan palm, Mediterranean (Chamaerops humilis) NCS
Lady palm (Rhapis spp.) CS
Lady palm (Rhapis excelsa 'variegata') CS
Madagascar palm (Pachypodium lamerei) S
Needle palm (Rhapidophyllum hystrix) NCS
Palm, pindo or jelly (Butia capitata) NCS
Palmetto, dwarf (Sabal minor) NCS
Palms, bamboo, parlor, etc (Chamaedorea spp.) NCS
Pygmy date palm (Phoenix roebelenii) CS
Sagos (Cycas spp.) NCS
Saw palmetto (Serenoa repens) NCS
Windmill palm (Trachycarpus fortunei) NCS

LANDSCAPING WITH FLORIDA SHRUBS

FRAGRANCE
Crape myrtle
Gardenia
Jasmine
Oleander
Rose
Sweet olive
Viburnum

SHOWY FLOWERS
Abelia   Azalea
Camellia   Crape myrtle
Gardenia   Hibiscus
Ixora   Indian hawthorn
Japanese privet   Lantana
Natal plum   Nandina
Oleander
Plumbago
Poinsettia
Yesterday-today-and-tomorrow

LIGHT SHADE
Abelia
Azalea
Boxwood
Camellia
Coontie
Croton
Japanese privet
Juniper
Nandina
Philodendron
Shrimp plants
Ti plants

Neither bears quality fruit. The one that does, *Phoenix dactylifera*, is too big for most yards.

HARDY TREES

Here are other trees familiar to former residents of states north of Florida:

Cedars. Here they are usually the southern red cedar (*Juniperus silicicola*) that ranges to lower central Florida or the white cedar (*Chamaecyparis thyrsoides*), also called false cypress, which grows in northern Florida. Both need sun.

Dogwood (*Cornus florida*) is native as far south as central Florida. I have planted several and have two survivors, one that is almost twenty years old and one that I've had for about three years. Both bloom variously every year, depending on the weather, and they are often only a shadow of the northern counterpart. Dogwoods are more reliable and seem to have larger flowers the farther north you live, but in central Florida, you can expect outstanding results only about one year in five. Other years they are mere reminders of other places, as their sporadic bloom throughout the winter takes away from the one glorious show in March. Chances of successful growth

are best, it seems, in a partial or lightly shaded site just under the edge of an oak canopy or under pines.

Dogwood or Cornus is plagued by several diseases. To help with disease resistance, give plants an acid, well-drained soil, plenty of organic matter, and good air circulation. Mulch to keep the soil cool, but don't let the mulch come in contact with the trunk.

Red and pink flowered dogwoods do not do well in Florida. Cornus kousa will grow in the northern counties, but the 'Stellar' series cross does not thrive. If you can get a named variety, 'Weavers White', discovered in Gainesville, is a good choice.

Elms grow in northern and central Florida and are most likely to be the native Florida or winged elm (*Ulmus alata*) that is easily identified by its winged twigs, or the Drake elm, a cultivar of the Chinese or lacebark elm (*Ulmus parvifolia*). The first is deciduous, the second evergreen. The Drake is one of my favorite shade trees. It always was resistant to Dutch elm disease. The graceful, spreading branches give it an interesting shape and a unique growing habit and it gives light shade so more kinds of plants will thrive beneath and around it. It only grows to 30 or 40 feet and then stays much the same for many years. The new growth on the ends tends to stand straight up, a good way to identify it. Often these are good climbing trees. It is said by some to be susceptible to storm damage, but author Michael Dirr, a true expert, says, "I have never seen extensive damage." He warns that it should not

be confused with the Siberian elm, *U. pumila*, which is inferior. These need sun.

Ginkgo (*Ginkgo biloba*) is hardy from zone 10 northward. I've read that it grows well in Florida, but the few I have seen have been very small, not at all like the tall trees they are in the northern states. It needs sun.

Holly (*Ilex* species). Holly trees and shrubs are quite lovely in most parts of Florida, with more choices from Zones 9 north and the Krug or Tawnberry holly growing from Zones 10B to 11. It takes a male and a female to have berries, but you can plant them both in the same hole and only we gardeners may notice that all the berries are on one side. Hollies are handsome for their shiny green foliage alone. Species vary from tiny to large leaved, spiny or smooth, mounded shrubs to tall trees. Most like sun to partial shade.

Linden or basswood (*Tilia floridiana*) grows from the central to the northwest section of the state and quickly reaches as tall as 45 feet. They like medium light and acid soil and bloom in spring and summer with inconspicuous flowers that are a good nectar source for bees. Medium light will do.

Magnolia. *Magnolia grandiflora* is a magnificent evergreen tree that has huge white flowers intermittently for much of the year, and

large, leathery, dark green leaves. The leaves have a brown underside that makes the tree seem somber to some people. I see a few of the saucer magnolias blooming pink in December or January, and get that old spring feeling, but they do not grow large. They probably do better farther north. Some of my friends have star magnolias, but I have not seen them in bloom. These are shrubs here. The sweet bay or swamp bay tree (*Magnolia virginiana*) grows wild from northern to southern Florida, and blooms with lovely white flowers all summer.

Maples in our area (*Acer barbatum* or southern sugar maple) are colorful with small red leaves in late winter and red seed clusters in early spring. They do not grow large or wide but they color the roadsides through much of the winter with red foliage giving way to red blooms and seeds. They need sun.

Mulberry (*Morus rubra*) grows as far south as Tampa and has delicious fruits in early spring. See chapter 8.

Persimmon (*Diospyros virginiana*) grows in northern and central Florida. Somewhat more heat tolerant are the many improved varieties of *D. kaki* with larger and better quality fruits than the native types. They are often grafted onto the wild rootstock. In the southernmost counties they do not fruit as well or grow as tall or wide, but in sunny spots in most of the state they make lovely, deliciously fruitful small trees.

Redbud (*Cercis canadensis*) grows in northern to central Florida, as it does in many northern states. But it is only a pleasant shadow of our northern memories, not nearly as showy, but nice. It is native to Florida, and every few miles to the north it improves in appearance. Big, heart-shaped leaves follow the linear sprays of rosy lavender flowers. It does best in sun to partial shade.

Sourwood (*Oxydendrum arboreum*) grows in northern and central Florida. Its other name is lily-of-the-valley tree for the flowers are

106

VINES FOR FLOWERS
Allamanda
Bougainvillea
Clerodendrum thomsoniae
Coral vine Cypress vine
Mandevilla
Moonflower
Morning glory
Passion flower
Petrea or Queenswreath
Thunbergia
Trumpet vine
Wisteria

FRAGRANT VINES
Japanese honeysuckle
Confederate jasmine
Star jasmine
Moonflower
Stephanotis

VINES FOR SHADE
Ivy
Honeysuckle
Smilax species
Virginia creeper
Philodendron
Pothos

strikingly similar. Leaves have a rich, dark red autumn color. Give it a sunny spot.

Sycamore (*Plantanus occidentalis*) has large, maple-like leaves and the trees may have a wonderful woodsy fragrance. Leaves turn brown about November and the trees are bare for about four months here. Tampa is their southern limit. They do not seem to grow as huge here as they did in the north, but they can still be larger than the average yard needs.

Sweetgum (*Liquidambar styraciflua*) grows all over Florida and has attractive red autumn color, but not as bright as in the north. It grows quickly with fair salt tolerance. For some people the prickly fruits can be a problem. You don't want this where children go barefoot. It also has high light requirements.

Weeping willow (*Salix babylonica*) grows along streams and lakes throughout Zones 8 and 9, but is not widely planted. I've seen a few. They grow quickly as in the North but never get as large, usually topping out at 25 feet. They are weak wooded. There are other weeping trees like the bottlebrush that are more decorative and choice.

IRRESISTABLE SHRUBS

Azaleas (*Rhododendron* species) bloom most abundantly and much more reliably at the same time as the flowering dogwood. They are beautiful together. They also have the same climate limit. More will grow in northern Florida, none in far southern areas. They do best in full sun in northwestern Florida but in shade in the rest of their range, and require fertile, acid soil. Varieties range from dwarf azaleas to some that get ten feet tall and spread almost as wide. They begin blooming while very small.

The yellow and orange-flowered types are mostly missing here. Most of the prevailing pinks, whites, roses, and lavenders can be mixed lavishly without any clash of color, although they make more of an impact with at least three of a single color. Some will begin blooming in the fall and continue until their grand show in March. Standard varieties are striking.

None are salt tolerant. In Florida they seem more problem free than the ones I saw farther north. They are shallow rooted so cultivate only with care and use mulch to control weeds and conserve water, of which they need much. Do any pruning shortly after bloom fades so as not to cut off next years bloom.

Camellia (*Camellia japonica* and *C. sasanqua*). Camellias are not the easiest plants to grow but many people have great success. A hard frost can take the flowers but will seldom hurt the plants. They thrive in partial

shade and grow slowly up to 15 or 20 feet. The lower part of Central Florida is usually their southernmost limit.

Give them plenty of water, excellent drainage, good air circulation, and a blueberry fertilizer since they like a slightly acid soil. Feed them before the spring flush of bloom, again in July and November. If you select your varieties carefully you can have bloom from November through March. Increase plants by cuttings (not easy) or air layering. Some of the *C. sasanquas* have a bit of fragrance. Leu Botanical Gardens in Orlando is a great place to see them. One of the best ways to succeed with them is to join the Camellia Society and learn from the experts.

Camellias grow slowly and do their best in enriched, acid soil and partial shade. They should be mulched, especially in central and southern counties, and watered as needed. Buds will drop from dry plants. Exquisite flowers of white, red, and pink, sometimes variegated, bloom for a few weeks each. They have poor salt tolerance and some pest problems, and can die back in hot summers.

Copper leaf (*Acalypha wilkesiana*) does best in full sun and in the central and southern counties. It grows quickly and can get 15 feet tall. The large, coarse, evergreen leaves can be mottled copper, shades of red and purple, or green and yellow. Mine dies back in frosts but always comes back and gets taller than the five-foot fence in no time. Flowers are catkins and tend to blend in with the colorful foliage. Copper leaf is salt tolerant behind the dunes and has few problems.

Crape myrtles (*Lagerstroemia* species) are shrubs or shrubby small trees that bloom all summer with pink, lavender, dark red, or white flowers. From a distance the clusters look like lilacs. That first summer I was so homesick that I resented the comparison, but now I appreciate the crape myrtles and even feel a little sorry for people who come to Florida every winter but never see this summer glory.

Crape myrtles grow quickly throughout Florida to about 20 feet tall. Species and cultivars vary in height. The leaf canopy is

Florida's native hibiscus.

umbrella shaped, above bare trunks with attractively mottled bark. They like full sun but will take some shade. They are not salt tolerant. Their deciduous, small, oval leaves have some fall color that improves the farther north you live. There are varieties that are hardy as far north as Philadelphia. Some cultivars don't smell at all but some have a delightful subtle fragrance. They bloom on new wood, are easy to propagate from cuttings, and start to bloom when very small.

Hibiscus (*Hibiscus* species) can grow with moderate speed up to 15 feet tall in central and southern Florida. Farther north, grow them in large pots. For best bloom, provide full sun, plenty of water, and slightly acid soil. The flowers resemble hollyhocks but are larger. The color range includes all shades but blue and purple. They bloom for much of the year on new growth. The large leaves are evergreen, toothed, alternate, and dark green. Even if they freeze to the ground, they usually come back. Because my plants have matured and our winters have been warmer, I have had little or no damage to my hibiscus for years. The similar looking, closely related rose of Sharon is hardy in northern to central Florida in shades of rose, white, blue, and lavender. Hibiscus species have few problems and root easily from cuttings, but are not salt tolerant.

108

Gardenias (*Gardenia* species) grow quickly in all of Florida and can get eight feet tall and equally wide, though mine stopped at five feet. They grow in full sun or high or light shade. Their shiny, evergreen foliage will have yellow markings if the soil is not acid enough; this is easy to correct with acidic or azalea fertilizer, though there will be some yellow leaves at bloom time no matter how much you feed the plants.

This was the first shrub I planted after moving to Florida. It is easy to grow here, but actually blooms for only a few weeks in the spring, and then seems to have as many old, faded flowers as new beauties. I wish now that I had put mine out of the limelight, but I do enjoy bringing the blooms indoors to float in a bowl and fill the room with fragrance. This is one of the few flowering shrubs that do much better on grafted plants because of nematodes. There are many improved varieties that will bloom much longer, have variegated foliage, or be more compact, even prostrate in form.

Nandina or heavenly bamboo (*Nandina domestica*) does best from central Florida north. It prefers clay soil and partial shade. It forms clumps of erect stems with large, fernlike compound leaves that turn a lovely orange-red in the fall and contrast dramatically with ter- minal clusters of scarlet berries. I have nandina in the Tampa area, where it is not remarkable. Nandina is more beautiful with every mile you travel north. Never judge a plant, especially in Florida, until you've seen it at its best.

Oleander (*Nerium oleander*) grows in full sun in all parts of Florida. Clusters of showy, single, five-petalled or double flowers bloom during much of the warm season in pink, red, white, cream, or yellow. Some varieties are fragrant. These shrubs can grow 15 to 20 feet tall, in time, but can be root- and top- pruned to stay smaller. All parts of the plant are toxic to humans. Oleander freezes to the ground at 26 degrees but will come back quickly from the roots. It has dark green, leathery, sword shaped evergreen leaves in whorls of three. The plants are poisonous to most insects but attract a strange oleander caterpillar that can defoliate them. Check plants closely. If yours are affected, dust them with Bt. or plant them where the pests and the imperfect leaves will not be noticed or minded. Otherwise they are easy to grow, for they tolerate both salt and drought. Cuttings are not hard to root in moist sand.

Pittosporum (*Pittosporum tobira*) is an evergreen landscape plant widely used for hedges and foundation plantings all over the state. It grows rapidly in sun or shade with whorls of leathery, dark green or variegated evergreen leaves that are about three-inch-long ovals, squared off at the outer end. Pittosporum can grow to 15 feet and tried to cover all our windows, but took to constant trimming much better than I did. We had it removed. Dwarf types are also available. The leaf clusters and foliage pruned off are attractive in bouquets. Where the plants do not have to be trimmed, they bloom with wonderfully fragrant terminal clusters of yellowish white flowers.

Plumbago (*Plumbago auriculata*) was blooming when we arrived in Florida in June. It has such beautiful light blue flowers that I decided to buy one at once. Luckily, two were already growing in our backyard, one under the family room window where it attracts a constant flutter of butterflies. Plumbago blooms best in full sun. It is hardy in central and southern counties, and dies back in a hard freeze. To keep it low, prune it to the ground. The small foliage is evergreen. Phlox-like flowers bloom all summer long and intermittently in warm months. It is used as groundcover in municipal plantings. I had never seen anything bloom for that many weeks per year before, but I've now grown used to that wonderful trait of Florida plants. The seeds of plumbago stick to clothing, so plant it where you need not brush against it.

gardenia blossoms

109

blue-flowered plumbago

There are several recent cultivars with deeper blue and white flower clusters. The plumbago is one of a small group of shrubs that will climb if given support and become well behaved vines. It makes a lovely combination with a white oleander.

There is also a red plumbago *(P. indica)* or scarlet leadwort, with terminal flower spikes. Both types are salt tolerant if planted well back of the dunes.

Podocarpus (*Podocarpus macrophyllus*) or Florida yew is another popular evergreen that is used in landscapes all over the state both as a shrub and as a small evergreen tree. Like pittosporum, the foliage is useful and long-lasting in bouquets. The plants grow in shade to full sun with long, slender, blackish green foliage and edible blue berries. It is a fairly upright and graceful plant, but like the yew, can be trimmed to any size or shape. It can grow to 50 feet, but fortunately it is not that fast a grower. It is somewhat salt tolerant.

Roselle (*Hibiscus sabdariffa*), or Florida cranberry, is a plant I couldn't wait to grow. Started from seed in early spring, it makes a large shrub by late fall that is momentarily both beautiful and useful. Its petioles can be pink,

green, or deep red, and most flowers are pink or red, though I had one that had yellow flowers with lime green calyces. It is the calyces that you pick for making jelly, tea, or juice. They are pretty but we don't much care for the taste that is supposed to be like cranberries but not as bitter. The plants die in the first breath of frost or else dry up and become ugly. Luckily they are shallow rooted and easy to remove. They also self sow for me. Plant them where their unsightly decline won't matter.

Roses (*Rosa* species) will grow in Florida as well or better than they do in the North, but they must be the types suited for this climate. Some of the old-fashioned roses like 'Louis Phillipe', 'Baroness Henriette Snow', 'Madame Lombard', and 'Mrs. Dudley Cross', most of the miniature roses, and some of the new roses such as the 'Knock Outs' do well here. Hybrid teas and floribundas must be grafted onto special Florida rootstocks to do well in central and southern parts of the state, so buy locally or from catalogs for Florida.

There are excellent rose gardens at many of Florida's public gardens. Visit them with notebook in hand and note the latest varieties you'd like to try. Also go to the local rose shows and rose society meetings and talk to the people who are growing them for the best and most detailed advice.

At home, I have 'Belindas Dream', 'Louis Phillipe', 'Smith's Parish', 'Knock Out', and 'Carefree Sunshine' that have done as well as mine in Iowa, but have had less coddling, especially regarding winter protection. I never spray. I have also had moderate success with rooting roses and growing them on their own rootstocks here as I never dared try before. They won't live as long, but my 'Louis Phillipe' has lived for 15 years and the cuttings were free.

Plant roses where they will have at least six hours of sunlight, preferably morning sun. Roses tend to grow taller here since they are never winterkilled and need to be pruned back severely. Prune dead wood any time, but do major pruning in January or February, even if plants are not dormant. I spray with water often to remove insects and disease spores, but early enough in the day for foliage to dry before

110

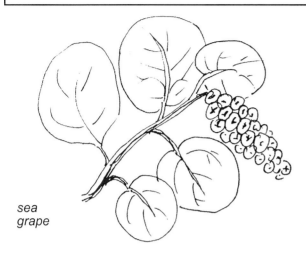

sea
grape

nightfall. With mulch, fertilizer, and water as needed, I enjoy six or seven flushes of bloom a year. With more precise care and weekly spraying, much like in the North, one can grow show roses. Roses are moderately salt tolerant.

Sea grape (*Coccoloba* species) is easy to recognize by its large, round, evergreen, often red-veined leaves. It is reliably hardy only in southern Florida, where it grows quickly to be a small, shrubby tree. Plants in our Tampa area have thrived ever since the 89 freeze. You can prune it drastically to keep it any size you wish.

This dramatic plant thrives in beach sand, loves full sun, and is completely salt tolerant. It can die to the ground in frosts in the central coastal area. It usually comes back, but never gets as large or as red as plants in the warmer zone. The flowers are inconspicuous on foot-long racemes, but the purple grapes that ripen in summer are very good for jelly.

Surinam cherry (*Eugenia uniflora*) has shiny dark green evergreen foliage with bright red new growth. It reminds me of abelia. It does best in full sun in central and southern regions, grows quickly, but will stand heavy trimming, even as a clipped hedge. The flowers are small, white, and starry, and can completely cover the bush in the south, though they are not so conspicuous on mine. Edible berries look like little pumpkins made of red or black jelly, and have a spicy taste and one or two large seeds in the center. Plants bear several crops a year.

Surinam cherry is related to clove and guava. Some plants are much more productive and have better flavor than others. They are, at first an acquired taste. We soon learned to love the red ones. The black ones are pretty but still too spicy for me. You can wash and freeze any extras for making jelly later. The seeds pop out readily as they thaw. They propagate easily from cuttings or layerings, and seldom suffer frost damage here in the Tampa area.

In fact Surinam cherry is on the invasive plant list and I have since discovered why. Almost every seed that drops or that a bird drops sprouts and grows with great vigor. When my first plant threatened to eat the whole front yard, I had the tree trimmers pull it out.

Vireya Rhododendrons. One of the stars of my garden was a "tropical rhododendron." I hate to pay high prices for plants until I'm sure I won't kill them, and I was plenty worried about this one. It bloomed in several flushes every year in light shade. Rare in Florida, the 300 species of vireya rhododendrons are found in the rainforests of Malaysia, New Guinea, and several southeast Asian islands.

This is always the first plant I cover when frost threatens. Vireyas are fine containers plants. They bear waxy-textured loose clusters of trumpet like flowers in exciting shades of yellow, gold, orange, vermillion, salmon, pink, white, cream, and bicolors. Some are scented.

Stephanotis

111

Species, named hybrids, and unnamed seedlings are offered by specialty growers including Bovees Nursery (www.bovees.com).

Cultural requirements include shallow planting, excellent drainage, good light but not full sun, regular light feeding and watering, protection from frost, a light mulch, undisturbed roots, and good air circulation.

VERSATILE VINES

Vines do so well in Florida that at first I found them threatening, with coral vine covering roadside shrubs in the summer and flame vine draping huge oaks in the winter. Many of them need control in your garden. Don't plant or encourage any vines until you know what they are going to do.

However, I've now learned to appreciate nature's ways of combining plants. I have gone so far as to almost sacrifice a pine tree in my front yard as a support for a moonflower that blooms at night for months on end, until a frost kills it back. Then it starts over from the roots and is blooming again by June at the latest. The moonflower is a native of the Florida wetlands with leaves that are coarse looking. The trick is to plant it close enough to see when blooms open at dusk, but not in the daytime spotlight.

I met one man who felt very strongly that all vines should be outlawed. Even after years of pulling unwanted miles of them off of my other plants, I still wouldn't want to do without them completely. I planted seeds of *Thunbergia alata* and the vines soon covered the banana trees, but only a third of them had the lovely dark orange flowers with black centers that I wanted. The others were pale in color. I've fought the decendents for years even while I admire those black-eyed flowers.

Another mistake was bringing home a cutting of the Mexican flame vine. I planted it in too much shade so it did what vines do—it grew wildly until it found the right amount of light. I pull it out constantly.

I also pull the pothos and philodendron that escaped from a dish garden. These are amazing the way the leaves increase in size as the vines climb trees and develop Swiss cheese holes in the giant leaves when they reach the first branches. As they hang down again, the leaves return to palm size and heart shape. But they can take over.

Most Florida vines can also be used as ground covers, and some can be trained as shrubs. They are usually easy to propagate from cuttings. Use them for color, fruit production, screening, quick shade, and privacy. Learn which ones are rampant and which are easy to control. Train them as they grow and prune ruthlessly when necessary.

Deciduous vines like the Virginia creeper on my porch are ideal for giving shade in summer but letting in welcome winter sun, saving both heat and air conditioning costs. I called them my green lace curtains and cherished them until we had other shade, by which time the creepers had become pests as well. Now I pull them constantly and sometimes find stems as thick as my wrist. And like the palms, after they grow so high, there is no way for a homeowner to prune them.

These vines or vinelike shrubs grow well in Florida:

Allamanda (*Allamanda* species) will capture your eye and your heart with its four-inch, waxy, yellow flowers. It is hardy in central and southern Florida, takes sun or partial shade, and grows quickly and easily to 10 feet in acid soil. Train it as a sprawling shrub or give some support to use it as a vine. Its salt tolerance is fair, but wind and drought tolerance are good. It is poisonous, so warn children not to taste. It freezes at 32 degrees but usually comes back from the roots. It is common here in the Tampa area, where it blooms mostly in the summer. Further south it blooms nearly all year. In winter, keep a few cuttings rooting indoors in a glass of water, for frost insurance.

Bougainvillea (*Bougainvillea* species) is one of the showiest vines in central or southern Florida. It is an evergreen with sprawling, thorny canes, alternate, heart-shaped leaves, and tiny flowers that come in showy clusters of brightly colored bracts, usually in the rose, red, orange, or purple range. There is a variegated cultivar with white flowers that is impressive also. They

Bougainvillea shades an outdoor garden room.

bloom during the cooler months, and some types change color as they age. The vines do best in full sun, grow quickly if well fed, die back in a hard freeze but usually come back from the roots, and are fairly salt tolerant. They bloom best when pruned often and need pruning in any case to remove dead wood and keep in shape. This is not an easy job with those thorns.

Bougainvillea can be kept in containers where growth is more controllable. Protect it from caterpillars and keep the soil on the acid side, or the leaves will yellow. Bougainvillea is lovely draped over a wall. A red one in Pompano Beach is skillfully and sparsely espaliered up to the top of a two story building. Another red one at Cypress Gardens grows as thickly as a waterfall and creates a breathtaking show. It is protected from frost to prevent dieback, which would thin the branches.

Coral vine (*Antigonon leptopus,* an-TIG-onon) grows all over the state. Plant in full sun for best flowering. It blooms with strands of bright pink or white little heart-shaped flowers for all the warm months. Use it to lure bees to your garden. Each flower spray ends in a curling tendril. In its native Mexico, it is called "chain of love" and the underground tubers are used for food. The foliage is light green, heart shaped, coarse-textured, and prone to caterpillar chewing. It is best to cut the canes to the ground each winter.

Clerodendrum (*Clerodendrum thomsoniae*) is called bleeding heart, glory bower, or bag flower in Florida. It is nothing like the bleeding hearts we had up north, but it has its own subtle beauty with evergreen leaves, opposite and prominently veined, and white calyces or bags with bright red corollas extending beneath them. The white fades to pink and then purple, and clusters remain showy after the flowers drop for a long season of interest. It blooms in summer and fall, climbs by twining, is hardy all over the state, and dies back at 28 degrees but usually comes back. This is one of the few flowering vines that prefers partial shade. It has fair to low salt tolerance.

Cypress vine and **cardinal climber,** cousins of the morning glory (*Quamoclit* species, *Ipomoea quamoclit* and *I. angulata,* and *Mina lobata*) grow wild in Florida. Also called star glory, these vines have multitudes of small white, red, pink, or lavender star-shaped flowers that stay open all day. They have either ferny or small, heart-shaped leaves, twine from ten to 20 feet, and bloom throughout the warm months. They thrive in dry soil and warm weather.

Cardinal climber is slightly larger than cypress vine in both flowers and foliage. It is usually listed in catalogs as *Ipomoea* x *multifida.* It has red flowers only. Plants come fairly true from seed and mine reseed freely whether or not I want them.

Jasmine. See chapter 6, ground covers.

Honeysuckle. See chapter 6.

Mandevilla (*Mandevilla splendens, M.* hybrids) has big flowers that look like hot pink allamandas. 'Alice du Pont' is one of several well-known, choice cultivars. This plant is sometimes listed as *Dipladenia.* Mandevilla is closely related to but vinier than allamanda, definitely more needful of support. It is hardy in central and southern Florida, with evergreen foliage. The vivid flowers are unusual in that they can double in size (three to six inches) after they open, and reach their richest color after

113

several days. The plants like full sun and acid soil, and have slight salt tolerance.

Morning glory (*Ipomoea* species) are wild and varied in Florida, but I still plant the annual 'Heavenly Blue' even though it seldom flowers as prolifically as in the North. It is best sown in early spring, just after the danger of frost passes, or indoors two weeks earlier for a head start, but I have had flowers at Christmas time, so plant a few seeds whenever you want and hope for the best.

Passion flowers (*Passiflora* species) come in many and varied kinds in southern and central Florida. I worked very hard to get them started and now work very hard to keep them in check. Only a few varieties give good fruit without hand pollination and those are definitely worth having. They seemed sensitive to frost those first winters, but since have proved too hardy. The lovely purple flower we cultivated in a Pennsylvania greenhouse grows wild around us and is an excellent butterfly plant.

The red passion flower, bold and beautiful with scarlet, recurved petals and rounded leaves with scalloped edges, looks so different from the delicate blue that it is hard to believe they are related, but they are and are equally invasive.

There are a dozen or more others, with at least three, including the giant granadillas, that produce edible fruit. In fact, Hawaiian punch is largely passion fruit juice.

The giant granadillas and yellow passion fruit do best in the south. Purple passion fruit will grow wherever it can be protected from

Aristochlea, or pipe vine.

hard freezes and even then it comes back. All the passion fruits need acid soil, trellising or other strong support, full sun, and pruning to keep them within bounds. They are easy to start from seed or cuttings, and can fruit in one year from cuttings.

Pipe vines. There are several species of *Aristolochia*: Marsh's Dutchmans pipe, plain Dutchmans pipe, woolly pipe vine, Virginia snakeroot, and Pelican or calico flower, all of which grow in Florida. Most are native, some evergreen vines, some deciduous. The flowers are more or less pipe shaped and begin blooming the second year, but the larvae of the gold rim swallowtail butterflies only need the leaves.

Caterpillars can eat a young vine to death. My friend Nancy Gaspermint started a pipe vine in her pool enclosure where the butterflies could not get in to lay eggs. When it was large she moved it outside where it has weathered all caterpillars since.

The plants are vigorous climbers and may require summer pruning to keep them in check. They can be grown from seeds or cuttings and in the ground or in containers. They vary by species in preferring full sun to light shade. Though moderately drought tolerant, they grow best in moist soil.

Queen's wreath or **sandpaper vine** (*Petrea volubilis*) is one of the most beautiful flowering vines we have. It is supposedly hardy only in Zones 10B to 11 but mine has been thriving for several years. Its best bloom comes in late January and February with intermittent bloom the rest of the year. It has yet to show frost damage although we are well above its recommended range. I have it near the south side of the house but know of two in the area that are out in the open and thriving. The purple or white flowers hang much like wisteria, but it has a longer season of bloom and is less rampant. It likes full sun.

Prune it back after each round of blooms. It has medium salt and drought tolerance. I have not been able to root cuttings. Most books advise air layers or suckers for propagation. The leaves are attractive, light green, four to six inches long, and feel like sandpaper. It is particularly gorgeous with maroon bougainvillea nearby.

Rangoon creeper or *Quisqualis indica* is a woody evergreen vine with abundant foliage, fascinating blooms, and nuts that are edible if you get them before the squirrels. I brought home a few nuts from a Rare Fruit meeting years ago and have had this plant ever since. I never saw a squirrel in my yard before this bloomed and, I assume, bore fruit. Now I have many squirrels and never again have tasted the nuts. Parts of this plant are poisonous.

It's a good thing the flowers alone make it worth having. They open white in the morning, turn pink by noon, and maroon by evening. They stay on the vine for several days, so each cluster is primarily maroon. Children in Cuba make the flowers into chains and necklaces as northern children do with daisies.

The six-inch leaves are bright green, opposite, and have smooth edges. The vine will quickly cover a strong trellis or wall and can make a natural cover for a porch. It quickly gets woody and thorny. It roots easily from cuttings, needs full sun to very light shade, and can be a pain to keep pruned.

Thunbergia, also called black-eyed susan vine (*Thunbergia alata*) is easy to grow from seed. The multitudes of funnel-shaped blooms may be cream, yellow, or orange. The ones with pale centers are not nearly as showy as the black eyed ones, but seed may produce either. You can weed out the paler ones after they start to bloom, if you wish. The vines bloom all year except after a frost, and grow as much as 30 feet, no problem. For more control, grow them in a hanging basket. I only planted seed once and I've been pulling them out ever since.

There are at least three other species of Thunbergia called clock vine or sky vine that have strings of much larger violet blue or white, orchidlike flowers that will take your breath away with their beauty but are quite rampant.

Trumpet vine (*Campsis grandiflora*) grows and looks much as it does in other states: massive vines with coarse compound leaves, and loads of large, tubular, red orange flowers. Although a rampant grower, it can be grown on strong supports, like wisteria, and trimmed regularly for a spectacular appearance.

Virginia creeper (*Parthenocissus qinquefolia*) looks and acts much the same in all of Florida as it does in states to the north. The whorls of five leaves are dark green, often with red markings. Some people consider this a rampant weed, others enjoy the graceful curtain it makes. It comes down easily when it needs to be controlled.

Wisteria (*Wisteria floribunda, W. sinensis*) grows here, but not nearly as rampantly as it did in states to the north. It blooms briefly, but makes a poor showing compared to what you remember. I planted one not long after arriving and grew it as a shrub, just in case, but after several years of its not blooming at all I had it removed. I prefer the Petrea with its similar but much more frequent blooms.

TREES AND HURRICANES

We lived here with hardly a worry about hurricanes for the first 17 years, but some seasons bring the problem into sharp focus. While we are now concerned, I have no plans to live anywhere else or to live without trees. Winter was a sure thing. Hurricanes may miss us forever.

In her book, *Stormscaping*, Pamela Crawford gives a lists the six most expensive landscape mistakes:

1. Not knowing the wind tolerance of your plants.

2. Neglecting routine tree trimming.

3. Bad trimming after the storm.

4. After the storm, throwing away valuable trees that could have easily been saved.

5. Planting large trees near power lines.

6. Planting wind-sensitive trees near buildings.

But there is good news, too. The right trees in the right places can help protect your home. Whatever trees you have, having them professionally pruned will help tremendously.

TREES WITH POOR WIND TOLERANCE
Acacia, ear leaf, *NCS
Australian pine NCS
Cherry laurel NC
Drake elm NC
Fig, Ficus benjamina S
Floss silk tree CS
Jacandra CS
Oak, laurel NCS
Palm, queen NCS
Redbud NC
Sand pine NCS
Tabebuia NCS
Water oak NC

TREES WITH GREAT WIND TOLERANCE

Small
Crape myrtle NCS
Dogwood NC
Ironwood NCS
Japanese maple NC
Lignum vitae S
Palm, pindo NCS
Palm, pygmy date NCS
Palm, sabal NCS
Palm, saw palmetto NCS
Palm, thatch CS
Oak, sand live oak NCS
SeagrapeSea grape CS
Stopper, redberry CS
Stopper, Spanish CS
Stopper, white NCS

Tall
Bald cypress NCS
Gumbo limbo CS
Live Oak NCS
Magnolia, Southern NCS
Palm, Canary Island Date CS
Palm, Date CS
Palm, Foxtail CS
Palm, Royal S
Red bay, NCS

* N=North, C=Central, S=Southern Florida.

CHAPTER ELEVEN
HOUSEPLANTS IN FLORIDA HOMES

Your houseplants, new or relocated, will celebrate your moving to Florida. Never again will they perish from living in a hot, dry, artificial atmosphere.

WHO NEEDS HOUSEPLANTS IF YOU HAVE THE GREAT OUTDOORS?

I thought that I wouldn't need houseplants in Florida. The same plants that people pamper in states farther north will grow outdoors for most of the year here. I would no longer need indoor greenery to help me through long winter months of cabin fever. Nor would the plants need my indoor nurturing to survive the months of cold. Since it was both warm and rainy when we arrived, the few plants that made the trip seemed to deserve the same outdoor summer vacation that I would have given them had we stayed in the North.

But even in Iowa I always kept the contented houseplants inside in the summer on the theory that a happy plant, like a sleeping baby, should not be disturbed. Looking back, that may have been partly an excuse.

For with the move I discovered that I need green living plants indoors. Some people can get by with silk ones, but for me every room needs some echo of natural, green, growing outdoor life. And I'm not alone. Should you doubt the appeal of indoor plants, look through the photos in any decorating magazine and just try to find one without any houseplants in it. Most of those rooms look so great precisely because they have about three times more green or blooming plants than most of us use.

People tell me that they want Florida to be lush and green and tropical, indoors and out. Rooms can seem artificial without them.

PLANTS ARE EASY TO GET IN FLORIDA

Plants are cheaper in Florida because it is a main source of foliage plant production, especially in "Foliage Capital" Apopka in Central Florida.

Some plants greatly treasured in northern climes, like lantana and Jerusalem cherry, show up as wildlings in our yards and can be invasive. This is not a problem indoors, where our choice of houseplants is large, and their need to readjust to the interior environment is small, but be careful when you set certain houseplants outdoors because they can quickly escape and become pests.

Growing plants indoors is easier here, for we have little drying heat and almost constant temperatures year-round in our houses. If plants need more light, we can rotate them to the lanai or outdoors under a tree until they form buds or green up, and then bring them inside again to show off their blooms.

By the time I had established my mulch pickup routine (see chapter 5) I sometimes came upon discarded plants as well. One of my favorites is a variegated Benjamin fig. This variety is expensive to buy, and I had read that they were difficult to grow, so I had passed them by even at garage sales. But whcn I found onc in its pot, about eight inches tall and only slightly wilted, I brought it home and set it under the oak tree, my intensive care area.

When the first edition of the book came out it was three feet tall and as lovely as lace. It sat by the front door where it could enjoy fresh air and sunshine when the door was open. When its leaves began to fall a few weeks after the air conditioning went on for the summer, I'd move it back under the oak tree where it enjoyed a growth spurt. It came back indoors happily when the air conditioning went off in September. When it outgrew our living room I gave it to son Mike who had just built a new lanai onto his house. After a good bit of neglect it is still growing in the shade of his bush sunflowers.

BUGS AREN'T REALLY ALL THAT BAD

You hear much about the abundance of pests and diseases in Florida, and all that is partly true. But we have advantages, too. Some experts disagree, but many people have long thought that insects are more likely to attack plants that are under stress, and houseplants in Florida homes don't suffer the lack of humidity that is their worst enemy in heated houses.

The ghastly pair, mealy bugs and spider mites, will still attack on occasion. Try insecticidal soap. One expert uses two different kinds and switches back and forth so the insects won't develop immunity to either. This soap is completely safe around people and pets, but bugs don't care for the taste.

If you have to use something stronger, systemic insecticides are safer because they go into the ground and up into the plant through the roots. Touching the leaves, even in a restaurant, won't hurt anyone. Neem and soap are safe enough to apply indoors. To see more about using neem see page 78. Neem works against mites and mealy bugs and a lot more. With anything stronger, take the plants outdoors to treat them. In either case, control may take a few treatments, several days apart.

I haven't had to use any insecticide on any houseplant since we moved to Florida. At the most, I put the affected plant outside in the intensive care area where natural predators, wind, and frequent spraying with the hose tend to wash off both insects and disease spores.

PLANTS STILL DO WILT AND DIE

The fact that plants sometimes just sicken or die causes more grief, guilt, and dissatisfaction in growing houseplants than is necessary. Once people take this into consideration, they are free to enjoy their successes with most plants and the challenge of a few difficult ones.

For even in Florida, indoor plants often get less light and humidity, more smoke and cooking smells, or less help in pest control from birds, little anole lizards, or beneficial insects than those growing outdoors. They are still vulnerable to too much or too little watering.

Many plants are naturally short lived or have cycles when they are not so attractive. For instance, dieffenbachia is a short-term plant that soon tends to get long and leggy.

Outdoors, we let our plants go to seed or go dormant and don't give them another thought. We lose some, but the loss does not seem so traumatic. Indoors, those same plants are always in the spotlight. It is unrealistic to expect them to be perfect all the time.

Anyone who remembers northern winters also remembers how some houseplants began to show the strain as the months wore on. The same plants perked up and grew lush again if they got to spend summer outside.

Here in Florida we can rotate plants from the indoor spotlight to the porch or to a sheltered, shady part of the yard for rest and recuperation (R & R). Before long we accumulate lots of plants in pots, indoors and out. Some will need protection from cold spells.

In northern Florida this means a few weeks of crowding all your potted plants indoors. Here in the central part of the state, I spread plastic on the porch and group containers just outside the sliding bedroom doors, where they are safe from all but the most drastic cold spell and I can enjoy seeing them. In southern

Florida the periods of threateningly cold weather are even rarer, and are usually brief.

Indoor heat and, to a lesser extent, air conditioning, are hard on plants because they lower indoor humidity. But this situation is much less dramatic at any time in Florida, even northern Florida, than in northern winters. Added to that is the recuperative power of our warm and humid outdoor climate. It is so easy to put a lagging plant outside for a few weeks of refreshment.

The ideal would be to have two of every plant, one for the indoor spotlight and one for outdoor recovery, to be exchanged as needed. For people like me who would rather have variety than perfection, a passing parade of different plants is more enjoyable. Though I am still experimenting, my houseplants are more successful in my Florida home than they ever were up North.

I am now finding that some herbs that will not survive summer outdoors because of high heat and humidity will live indoors or on the porch until cooler weather arrives. Then they go back into the garden. Indoors or behind screens, they are protected from insects, and the constant shade makes the heat and humidity easier to bear.

PLANTS NEED TO ADJUST TO NEW PLACES

Plant owners should be aware that drastic changes are hard on plants. In any new spot, the combination of light, humidity, temperature, and soil gives the plant an entirely new world. People cannot move into anyone else's house, or even a new house of their own, without some adaptations. Neither can plants. Some of their adaptations include dropping a few leaves or buds. Give a plant a few weeks before expecting it to resume normal growth.

It is a good idea to put a new plant into isolation until you are sure there are no disease spores or insect eggs hiding in the crevices and waiting to spread to your other plants.

DON'T LET THE TERM "DIFFICULT" DETER YOU

If you choose the right plant for the right place, the plant's adjustment will be minor and it will soon begin to thrive. If it does not, move it to other windows or rooms until you find the place where it is happiest.

If some of your plants die, it is not because you are a bad person who is sure to kill all plants. Just try another kind of plant or another place for the same kind. One lady I knew in Iowa had magnificent plants and was the only person I'd met in the North who could bring poinsettias back into bloom, but she couldn't grow philodendrons. Another told me that orchids were as easy as African violets, so I got some and found her right. I've killed many African violets since, but orchids keep on growing for me.

Incidentally, African violets and their many cousins in the Gesneriad family do very well in Florida and African violet and Gesneriad societies abound. I have interviewed people who have blooming plants in every room of their house including the bathrooms.

Success with any plant depends largely on the light, the house, and one's own tendency either to overdo the care of or to neglect plants.

HOW TO HAVE FEWER PLANT PROBLEMS

* Pick the right plant for the right place. If your first pick fails, try again until you find plants that like your lifestyle and thrive in the light you can provide.

* Water only when needed. The smaller the pot and the brighter the light, the more often the soil will dry out. Provide drainage and never let most plants sit in saucers of water for longer than 20 minutes.

* Fertilize only as needed. That will be more often during active growth, very little or not at all during short winter days.

* Watch for little white mealy bugs in the leaf and stem crotches. Spider mites are almost invisible; showing as a red dust on the undersides of the leaves. Their little webs don't show until the infestation is far along. If the leaves look pale or tarnished and the plant suddenly stops drinking as much water as it used to, treat for spider mites.

* An occasional shower, indoors or out, is a good pest prevention measure that removes dust and perks up the plant.

* Young and rapidly growing plants need to be shifted to slightly larger pots as needed.

* Because they like humidity, plants tend to thrive in kitchens and bathrooms, all other things, like light, being equal.

* If a large plant starts to wilt more often or grow more slowly, it may be root bound. Turn it out of the pot to check by holding the pot upside down and knocking it firmly on something solid. If the pot has more roots than soil, repot in a larger container or divide if possible. Be sure to leave 1/2 to 1 inch of pot above the soil line for watering.

Overwatering is a common error that leads to root rot. Sometimes moving a plant to a room where you won't remember it so often improves its chances.

MOST PEOPLE TEND TO OVERWATER AND OVERFEED

Professionals who work with plants in pots six inches wide or larger almost never water more often than once a week. Many plants, especially in low-light situations, will go three or four weeks between waterings. For most of us the finger-to-the-soil test is the best way to tell if the soil is damp enough or not. Some plants like to dry out between waterings, and others prefer their soil evenly moist all the time. Still others, like hibiscus and hoya, need quite a lot of water when they are in bud and bloom and very little the rest of the time. All plants need more water when they are in active growth than they do when growth slows down for winter. That is not as sharp a contrast here, but the shorter days of winter make a difference, even when they are warm.

You can use a moisture meter that you insert into each pot. A dial on the top registers water needs. Water or not accordingly, and then pull the meter out and stick it in the next pot. They are not supposed to last over six months, but one professional used the same one all day three days a week for as long as two years. I bought one and it works well, but mostly I don't bother except for periodic checks. Something in the rod registers the moisture level on the meter.

INTERIORSCAPING

People want plants indoors, lots of lush plants. And if they can't grow them themselves, businesses know the value of plants both for decoration and for morale in the workplace, and are more than glad to hire a professional plant service for their "interiorscape." Indoors as well as out, plants add charm, vitality, and individuality.

The rest of us enjoy growing our own houseplants. Some people succeed with everything from orchids to indoor trees. If you are not experienced, you may want to choose pothos, bamboo palm, Chinese evergreen, and spathiphyllum as the most reliable and easy to grow, even in dark places. Some plants can stay in the same place for as long as four years. Often, when you do have to replace them, it is because they have grown too big.

THE R & R AREA

The greatest blessing for houseplants in Florida is being able to be put outdoors for rest and recuperation occasionally or on a regular rotation basis. I have an area under a large oak where I am sure to be using the hose every day or so. The plants can survive with very little care during the rainy season and much less frequent watering than if they were in the sun. But plants in pots always need more watering than those in the ground.

Be sure that pots do not fall over (mine can get lost in the ferns). If necessary, repot them, including more sand in the mix to anchor them. Or drive a small metal stake into the ground and push a side pot hole down upon this. Feed these plants the same way you would indoors, more often during the summer of active growth and frequent, leaching rains. Watch for insect damage or disease and prune as needed.

Don't be surprised if some plants escape the pots. I now have pothos, philodendron, Chinese evergreen, and several other house-plants growing as ground covers in that shady area. The Christmas freeze of '89 seemed to wipe them out, but they came back again from the roots.

All these years later I realize that many of these plants can become invasive and need to be controlled. I spend probably as much time ripping out what I once started as I do weeding true weeds. This much growth is hard to believe in your first five or even ten years, but all the while those vines, especially, are growing and rooting wherever they touch the ground. And there comes a time when you even realize that a big freeze is not all bad.

PORCH AND PATIO LANDSCAPING

Even more than indoor rooms, any transition room between outdoor and indoor living cries out for plants. What is more, it offers a fine haven for them. Porches and

screened-in patios offer additional advantages. Depending on location, they can get enough sunshine for most sun loving plants, enough shade for those that prefer shade, and in some cases, both!

In fact, a sunny, screened area is a lot like the shade cloth structures used by professionals to grow foliage plants for sale. The screening cuts the sun's intensity a bit, maybe ten percent, without putting the plants in the shade.

Porches will offer protection from wind. On the coast they can cut down on salt spray. If the porch or the entire pool area is screened, there will be no pests to do damage.

One of my neighbors, Ruth Feinberg, has a typical Florida room with the usual porch furniture for relaxing and a table and chairs for eating. But her porch also has unique decor: floor to ceiling, wall-to-wall potted plants. I find it enchanting, but it seems very labor intensive.

"No, it's easy," Ruth says. "I bring the hose in to water them. And the plants never freeze in the winter."

Our porch has a natural shelf all around the edge that holds window box type planters. A wicker plant stand in the corner holds a changing parade of accent plants, currently a rex begonia, another of the types that died for me in the North but thrives with little care here.

HANGING CONTAINERS

Plants in pots take more water than those in the ground, and plants in hanging containers take more yet, for evaporation is occurring on all sides. This is where water retaining gels (chapter 5) can make a great deal of difference. Hanging planters that normally would need watering as often as twice a day can go two days or more between waterings when they have gel in the soil.

Chains from the ceiling in the other corner hold either hanging baskets of plants or ripening bunches of bananas from our trees. Our indoor-outdoor carpeting survives drips well, but when I bring in the crowd of tender plants for their winter stay, a few weeks long, I put down a sheet of plastic first so I can water without worrying.

Don't let your plants give a feeling of encroaching upon your space. The population of plants on Ruth's porch does not. But it would only take a single hanging frond to make a few taps on my spouse's shoulder for him to send the plant outside or me for the pruning snips.

I like to keep some fragrant herbs like rosemary on the porch because it is such a handy place to rub them with my fingers as I pass or sit. And days when it is raining or dark, there they are, available for adding to the supper stew or salad or as a garnish.

BALCONY GARDENING

If your entire garden is only a balcony, you will want to use as much vertical and horizontal space as possible. Select shade or sun loving plants depending on which side your balcony faces. You can grow blooming plants like verbena, vegetables like tomatoes, and fruits like kumquat on a balcony that gets six or more hours of sun a day. With limited space and time, planting whatever culinary or healing herbs you will use may be the most rewarding.

If your balcony gets less than six hours of sun a day, grow houseplants like the Gesnariads or the Bromeliads, shade lovers like coleus, leafy vegetables like lettuce and spinach, or blooming plants in containers on casters that you move with the sun.

Wind can add stress and cause more frequent watering, but it is amazing how much stress plants can survive, and how much they improve the area's ambiance. If your balcony is crowded with furniture and people, put the

Coleus contained.

plants in corners or on shelves, or hang containers of them from the walls.

PATIO AND DECK LANDSCAPING

Unscreened patios and decks should blend into the landscape as much as possible. Surrounding shrubs or vines in the yard beyond may help you achieve this. Here again, use plants and planters to hide undesirable views and frame the ones you treasure. Trellised vines are useful and beautiful, an easy way to add height to your plantings. In-ground planting areas within the patio or deck allow you to feature certain plants or trees and enjoy their shade as you sit.

Other planters with trees or shrubs can add to the feeling of privacy. Most of us don't mind if others can see us walking or working, but we'd prefer to be hidden while we sit and rest. Raised beds or large planters full of flowers can provide screening for this effect.

If your patio is sunny, it is an excellent place to grow the fruit trees and shrubs that are too cold sensitive to plant in the ground. They can provide shade, screening, flowers, fragrance, and the interest and taste of ripening fruit close at hand.

For colorful accents, nothing beats smaller containers of blooming plants on tables, steps, or in corners. Some of these, with petunias or pansies for winter, portulaca or vinca for summer, will have to come and go on a rotation basis. Others with long lasting plants like begonias or impatiens can stay for months before they need pruning back and R & R out of the limelight.

PATIO AND DECK TIPS

* Patio plantings are always in the spotlight. Avoid using plants with messy parts: flowers and fruit that drop and make litter or stains, like mulberries, and flowers that look bad when they begin to wilt, like gardenias. If you use the patio mostly early in

CLEVER CONTAINERS

Check your own attic or upper cupboards as well as garage sales for bean pots, crocks, buckets, tool boxes, baskets, wooden boxes, and wooden or ceramic planters that will hold plants and add to the decoration or mood as well.

I once had a cheese-making box but I never got around to making cheese. And at a farm auction an old wooden grocery box with old-fashioned labels on the side was thrown in with something else. Now I realize how perfect both would have been for plants, had they not gotten lost in one of the moves.

So now I look through my own and other people's "junk" with planting possibilities in mind. If a box has lots of character but no bottom, just put a plastic container inside.

One lady used her grown children's old wagon to hold a collection of potted plants. Rug tubes covered with adhesive paper will hold plants at various handy levels. An old birdcage will turn a pot into an interesting hanging planter.

You can buy or make wreaths full of sphagnum moss and soil mix to hold living herbs and succulents, then use them as wall decorations.

You can also buy or make "living wall" vertical units that hold a soil substitute in which all sorts of flowers, vegetables, or herbs grow. These columns, arches, or walls can be used on a rooftop, balcony, or even a boat deck.

Son Mike once gave me a new garden cart, painted in his car-bright shade of red. When it started to fall apart years later, I couldn't bear to chuck it. It still stands in the far view of my family room window with matching red impatiens growing in a container along the edge by the handles, the only solid horizontal strip left, but it still looks good from a distance and lifts my heart to see it. Choice coleus and aroids grow in a large plastic container where the cargo once rode.

---

the day, plants that bloom only at night, like moonflowers and daturas, could be depressing. If you use it mostly in the late afternoon or evening, they are sensational.

* Save space and work in sunny areas by setting plants in pots on top of the soil of larger plants in pots. On top of the huge pot that keeps my black sapote ready to be moved away from frost, I set several gallon-size containers of other fruits all around the trunk. If I come home with a plant in a four-inch pot, I set that on the soil in one of the gallon pots. In full sun, all the plants get enough light, but this helps keep the roots shaded. I never lose or forget any of them, but feed and water them all at once. They grow fast, look great, and can even be decorative if you add several pots of petunias or marigolds to bloom and cascade over the sides.

* In larger pots in sunny areas, use more water-retaining material like peat, vermiculite, or gels in the soil, inside terra cotta pots. Terra cotta looks great and keeps the plant roots cooler. Be sure to check for water needs every day or two, at least.

* Plants that will survive in low light will grow even better in medium to slightly higher light. Good drainage and drainage holes are really essential with shade plants which can be prone to rotting.

* Turn your plants counterclockwise every few days if light from one side is stronger. This will keep them well rounded and prevent their leaning toward the light or having one bare side.

* Most houseplants that we grew in the North will not survive full Florida sun but will thrive in partial shade.

* Dracaenas and crotons will have less color in deep shade than in partial sun. On the other

hand, coleus and Joseph's coat will fade in full sun and have deeper color in partial shade. Most flowering and fruiting plants will do more of both with full sun.

TIPS FOR ELEGANT CONTAINERS

I never expected or meant to spend money on elegant containers...until I saw the golden leaved 'Blanchetiana' bromeliad in a royal blue pot. I already had the plant and an itchy gift certificate. So now I have a royal blue pot and a new outlook about the wonderful new containers that are on the market.

Some containers are so dramatic that they don't even need plants. They are a garden accent all by themselves, but why waste the growing space? It is important to choose container styles and materials that are in keeping with your garden. Plant colors can echo the colors of the containers for a unified look, for instance having some blue pansies or petunias in or near those blue glazed pots.

Tall containers can lift a plant into the spotlight or to the point where the grass plumes dance in the rays of the sun or the fragrance of the orchid is much closer to eye level and you can sniff with little stooping. They also present columns of color.

Plastic versus Terra Cotta. Plants will grow well in plastic, and some of the plastic containers look good, especially from a distance or beneath a curtain of cascading foliage and flowers, but in themselves they have less character to add to the scene. Okay, I find myself saving my clay pots for special plantings. In theory they may not be as decorative, but they seem to belong in my landscape and the plants love them. Terra cotta containers have a natural look and have long been treasured for portable gardens.

Ceramic Glazes. Clay pots with ceramic glazes add dramatic color to the garden scene while they are easy to keep clean. They are fairly expensive and fairly durable, but they can break. In northern states you'd have to empty them and bring them indoors for winter to prevent ice from cracking them, but not in most parts of Florida.

Cast Stone and Garden Troughs. I've been planting cast stone containers since the time we had a greenhouse and filled orders at the local cemetery. These planters are decorative in themselves but

> Repot plants that dry out too fast. Plants that wilt quickly and need water more than twice a day may be in pots that are too small and are overfilled with roots.

not enough to detract from the plantings. Still you might want to keep the plantings simple, perhaps all the same plant of the same color or with a center plant a bit taller of a contrasting color. Most are too heavy to really be portable and are considered dual purpose garden statuary.

Garden troughs can be a form of cast stone (concrete) or even real stone. Originally recycled from old farm feed or water troughs, they now are made just for garden purposes and have drainage holes. They are good at helping to keep plant roots cool and are weatherproof, which makes them especially nice for herbs.

In all sizes, you can buy them ready made or make your own. Many troughs are made from hypertufa, a relatively lightweight variant of concrete that is composed of peat moss, perlite, and Portland cement. Some people including my friend Betty Mackey are making them out of papercrete, a form of concrete made with paper shreds, perlite, and Portland cement. She has free directions for making planters of both papercrete and hypertufa posted on her website at www.mackeybooks.com.

Fiberglass Lookalikes. Because I worry about breakage, I am drawn to the new fiberglass containers that sometimes look like stone or metal but are actually so lightweight that wind can be a problem, especially if you live near the coast. Add a few rocks or concrete chunks to the bottom before filling them to weight them down. Bring these containers inside when hurricanes threaten or they might blow away. Otherwise these last indefinitely, are easy to maintain, and are well worth the cost.

Metal Containers. Many of the metal containers (brass, iron, etc.) are meant for indoor use and will rust or turn black with Florida}s rains and humidity, not to mention frequent watering. Ore iron ones are supposed to rust.

They look great but may last only five to ten years.

Painted Containers. Hand-painted containers are especially popular because each one is unique and the colors are often bright and fit right in with our tropical flair. Again simple plantings, perhaps foliage plants or all the same flowers of a color that echoes one of the colors of the painting, look good in these and don't detract from the artistic design.

Tubs and Water Gardens. Water gardens do well in plastic, glazed ceramic, resin or fiberglass containers. Such a pot should hold about 35 gallons of water. It is quite amazing to discover which plants do better in the water, near the water, or away from the water. I have one green colocasia (elephant ear) that does well in all three types of places. In three years it has multiplied to dozens of attractive plants. This species loves constant moisture. A variegated colocasia did less well, possibly for lack of chlorophyll in the leaves' white portions.

DESIGNING WITH CONTAINERS

When combining plants in pots, you get more effect if you have something upright, something trailing, and something bright and wide in the middle to tie it all together. A classic combination is geranium (upright) with wandering jew (trailing) and petunias (flowery and wide).

Bold foliage and striking floral colors looks great in pots. Cannas, coleus, begonias, dwarf bananas, dwarf citrus, petunias, impatiens, and hibiscus are good pot plants.

Florida gardeners and landscape designers truly enjoy the Florida climate and find inspiration in the wonderful, sometimes exotic plants, with their striking textures and colors, that thrive in it. And so will you, as you adjust to gardening in Florida.

RESOURCES AND SUPPLIERS

Here are some helpful places for Florida gardeners.
Please note that this data changes frequently.

American Camellia Society, Massee Lane Gardens, 100 Massee Lane, Fort Valley, GA 31030478-967-2358. www.camellias-acs.com.

American Hibiscus Society, POB 1580, Venice, FL 34284-1580. www.americanhibiscus.org.

American Horticultural Society, 7931 East Boulevard Drive, Alexandria VA 22308. 703-768-5700. www.ahs.org.

Going Bananas, 24401 SW 197th Ave, Homestead FL 33031, 305-247-0397. www.going-bananas.com.

Better Lawns and Gardens. Radio show with Tom MacCubbin. 7-9 Saturday mornings in Florida, Phone 888-45LAWNS. www.betterlawns.com.

Brudy's Exotics, P.O. Box 820874, Houston, TX 77282. 800-926-7333

Burpee, W. Atlee & Co., 300 Park Avenue, Warminster, PA 18974. www.burpee.com. Seeds, plants, supplies, informative website.

Crosman's Seeds, 511 West Commercial Street, P.O. Box 110, East Rochester, NY 14445. 1-800-446-SEED (7333). www.crosmanseed.com. Flowers, vegetables and herb seeds.

Echo Seeds, 17391 Durrance Road, N. Ft. Myers, FL 33917. 239-543-3246. www.echonet.org.

Exotic Hibiscus, 4660 Crescent Ave. SW, La Belle, FL 33435. 941-322-2841. www.exotichibiscus.com

The Exotic Plumeria, 453 MLK Blvd. W., Seffner, Florida 33584-5016. 813-653-2496. www.exoticplumeria.com/

Fancy Hibiscus, 1142 SW First Ave., Pompano Beach, FL 33060, 1-800-432-8332. www.fancyhibiscus.com. 250 varieties.

Florida Colors Nursery, 23740 SW 147 Ave., Homestead, FL 33776. 1-800-527-8308 www.floridacolors.com. Hibiscus, plumeria.

Florida Federation of Garden Clubs, Inc., State Headquarters, 1400 South Denning Drive, Winter Park, Florida 32789-5662. 407-647-7016. www.ffgc.org. This is the parent group of 280 active garden clubs, publishes a federation magazine for all members.

Florida Gardening (Magazine), POB 500678, Malabar, FL 32950-9902. 321-951-4500. www.floridagardening.com. Just for us, a magazine dedicated to gardening in Florida. (1 year, $21.00).

Florida Keys Native Nursery, Inc., Mile Marker 89, Bayside, Plantation Key, FL 33070. 305-852-2636.

Florida State Horticultural Society, 700 Exp. St. Rd. Lake Alfred, FL 33850. 863-956-1151.

Garden of Delights, 14560 SW 14th St., Davie, FL 33325. 1-800-741-3103. Exotic and tropical fruit trees.

Gardens Alive!, 5100 Schenley Place, Lawrenceburg, IN 47025. 513-354-1482. Organic supplies.

Gardener's Supply Company, 128 Intervale Road, Burlington, VT 05401. 1-888-833-1412. Tools, supplies, innovative earth-friendly products.

Glasshouse Works, P.O. Box 97, Stewart, OH 45778. Tropical plants.

Great Outdoors Publishing Co., 4747 28th St. N., St. Petersburg, FL 33714. 1-800-869-6609. Florida and tropical garden and nature books, catalog. www.floridabooks.com.

Harris Seeds, P. O. Box 24966, 355 Paul Rd, Rochester, NY 14624-0966. 1-800-514-4441, www.harrisseeds.com.

Hartley's Herbs and Everlastings, 935 Tolhurst Rd, Cleveland, GA 30528. 1-888-206-9942, www.hartleysherbs.com.

J. L. Hudson, Star Route 2, Box 337, La Honda, CA 94020. www.JLHudsonSeeds.net, one of my favorites.

Holland Bulb Farms, W162 N4914 Graysland Drive, Menomonee Falls, WI 53051, 1-800-689-BULB. (2852), www.hollandbulbfarms.com. Remember that tulips and such will not grow in Florida without refrigeration.

Johnny's Selected Seeds, 955 Benton Avenue Winslow, Maine 04901. 1-877-564-6697. www.johnnyseeds.com.

Le Jardin du Gourmet, POB 75, St. Johnsbury Center, VT, 05863, www.artisticgardens.com. Tiny sample packets of international seeds of edibles. 35 cents a pack, more for larger packs.

A. M. Leonard, Inc., 241 Fox Drive, Piqua, OH 45356 (tools). 1-800-433-0633.

Logee's Greenhouses, 141 North Street, Danielson, CT 06239.860-774-8038 . Exotic Plants and Flowers; Fertilizer, .

Mellinger's, Inc., 2310 W. South Range, North Lima OH 44452-9731. 330-549-9861. www.mellingers.com, a catalog I consult often.

Neem Tree Farms, 601 Southwood Cove, Brandon FL 33511, 813-661-8873. www.neemtreefarms.com. Neem trees and neem products.

Our Kid's Tropical, Nursery and Landscaping 17229 Phil Peters Road, Winter Garden, FL 34787.407-877-6883. Many varieties of fruit trees, gingers, bamboos, and more

Park Seed, Cokesbury Road, 1 Parkton Ave., Greenwood, SC 29647. 800-213-0076. www.parkseed.com. Seeds, plants, supplies.

Pinetree Garden Seeds, Box 300, New Gloucester, ME 04260. 207-926-3400. www.superseeds.com. Seeds and supplies.

Roses of Yesterday and Today, 803 Brown's Valley Road, Watsonville, CA 95076. 831-728-1901. www.rosesofyesterday.com.

Seminole Springs Antique Rose & Herb Farm, 34935 W. Huff Rd. Eustis, FL 32736. Healing and culinary herbs, antique heirloom roses, perennials.

Seeds Blum, HC 33 Idaho City Stage, Boise, ID 83706.

Seeds of Change, P. O. Box 15700, Santa Fe, NM 87506-5700. 1-888-762-7333.. Organic flower and vegetable seeds. www.seedsofchange.com.

Smith and Hawken, P.O. Box 8690, Pueblo, CO 81008-9998, 1-800-940-1170. www.smithandhawken.com

Southern Exposure Seed Exchange, P.O. Box 460, Mineral, VA 23117. 540-894-9480. www.southernexposure.com.

Stokes Seed, POB 548, Buffalo, NY 14240-0548. 716-695-6980. www.stokeseeds.com.

Stokes Tropicals, 4806 E. Old Spanish Trail, Jeanerette, LA 70544, 1-800-624-9706.

Thompson & Morgan, Inc., 220 Faraday Ave, Jackson, NJ 08527-5073. 1-800-274-7333. www.seeds.thompson-morgan.com. All kinds of seeds.

Tomato Growers Supply Co, P.O. 60015, Fort Myers, Florida 33906, toll free orders 1-888-478-7333 , www.tomatogrowers.com.

Jene's Tropical Fruit Trees, 6831 Central Ave, St Petersburg, FL 33710, (727) 344-1668.

Tropiflora, 47770 Bermont Rc., Punta Gorda, FL 33982, toll free1-866-897-7957. www.tropiflora.com.

University of Florida Cooperative Extension Service. Branches in every county, for help with all aspects of Florida gardening. www.edis.ifas.ufl.edu/. Link to all the IFAS county extension agency homepages, for urban horticultural and agricultural information.

Van Bourgondien & Sons, Inc., P.O. Box 2000 Virginia Beach, VA 23450. 1-800-622-9997. www.dutchbulbs.com/bulbs

Wayside Gardens, 1 Garden Lane, Hodges, SC, 29695-0001._800-213-0379. www.waysidegardens.com.

http://www.ahs.org/. Website of the American Horticultural Society with many features.

www.botanicalgardening.com. Carlo Balistrieri's informative website which includes info on growing orchids and much more.

www.floridagardening.com. Website for garden information.

www.google.com. Search engine. Find any plant, or anything else, for that matter.

www.gardensflorida.com. Monica Brandies' website with columns, featured plants, books, events.

www.mackeybooks.com. Books for Florida and regional gardening. Trough-making information, free. Tips, events, garden links, garden info.

www.nationalgardening.com. Clearinghouse of horticultural information.

www.plantcare.com. Expert information on greenhouse and indoor plants, many of which grow outdoors in Florida. Huge database available to the public, free.

http://www.publicgardens.org/. Website of the American Public Gardens Association, with links to notable public gardens and arboreta all over the United States. Find information, events, and places to see.

RECOMMENDED READING

This is only a sampling of the many great book resources available. Prices and availability are subject to change. New books appear every year.

A Cutting Garden for Florida, Third Edition. By Betty Mackey and Monica Brandies. Here are annuals, bulbs, perennials, flowering shrubs, and trees with which to fill your house with flowers. Month-by-month planting guide, bulb chart, flower conditioning info. B.B. Mackey Books, Wayne, PA. www.mackeybooks.com.

Container Gardens for Florida. By Pamela Crawford. An extensive reference book on container plants, planters, and cutting-edge instructions on how to get great results and maintain container gardens or garden accents. Color Garden Inc, Lake Worth FL. www.easygardencolor.com.

Florida's Best Fruiting Plants: Native and Exotic Trees, Shrubs, and Vines. By Charles S. Boning. How to select fruits for Florida's growing conditions, to plant, cultivate, treat pest and disease problems, and give cold and wind protection. Fruit profiles for nearly 100 possibilities. Pineapple Press, Sarasota, FL. www.pineapplepress.com.

Florida's Gardening Guide, Second Edition. By Tom MacCubbin and Georgia B. Tasker. Cool Springs Press, Nashville, TN. ***Florida Home Grown Series*** and other books By Tom MacCubbin. Clear and practical advice from this popular public radio host. ***Landscaping*** and ***Edible Landscaping***. Sentinel Communications, Orlando, FL.

Florida's Fabulous Flowers and ***Florida's Fabulous Trees.*** By Winston Williams. Each is a full-color, beautifully photographed guide to native and exotic plants that thrive in Florida. World-Wide Publications.

The Florida Gardener's Book of Lists. By Lois Trigg Chaplin and Monica Moran Brandies. Lists the kinds and varieties of trees, perennials, ferns, annuals, vines, shrubs, and groundcovers that will do best and just how far south. Taylor Trade Publishing, Lanham, MD. www.rlpgtrade.com.

Florida Gardener's Guide, Revised Edition. By Georgia Tasker and Tom MacCubbin. On gardening in Florida with annuals, cycads, ground covers, orchids, ornamental grasses. Palms, perennials, roses, shrub, trees, tropcials, turf grasses, and vines. Cool Springs Press, Nashville, TN.

The Florida Lawn Handbook. Edited by Laurie E. Trenholm and J. Bryan Unruh. Detailed information for homeowners on lawn grasses and turf care. University Press of Florida, Gainesville, FL. www.upf.com.

Florida Plant Selector, Florida Trees and Palms, Florida Lawns and Gardens, Florida Vegetables, Florida Insects, Florida Fruit, Florida Flowers, and other titles. Widely available at local nurseries and Home Depot. Small, useful, inexpensive reference books, well illustrated. Published by Lewis S. Maxwell, Tampa, FL. Lewis was a fellow member of the Tampa Chapter of the Rare Fruit Council International. We sold our books together two weeks before he died in 1998 at the age of 89. I still keep his books, especially Florida Fruit, within arm's reach at my desk and cherish his autograph, the memory of his humor, and his great store of gardening information and enthusiasm.

Florida Top Ten Garden Guide. By Robert Bowden, director of Leu Gardens in Orlando. Focuses on plants naturally suited to the climate zones and seasonal conditions of Florida, readily available and most reliable. Includes a calender of tasks for each season and fantastic color photos. Sunset Books, Menlo Park, CA. www.sunsetbooks.com.

Gardening for Florida's Butterflies. By Pamela F. Traas. This book tells you how. Great Outdoors Publishing, St. Petersburg, FL. www.floridabooks.com.

Growing and Using Exotic Foods. By Marian Van Atta. Complete guide to growing fruits and vegetables in the subtropics by "Florida's Mother Nature." Pineapple Press, Inc. Sarasota, FL.

A Handbook of Landscape Palms. Edited by Jan Allyn. What palm is that? A great guide with facts and photos. Great Outdoors Publishing Company, St. Petersburg, FL. www.floridabooks.com.

Herbs and Spices for Florida Gardens. By Monica Moran Brandies. Grow herbs and spices for flavor, health, beauty, crafts, scent, and garden color. B. B. Mackey Books, Wayne, PA. www.mackeybooks.com.

Landscape Plants for the Gulf and South Atlantic Coasts. By Robert J. Black and Edward F. Gilman. Comprehensive guide to the selection and care of 500+ seaside plants. Color photos. Invaluable to coastal gardeners. University Press of Florida, Gainesville, FL. www.upf.com.

Landscaping With Tropical Plants. By Monica Brandies. How to use tropicals and tropical look-alikes to create a lush and fascinating landscape in Florida or anywhere. Sunset Books, Menlo Park, CA. www.sunsetbooks.com.

Native Florida Plants, Revised Edition, Low Maintenance Landscaping and Gardening. By Robert G. Haehle and Joan Brookwell. Create beautiful, inexpensive, and easy-to-maintain landscapes. Color photos and profiles of 281 native plants, landscape plans, and more. Taylor Trade Publishing, Landham, MD. www.rlpgtrade.com.

Natural Florida Landscaping. By Dan Walton and Laurel Schiller. How to Create a beautiful, healthy, and environmentally-sensitive landscape. Helps with planning, native plant choices, even growing edibles. Pineapple Press, Sarasota, FL. www.pineapplepress.com.

Shade Gardening For Florida. By Monica Brandies. A book with Florida methods and Florida plants. Tells you what and how to grow in the shade, how quick and easy it is to get shade here, how to manage the shade level, the difference in kinds of shade, and what to do if you get too much shade. Great Outdoors Publishing. St. Petersburg, FL. www.floridabooks.com.

Stormscaping, Landscaping to Minimize Wind Damage in Florida. By Pamela Crawford. How and what to plant for minimal damage during storms and hurricanes. A unique book, the research for which started with Hurricane Andrew and came out in the middle of the bad hurricane years of 2005 and 2005. Many photos, some beautiful, some scary. Lake Worth Florida, Color Garden Inc, www.easygardencolor.com

Xeriscaping for Florida Homes. By Monica Brandies. A resource for creating a colorful, efficient, beautiful, water-saving garden. Charts of grasses, groundcovers, shrubs, vines, and trees. 181 pages. $18.95. Great Outdoors Publishing, St. Petersburg, FL. www.floridabooks.com.

Your Florida Guide to Perennials. By Sydney Park Brown and Rick K. Schoellhorn. Principles of perennial gardening in Florida zones and conditions, and a great plant directory of perennials for Florida. University Press of Florida, Gainesville, FL. www.upf.com.

INDEX

troughs, garden, 124-5
trumpet vine, 115
tufted palm, 104
Tulbaghia violacea, 62
turf, 20. See also grass and lawn.
turf, reduction of, 42,51
Ulmus species, 105

U-Pick farms, 77
USDA Plant Hardiness Zones, 40

Van Atta, Marian, 75,87,91,96
Vegetable Gardening Guide, 77
Vegetable Gardening in Florida, 76, 78
vegetables, 5,75-88
Vidalia onions, 84
Vigna unguiculata, 85. See also Southern peas.

vines, 22,33,34,112-115
Vireya rhododendron, 31,111
Virginia creeper, 33,115

wandering Jew, 62
Washington palm, 103
Washingtonia robusta, 103
water gardens, 14,125
water,
    and pavements, 21
    rain, 25,26
    restriction of, 42
waterfront, and gardens, 39
watering, 6,38,39,120
waterleaf, 67
weather, Florida, 5
    and fruit, 95-6
weeds, tree seedlings, 29,30
Whisenant, Blake, 85
willow, weeping, 107
wind tolerance, and trees, 116

Wisteria species, 115
wood chips, 22-24,45
woody plants, 99-116

xeriscaping, 21, 42

yard care services, 28
yard waste, 44-46

Zamia floridana, 104
Zebrina pendula, 62
Zoisia species, 53-4
zones, of hardiness, USDA, 40
Zoysia grass, 53-4

Notes

Monica Brandies, Author

For links to more information about Florida gardens, lots of fascinating free garden columns, and color photos associated with this book, visit Monica Brandies' website at **www.gardensflorida.com.** You also can find out her schedule of events and see how to contact her about speaking to your organization or garden club.

Monica Brandies, who has been gardening all her life, is the author of many books and the coauthor of several. Her articles appear weekly in the Brandon News (Florida) and are often seen in magazines such as Florida Gardening.

Monica has spoken to church groups, plant societies, garden clubs, and other groups in five states with talks that combine inspiration, entertainment, and information. Favorite topics include adjusting to Florida gardening, watersaving gardening, tropical plants, growing and using herbs in Florida, cut flowers in Florida, edible landscaping, shade gardening, easy flower arranging, butterfly gardening, earth-friendly gardening, veggies in Florida, plant propagation, and many others.

A Note from the Publisher

This book was published by B. B. Mackey Books, a specialist in regional and niche gardening literature. Our books and CD's are available online at **www.mackeybooks.com.** Books are also sold at many Florida bookstores, herb stores, and garden stores, and can be specially ordered from any full-service bookstore. They are available from www.amazon.com and are at many libraries, too.

New books on deep south gardening and formal garden design are in development now. Our current books available include:

___*Bless You for the Gifts*, by Monica Brandies. Wonderful autobiographical stories.

___*Creating & Planting Alpine Gardens*, by Rex Murfitt. Winner, silver award of achievement, Garden Writers Association of America.

___*Creating & Planting Garden Troughs,* by Joyce Fingerut and Rex Murfitt. Winner, Book of the Year (2000) from the American Horticultural Society. Make and plant hypertufa garden troughs.

___*A Cutting Garden for Florida*, by Betty Barr Mackey and Monica Moran Brandies. A fantastic compendium of flower lore on growing, using, conditioning, and arranging.

___*Herbs and Spices for Florida,* by Monica Brandies. Here's the Florida herb growers' most complete source of information on growing and using herbs in a semi-tropical climate.

___*Florida Gardening: Newcomer's Survival, Second Edition,* by Monica Brandies. This beloved title now offers more information than ever. Avoid mistakes and perils and grow all kinds of plants successfully, right from the start of your efforts in a new region.

___*Questions & Answers for Deep South Gardeners, by Nellie Neal.* In the Deep South there are special ways of coping, and here is Nellie's wise and witty guide. You are in the Deep South if you are in steamy Mississippi or other parts of the lower Southeast USA. If you're not sure, there's a map.

___*Who Does Your Garden Grow,* by Alex Pankhurst. The North American edition of this classic British book of tales of famous garden cultivars and the amazing people of many eras for whom they were named.

For a free booklist and order form, write to **B. B. Mackey Books, P.O. Box 475, Wayne, PA 19087.**